The
Compact History
of the
United States Navy

FLETCHER PRATT

Illustrations by **LOUIS PRISCILLA**

HAWTHORN BOOKS, INC. ★ *Publishers* ★ **NEW YORK**

THE

COMPACT HISTORY

OF THE

UNITED STATES

NAVY

★ ★ ★ ★ ★ ★ ★ ★

First Edition

Introduction

THERE HAVE BEEN many books telling the story of American naval strategy and tactics and the influence of the United States on world sea power. Here, however, is the story of the Navy itself—how it began; what it has been; and what it is today. Here, too, is the story of the American sailor—who he has been and who he is today; where he came from at first and where he comes from today; what he has done to the Navy; and what the Navy has done to him.

This book, then, is an American naval review, in which almost two hundred years of American ships and sailors pass by. From the privateers and their men without uniforms to the atomic-powered ships now being built and their crews of technicians, this is the story of how the United States Navy—afloat, ashore, underwater, and in the air—fulfilled its mission as America's first line of defense.

Such a book is of particular significance in today's world when each of our Armed Services is subject to almost daily revaluation not only by civilian political leaders, the press, and the public at large, but also by the other branches of the Armed Services and, last but not least, its own members. This revaluation must be not only in terms of its historic role but the particular place of that role today when technology is changing the rules almost faster than the experts can formulate them.

Fletcher Pratt was a man interested not only in the Navy's past but in its future. This history reflects his appreciation that the future of any institution is necessarily the product of its own past. It is a sad thought that this is Fletcher Pratt's last book; he died a few days after completing his manuscript. It would be difficult, however, to conceive a book that better expresses his life. Over many years Fletcher Pratt gave to the Navy not merely his devoted personal interest but also the most valuable of all gifts, a friendly yet critical appreciation of the Navy's place in our democracy.

Because of the author's death, the final work on *The Compact History of the United States Navy* had to be carried out by other hands. The late Captain Walter Karig, USN, lent his intimate knowledge of the Navy and its history to make this book as authoritative as possible.

It was prepared for publication by Commander Hartley E. Howe, USNR, who incorporated Captain Karig's suggestions, added several passages to bring certain portions into better balance and, in particular, expanded the last chapter to reflect the Navy's position in the world today. Any material he has added, of course, expresses only his own views and not those of the Navy.

The illustrations, by the late, talented Louis Priscilla, are largely based on photographs and drawings in the United States Navy's own possession.

THE PUBLISHERS

Contents

The
Compact History
of the
United States Navy

★　　★　　★　　★　　★

1

The Revolution

AT THE TIME the troubles broke out in Boston in 1775, there were not a few officers of the Royal Navy who came from the colonies, but since naval men of sailing-ship days were so frequently and so long from home, their real life was the service. As usual in periods of civil disturbance, these officers stayed with the flag rather than join persons in revolt against due authority. A few men were available for the Continental Navy who had served with the Royal Navy earlier in their careers, but only one man is reported to have left the King's service to join the colonists in revolt, and his name has not survived.

Thus the naval activities of the colonials were necessarily a matter of improvisation from resources locally available, both in personnel and materiel, and this has left on the American Navy and its history marks that have never been erased. The resources themselves were by no means insignificant. The colonists had little sense of the vast continent that lay behind them; they faced outward, toward the sea. Whatever they produced above the subsistence level was intended for shipment abroad, and articles not locally produced came from overseas. In effect, colonial America was an archipelago with a thin veining of roads in the backland, and over many of these roads there hung the shadow of the Indians. The normal trip from New York to Philadelphia was around by water, and even when it was made by land, it involved crossing the Hudson in a sailing ferry and the Delaware by one with sweeps. Almost everyone in the seacoast towns knew something about building or handling a ship, and, as a corollary, something about handling guns, since there were pirates and foreign privateers on every sea.

The colonials were thus a race of seamen and potential sea-fighters, but the concept of naval defense never entered their minds. In the terms of the age, naval defense required a fleet of battleships, strong enough to keep the enemy from landing expeditions on one of the islands of the archipelago, and everyone knew it took from three to five years to build ships like that. You fought the major actions of a naval war with substantially the ships you had at the start of it, and there was no real chance of breeding such a herd of elephants before the dynamic issues were settled.

Moreover, in the series of wars with the French that began in 1689 and did not really end until 1763, the defense of the colonies had been very competently supplied by the Royal Navy. The colonials' own efforts afloat were devoted to taking the offensive in areas where the elephants did not operate—attacks on the enemy merchant marine, principally by privately armed vessels, which made a very good thing out of it, since the law allowed them to keep everything they took. Convoy was almost never supplied except for military expeditions and the valuable sugar fleets that left the West Indies for Europe in the spring, usually more than two hundred ships in number. The vessels of ordinary commercial traffic sailed by themselves; they mounted a few guns and took their chances, and beating off a French privateer became a standard item in any tale of a sea voyage of the period.

The seamen of the colonies thus thought in offensive terms; what they could win from the enemy. They also thought in terms of private enterprise. There was what moderns would call a lack of investment capital in the colonies; the custom in both building and managing ships, particularly privateers, was to go shares, and at least in New England, it was not uncommon for the shareholders to choose their captain by free election. The result was a race of independent and cantankerous, if skillful, seamen; by Geekus Crow, they were as good as anybody, and discipline had to be salted with a demonstration of the necessity of a given order, even when the men were not sharers, but hired hands.

American seamen were, as a rule, a cut above the British of the same period. The latter had frequently drifted into the merchant marine from the Royal Navy because they found it difficult to enter any other profession after discharge; and they had often come to the

King's ships out of crimping-house, jail, and vagabondage. In war-time, the Royal Navy was always desperately short of men and adopted the most frantic methods to fill its crews with anyone who had muscle enough to pull a rope.

The American seaman was an independent operator. If he could not find a captain who suited him, he was just as likely to hire out as a farmhand for the season. A typical background enterprise was that of Samuel Welles of Connecticut, father of Lincoln's Secretary of the Navy, Gideon Welles; he owned a large farm, a general store and a shipyard beside his own exporting business, and his hired hands worked for him indifferently in all these. At sea, employment was on a voyage basis; when the trip was over all hands were paid off. Aboard ship men led a reasonably hard life, with poor food, cramped quarters and heavy labor; one hears of retired seamen, "too broken to work" at the age of forty-five. But it was probably not much harder than life on the frontier at the same time, and there was about it all the attraction of far lands and high adventure in a little-traveled age. Instead of working on a space ship for the moon, boys ran away to sea, sometimes with extraordinary success, like Joshua Barney, who became master of a ship at the age of sixteen. A sailor was something between a knight-errant and a compendium of useful information.

It is also to be noted that this seaman, in spite of his willingness to take goods from the enemy and to defend his own against pirates and privateers, was not a professional fighting man. He had often been impressed into the Royal Navy, or had heard from others about it, and he hated everything connected with the regular service—the dis-cipline, the brutality, the food and quarters worse than those on any merchant ship, the fact that he was cheated by rascally paymasters and subjected to the regime of the cat. It required quite another order of being than the American seaman to stand up under this and be-come a man-o'-war's man.

These independent, hard-bitten, violent seamen had developed some remarkable instruments of their trade by the time of the Revo-lution. One of the great economic facts of the history of the American colonies was the inexhaustible (or so it seemed) supply of ship tim-ber all along the coast from Maine to Georgia. Nearly every river had its shipyard and shipbuilder, and though these individuals rarely pro-duced more than one vessel a year, the total number was very considerable, especially in New England and Pennsylvania, where skilled labor was easiest to come by. The ships were frequently built of green timber, which caused them to have pains and aches in service, but this was probably not much worse than contemporary British practice, which called for a half-built ship to be left open to the weather for a long time for "aging," and resulted in vessels that were already half rotten when launched. American yards had built some considerable warships for the Royal Navy during the French wars of a generation before, but their major output was always merchant vessels, and these ships were nearly all small. Probably a 75-tonner would be average—but this was an economic size, both for fishing and the other great business of commercial craft—which was smuggling—in the period just before the Revolution.

The various sets of Navigation Acts were based on a theory usually attributed to Colbert, Louis XIV's chief minister—that colonies existed solely for the benefit of the mother country, that there was only so much in the world, and that any part of colonial commerce that went elsewhere than to the homeland unjustly deprived the latter of something that belonged to it. The British Navigation Acts thus prescribed that anything produced in the West Indies had to pass through a British port before going to Boston or Virginia, and in British, not colonial ships. The Spanish Navigation Acts prohibited ships of other nations to engage in trade with her colonies on any terms. Now precisely the most lucrative trade of the age was that which brought West Indian sugar to New England, where it became rum for export, and there was an overtone of triple trade which took the rum to Africa, where it was exchanged for slaves for the sugar colonies.

To men who saw the profits in these traffics the Navigation Acts were simply ridiculous, especially in view of the fact that the enforcing agencies were so ill-supplied with both ships and men that actually catching a smuggler was pretty much a matter of chance. Indeed, the attempt to enforce was regarded with so much indignation by the colonists that "cutting off our trade with all parts of the world" was one of the specific aggressive acts charged against George III in the Declaration of Independence.

But the existence and dimensions of the smuggling traffic had certain effects on the ships as well as the men who engaged in it. It placed an emphasis on boldness and disrespect for law; it called for small ships that could work into narrow inlets and hide themselves anywhere; and it demanded handy and weatherly ships that could operate in crooked channels and sail close to the wind.

The sum of these requirements was the schooner, of less load capacity but more adaptability than the brigs that were the usual carriers of British trade. By the date of the Revolution there were more schooners in service in America than all other ship types put together. It is not true that the schooner was invented in the colonies, as sometimes said; but American builders put so many alterations into the standard design that it became something quite new. The profession in which these schooners were engaged imposed speed as one of the requirements, and speed the builders sought above all else. The high poops of earlier vessels came down and the American schooner was soon a flush-decker. Her masts went up to carry more sail and the bowsprit and its attendant spars leaped forward to give her a cloud of jibs. There was constant, if slow experimentation with the hull form—"taking off the lines" of a vessel known to be fast and adding a little here, whittling off a little there from the previous model to make the next one faster still.

The schooners of the smuggling trade were thus notably fast ships, though that most wonderful achievement of American shipbuilding, the Baltimore clipper, was still in the egg, and it would take two wars fully to hatch it. The guns these ships carried in their peaceful (and privateering) pursuits were mostly 3-pounders, more rarely 6-pounders —terms that referred to the weight of the solid iron ball they fired. All ships had a certain number of swivels, which were just what their name indicates—small guns of about an inch-and-a-half bore mounted on a swivel and firing a charge of something like buckshot.

These were the ships and men behind the unborn navy of a nation not yet independent. They had many assets—courage, initiative, good seamanship, fast ships. But then as now, it takes more than good raw material to make a navy.

The smoothbore cannon of the Revolution may look small today, but they were crammed into fighting ships in such numbers as to impose real problems for the designers. Guns had to be reasonably high above the waterline if they were to carry any distance—and if the ports were to be opened when the ship rolled in open ocean. And that much weight high in a ship could make it unstable unless the hull was designed to take it. A warship was heavier built than a merchant vessel, reinforced in her decks to carry the weight of guns, with heavy sides to withstand pounding shot. Converted merchant ships—which was all the Continental Navy had to depend on at first—could neither carry the guns, provide a stable and safe firing platform, nor withstand enemy roundshot as successfully as a ship which had been designed for fighting.

And there were similar problems with the human element. A ship of war was necessarily crammed with the men needed to work and fight her, with men sleeping wherever there was room to swing a hammock. A ship of the line—the big battleship of the day with two or three tiers of guns—might have as many as five or six hundred men crammed into 200-odd feet of ship. Firm discipline was necessary under these conditions to keep the ship clean and orderly—discipline enforced with colt and cat, and equally essential in keeping the men at their guns when solid shot sent showers of deadly splinters spraying across the decks. And whether this discipline degenerated into tyranny depended primarily upon the leadership of the quarter-deck, the officers who ruled like kings but upon whom the survival of the ship depended in storm and battle.

Ruler of the seas was the ship of the line—the largest class of fighting ship, strong enough to hold its place in the line of battle against similar vessels of the enemy. The Continental Navy never possessed such a vessel: the only one completed by American yards being turned over to the French as a gesture of good will to replace one of theirs lost in America. As a result, the American Navy never seriously challenged British control of the seas off our coast, and British troops were able to take full advantage of sea transport in moving from state to state. It was only when the French alliance sent fleets of French battleships to our assistance that the score became more even, and these vessels played a major part in the final triumph at Yorktown.

Ship of the line or frigate, an eighteenth-century warship was likely to prefer to fight at close range. The heavy smoothbore cannon, wheel-mounted so they could be pulled back in through the ports and loaded through the muzzle, had only the most primitive aiming mechanisms—and ships at best were an ever-moving gun platform. A few hundred yards was maximum range except for the extra long guns mounted fore and aft where the broadside could not be brought to bear. As a result, while the frigates—lighter ships, usually with only one full row of guns and designed primarily to cruise alone—might maneuver for position in single-ship actions, the general trend was to fight at extremely close range, often muzzle to muzzle. The heavy ships' sides could take it—a ship was sunk in battle surprisingly rarely provided she did not catch fire or blow up—but flesh and blood suffered heavily, not only from cannon balls and musket fire—every ship's tops carried marine sharpshooters who picked off personnel on the enemy's deck—but from the deadly splinters that flew everywhere. There was a grimly practical reason why the interiors of fighting ships were often painted red: the color scheme hid the bloody smears of battle.

Three great weaknesses of the Continental Navy were in trained officers, in ordnance, and in money. There was more to commanding a fighting ship than good seamanship; the naval officer was required to be an expert in naval tactics, in the day-to-day leadership of several hundred men cooped up in darkness and damp, in administration of complex supply problems. Personal courage was important—and many seamen had it. Professional courage—the ability to know when to take a risk and when to avoid one—was to be gained only in hard experience.

And if the American forests provided plenty of raw material for American shipwrights, there was no such happy situation for the gun foundries. American ironmasters were rare birds and gun-casting not a native art—partly because the mother country had tried to keep it as a monopoly for home industry. Throughout the war, American ships had to be armed with what cannon could be scraped together— taken from old forts ashore, captured from the enemy, borrowed from the French.

But worst of all was the lack of money. Afloat as ashore, there was a constant struggle to obtain funds for pay, for ammunition, for food and clothing. Racing inflation cut the value of the dollar until it wasn't worth a "Continental." There were no easy answers to these problems. It is a tribute to the tenacity and ingenuity of the Continental Navy that it succeeded in evading them as long as it did.

II

The first naval transaction of the Revolution illustrated the type of opposition the British were to encounter. The people of Machias, in the Maine district of Massachusetts, ran short of provision in the spring of 1775, their crops having failed. News of this reached British-occupied Boston. A certain Captain Ichabod Jones accordingly went to Machias with two sloops loaded with food (being covered by the armed schooner *Margaretta* of four 3-pounders, under Midshipman Moore) to exchange for lumber for the use of the British troops, doubtless with a handsome profit for Ichabod Jones in the offing. A Machias town meeting voted to make the exchange as the only means of obtaining something to eat, but Jones ruined his own game by passing out his provisions only to members of the majority who had voted for him.

The result was that an indignation meeting of patriots tried to catch the British officers in church on June 11, and failing that, went to the wharf, where they stripped the sloop *Unity* of her cargo. Midshipman Moore, not liking the look of things, dropped down to the harbor entrance, where he raided a small sloop of her captain as a pilot, and next morning made sail. The patriots assembled around *Unity* at dawn, gave three hearty cheers to rouse out local talent, which appeared to the number of some thirty-five men, armed with "guns, swords and pitchforks," and set out in pursuit. On the way they built breastworks of pine boards around the sloop and, deciding to have a captain, elected Jeremiah O'Brien, one of five brothers aboard. *Margaretta* was a dull sailer and as *Unity* hauled up fast on her, not much better with the guns. Her shot only cut the sloop's sails, and when a well aimed swivel discharge killed the man at the schooner's wheel, she broached and the vessels came into contact. Midshipman Moore caused about nine casualties with hand grenades, but he was shot through the body by the return fire, and when the colonials boarded with clubbed muskets, resistance collapsed.

This was the first naval battle of specifically American history, and the interest that attaches to it is less in the action itself, which worked out about as might have been expected from the forces engaged, than in the sequel. It established a graph of the effort to form a naval service from the materials at hand. The Massachusetts General Court thanked O'Brien and directed that *Unity* be fitted out with *Margaretta*'s guns under the name of *Machias Liberty;* presumably the schooner was sold and the captors pocketed the prize money. About a month later, when the sloop's fitting out was complete, the British schooner *Diligent* of eight or ten guns appeared off Machias, with a tender. Her captain went ashore on some business of his own, was seized by a band of patriots, and when *Machias Liberty* dropped down the stream, the leaderless British surrendered without firing a shot. The General Court assented to a petition that a "company" be formed to man both ships at the expense of the province to relieve unemployment, and sent them to cruise in the Bay of Fundy, where they captured a number of small British merchant ships before October, 1776. By that date the small British merchants had mostly vanished from the area and been replaced by small British cruisers; O'Brien was captured and taken off to Old Mill Prison.

In other words, the amateurs did very well in casual encounters with people trying to carry out normal commercial and regulatory functions in an area where few yet realized that there was a genuine war on; but when these amateurs encountered professional fighters, they melted.

Projected and enlarged, this was the story of local naval effort in the Revolution. Every state except New Hampshire put some ships in commission, Virginia and South Carolina considerable squadrons. Nearly all the ships were small, nearly all operated close in territorial waters for the prevention of plundering descents on the coast, of which the British became particularly fond. Many were row-galleys. Their officers were as irregular as O'Brien and tended to slip easily into and out of privateering, especially as financial stringency made it hard to keep up ships at the public expense. Their actions have left little record and were not long remembered even in their own time. Many of the men were taken and died in prison hulks or British jails. But these fishermen, seashore farmers, and country bumpkins rendered a service not told in statistics and rarely recognized. As an irregular light cavalry of the coasts they made it difficult for British ships hovering offshore to get supplies, in spite of the willingness of the colonials to behave like members of revolting communities everywhere and sell out for personal profit. More important still, the little ships kept functioning that network of inshore water communication on which so much of the life of the colonies depended.

The major overseas commerce of the colonies took paralyzing losses from the start. There were no more of the lucrative trips to the West Indies for sugar or out of Carolina with indigo, rice, and tobacco, and the economic pinch this brought about contributed in no small degree to the inflation and money shortage that made it so difficult for the united colonies to keep ships afloat and armies afield. But the mosquito traffic continued practically unhindered; the British found it impossible to maintain small craft inside the inlets and shoals in numbers sufficient to stop it. Even while the British held New York, coasters continued to ply Long Island Sound.

III

The idea of colonial operations at sea began with General George Washington, besieging Boston, as head of the Army of the Continental Congress. His main trouble was arms and powder to shoot them with: there were not enough muskets for the men in the circling camps, and as their terms of enlistment expired, the troops evinced a cheerful disposition to take their weapons home as souvenirs. As for artillery, there was none at all. And how do you run a siege without powder?

Washington had no sea experience, but he possessed not inconsiderable powers as an analyst of naval matters, as he was later to demonstrate on a larger scale, and he could see supply ships beating into the harbor, carrying the very things he needed. Early in September, 1775, he had the schooner *Hannah* fitted out, and placed in charge of Captain Nicholas Broughton of the Marblehead regiment, whose men were seamen all. She caught one ship, with naval stores and lumber, and Washington gave army commissions to six more schooners and brigantines, sending two of them under Broughton to the mouth of the St. Lawrence to intercept two brigs with military stores that had been reported on their way to Quebec. This was in November. Broughton missed the brigs, hailed and examined fourteen sail of British merchants, but as he considered it as yet a war with the King's ministry and not with England, let them go; then kidnapped the governor of Prince Edward Island, whom Washington released.

There was constant trouble with the crews of this little Navy, "a set of unprincipled abandoned fellows," who complained they had "enlisted to serve in the Army and not as Marines"; they deserted two of the ships en masse. Some of the reason and the cure for it appear in the story of Captain John Manley of the schooner *Lee;* he mustered his men and asked them their troubles. When he found they related mainly to a lack of sufficient clothes for the high stormy season, he made good the deficiency at once, and was received with three cheers and an expression of willingness to go anywhere. Manley was Washington's favorite captain; he followed up his conciliation of the men by capturing an extremely valuable storeship with more than two thousand muskets, a lot of ammunition, and a brass mortar, "pronounced to be the noblest piece of ordnance ever landed in America," and took several other prizes.

His successful cruise supplied a much-wanted stimulus to the little Washington navy, whose crews were always ready to give three cheers over the prospect of prize money. All that winter and down past the British evacuation of Boston in March, 1776, they cruised the Massachusetts Bay approaches and gave a good account of themselves. But most of the ships were not physically fitted for deep-water work, it became increasingly hard to find men, with privateering so attractive, and toward the end of 1776 it was decided to formalize an existing state of affairs by selling out the few ships that remained. At this date neither officers nor men cared very much.

IV

These were the beginnings, and they were all part of a pattern before a sail was hoisted; a pattern of revolt along the seaboard, with overtones of semi-piracy. Men deprived of their normal livelihood by the fact that they could not sail under the Royal flag without having trouble at home, nor under the colors of the colonies without having trouble with the King's ships, became pirates willy-nilly.

The beginnings of the national navy came in October, 1775, when a motion was brought in to the Continental Congress for the fitting out of two vessels, one of which should carry ten carriage guns, for the interception of the enemy's transports. Note the detail—the size of only one ship specified, and that to be used for the interception of transports, which was what Washington was already doing, under no authority but that of a general supplying his troops. It was not really a bill for a navy at all. Nevertheless there was a long, acrimonious debate, in which the agrarian opponents of spending money on ships for any purpose were joined by a not inconsiderable number of delegates like Mr. Dickinson of Pennsylvania, strongly opposed to acts of aggression that might make it difficult to conciliate matters with His Gracious Majesty.

The proposal carried by "a very narrow majority" and a Naval Committee of seven was appointed, on which the most significant name was that of John Adams of Massachusetts. With this victory under their belts the pro-navy men carried through a bill authorizing two more ships, of 20 and up to 32 guns, and another provision for naval regulations to be drawn. Two ship-rigged commercial vessels and two brigs lying at Philadelphia were immediately taken in hand for conversion, with two little schooners and two one-sticker sloops soon added; and while the committee steered its way through such details as a Marine Corps, courts-martial and pensions, there arrived a piece of news that broke the back of the resistance to naval activity.

A British force from Halifax had appeared off Falmouth (now Portland), the most considerable town in the Maine district, and in reprisal for the taking of *Margaretta* and *Diligent,* drove the inhabitants into the November woods and burned every one of the four hundred houses. On the wave of indignation over this Congress carried through a provision for the construction of thirteen frigates, five of 32 guns, five of 28, and three of 24. The previous vessels, provincial or colonial, were armed ships whose main purpose was the interception of stores; but a 32 was the standard cruiser of the day, with 12-pounders on the gundeck, and these new ships were to be built from the keel up as warships, not raiders. The United Colonies were going to have a regular navy—and there immediately ensued among members a scramble to get captains' and lieutenants' commissions for friends, relatives, and acquaintances. Four grades of officer were created—captains, lieutenants, masters (professional navigators concerned with sailing the ship rather than with fighting), and midshipmen, with a pay scale ranging from $60 a month for the captain of a ship of more than 20 guns down to $12 a month for a mid. Warrants—boatswain, sailmaker, carpenter, gunner—were to receive $15 a month: their mates, $9.50. Petty officer pay ran from $8.50 to $10; seamen drew a flat $8 a month. Uniforms were prescribed for officers but not for men; blue coats and britches with red lapels and waistcoats, with rank indicated by such details as the amount of lace on the waistcoat, the shape of the cuffs, embroidery around the buttonholes, and so forth. The officers were not too happy about this Quaker plainness: they petitioned for gold epaulets and some, such as John Paul Jones, went right ahead and wore them anyway.

Among the bills setting up the new service was one that would prove absolutely fatal. It provided that when a transport or supply vessel was taken, two-thirds of the proceeds went to the government; when a vessel of war, one-half. The proportions were changed later, but much too late. What was worse, privateers did not have to share with the government at all.

As everyone tried to get into the act, the administrative side of this new Navy rapidly became so complicated that it is almost impossible to trace a way among the various committees and boards. The work became so boresome that the members did not attend meetings or understand what was being said when they did. At sea matters were necessarily more simplified. The converted ships at Philadelphia were intended to sail as a squadron—*Alfred,* 24, *Columbus,* 20, the brigs *Andrew Doria,* 14, and *Cabot,* 14, the sloops *Providence,* 12, and *Hornet,* 10.[1] Mr. Adams was above jobbery, but his fellow member of the committee, Stephen Hopkins of Rhode Island, was not, and the latter state had contributed one of the ships as well as a considerable contingent of the crews. Therefore, Rhode Island got first choice of the command plums. Stephen's brother Esek Hopkins became commander-in-chief, "a most experienced and venerable officer," who was just past fifty-seven, an age which qualified him as venerable at the time. He had been in retirement for four years. Another Hopkins, John B., commanded *Cabot;* Abraham Whipple of Rhode Island, *Columbus;* and Tom Hazard from the same state, *Providence.* Hopkins' flag captain aboard *Alfred* was Dudley Saltonstall of Massachusetts; Nicholas Biddle of Pennsylvania received *Andrew Doria,*

[1] The number of guns was always given after a ship's name in sailing-ship days; it expressed her "rate." That is, she was equal in force to a standard ship carrying that number of guns. That the armaments often changed and the figure did not represent the exact number of guns carried did not affect this rating.

and William Stone of Maryland, *Hornet*. Thus the commands were distributed on the combined principles of geography and nepotism, modified by political maneuver.

On December 22, 1775, as the fleet lay among floating ice in the river, the first American naval flag was broken out from *Alfred* by the only North Carolina contribution to the officer list—First Lieutenant John Paul Jones, more or less a man of mystery, about whom it was whispered that he had been a pirate and openly stated that he did not believe in God. It was February 17 before the fleet could sail, under orders to clear out the small craft fitted out by the loyalist governor of Virginia, then to repair to South Carolina, where there were simillar troubles.

Now Esek Hopkins was one of those Yankee sea-captains who had come up through the highly practical school of the old wars. The doctrine of that school rested on the absolute responsibility and absolute authority of the skipper. If he were carrying a cargo of tobacco to a consignee in Alicante and on the way found that Spain had gone to war, it was not merely all right for him to take his goods to Leghorn and sell them there instead; he was specifically expected to do so. Sometimes he sold the ship in addition, paid off his crew, and made his way home with a pocketful of drafts, whose real value might not be known for months. To a man educated in this tradition, it was simply silly that a group of Congressional delegates ashore, who did not know a spritsail from a marlinspike, should direct his operations. Instead of heading for Chesapeake Bay, Hopkins took his squadron straight to New Providence in the Bahamas, where there was reputed to be a great stock of ordnance stores and powder.

On March 3, 1776, the marines were landing; the place surrendered without a fight and Hopkins got eighty-seven pieces of artillery and a quantity of powder, very acceptable to the ill-supplied Continental forces. He intended to put into Newport, but on the way a British schooner and a couple of merchants were taken, and it was learned that the enemy had set up a naval station in Narragansett Bay, with strong frigates, so Hopkins bore away for New London. Just after midnight of April 5 a ship was seen standing down; she showed lights and then British colors, and fired into *Cabot,* which was nearest. The brig sheered off, badly hurt; *Alfred* drew alongside the stranger under a press of sail, and they fought it out for nearly three hours, when the flagship's wheel-ropes were shot away. *Doria* fired only a few guns, *Columbus* a single broadside, and *Providence* never got into action. The Britisher escaped.

It turned out that she was only the little 20-gun corvette *Glasgow*, one-fifth the force of the Continental squadron, and explanations were in order. They were various and of a character to indicate what kind of Navy the United Colonies had set up: many of the men had got drunk on liquor taken out of the prizes; a contrary puff of wind had kept *Columbus* out of action; the *Alfred* had lost her wheel-ropes. But when pieced together they added up to the fact that the captains were at best privateersmen, who did not know how to keep discipline, teach their men gunnery, or handle ships together. One of them, Tom Hazard, was dismissed for cowardice and his *Providence* given to the mysterious, sharp-nosed Lieutenant Jones; more would be heard of her, and of him.

A few weeks later Hopkins ran his squadron down the coast to Providence and troubles began to pile up. The ships were not up to specification, *Alfred* a bad roller and leaky, *Columbus* too weak to bear the weight of her artillery. An epidemic of smallpox sent one hundred men ashore. General Washington had loaned one hundred men to the fleet and wanted them back. There was no money to pay those who were left, not even the prize money from the captures. It was absolutely impossible to enlist men for such a service when the free-lance work of privateering offered better shares and cash on the barrel-head.

This was effectively the end of American fleet operations, of any attempt to influence strategy by naval action. Hopkins could get his ships to sea only as individuals, when men and supplies became available to send one out.

After he had been at Providence for a while, unable to execute peremptory orders to send a squadron to the Carolina coast and to break up the Newfoundland fisheries, Congressional tempers ran short, and he was summoned to Philadelphia with Whipple and Saltonstall to explain the actions of his only cruise. John Adams, who understood something of the independence a sea commander must have, spoke warmly in Hopkins' defense, but the honorable delegates voted a censure on him and sent him back—a step which did not improve discipline in the squadron. The Commander-in-Chief tried to restore it by severity. He had men flogged for the slightest cause and had them beaten about the head when they did not jump. But this did not prove to be much help and Hopkins was still at Providence with insufficient crews in the month of December, 1776.

The first commander-in-chief of the American Navy made a quaint end of his career.

At this date he had two of the new frigates, *Warren*, 32, and *Providence*, 28, in addition to *Columbus* and the sloop *Providence*. The British appeared in the bay below to take Newport and set up a naval station there, with a fleet that included battleships. Hopkins warped up Providence River to safety; on New Year's Day of 1777 the enemy sent the light frigate *Diamond* up to investigate, and she went aground on a shoal. At this point the wind came strongly from the north, which would prevent the Britisher being helped by the fleet below. Hopkins did not judge it prudent to take one of his own frigates down to attack the grounded vessel, but boarded the sloop *Providence* and with her took station under *Diamond's* stern and began firing her little 6-pounders, not very accurately or effectively. In the meanwhile, some militia had brought up some 18-pounders ashore, guns which could really hurt, but after twenty-six shots, all of which missed, they hailed *Providence* to say they were short of powder and hungry. Just why Hopkins should have found it necessary to take them ship's biscuit and powder in person is not clear, but he did, and while he was picnicking with the militia and *Diamond's* people frantically pumping out water and throwing spare spars overboard to lighten ship, Hopkins' boat drifted away and he was marooned on a sandbank.

This was the last straw. Hopkins was dismissed and the process of disorganizing the Continental Navy was complete from top to bottom. The ships were become individual raiders, a privateering service in all but formal designation, with the captains obtaining their appointments through favor of the management (one of the various government boards or committees), and readily slipping out of the service into purely private employ or back in again. The basic good material was never assembled or its energies channeled toward the achievement of a common purpose. Which is to say that Hopkins, in a position at sea analogous to that of Washington on land, had none of the latter's ability for drawing and holding together a service. The Naval Committee had picked the wrong man.

In the meantime the Continental Army carried out two naval operations. Neither was successful, but one was a notable example of impact of war on naval technology—which has been a continuing thread in our naval history from the start. The other provided an excellent example of a case in which even a defeat paid great dividends in terms of the over-all strategy of the war.

The *American Turtle* was never carried on a naval register, but she embodied more significant advances in marine warfare than any ship before the *Monitor*. When she set boldly out to attack the British ship *Eagle*, 64, in New York harbor, she was the first practical submarine, the first screw-propelled vessel, and a pioneer in mine and torpedo warfare.

The *Turtle* was born in the ingenious mind of a Connecticut Yankee named David Bushnell, who persuaded Continental leaders to back his attempts to put engineering science to work to challenge British sea power. His vessel was little larger than a big barrel, just room enough for one man to sit in it and drive it by turning a crank connected to a propeller. The *Turtle* submerged like a modern submarine by flooding her tanks, and she carried a mine towed behind to blow up the enemy ship.

Sergeant Ezra Lee of the Continental Army manned the *Turtle* on her historic cruise. He succeeded in submerging beneath the *Eagle*, but the design called for him to screw a support for the mine into the ship's bottom (the mine would then be armed to go off by clockwork after giving the *Turtle* time to get away). However, the current kept sweeping Lee away; his screw attachment ran into the copper sheathing on the ship's bottom. The air supply in the tiny craft gave out before Lee could complete his mission—and the *Turtle* was never successfully used to destroy an enemy ship. It was eighty-five years before another submarine carried out an attack—and once again it was manned by Americans.

The Army's other venture into naval activity was far to the north. Sir Guy Carleton was leading a British army south from Canada, invading New York via Lake Champlain. The lake was a vital sector of the invasion route since there were no roads through the wilderness ashore. Benedict Arnold, in command of the defending

American army, hastily built a tiny fleet of sloops and galleys while the British assembled one of their own at the north end of the lake. Heavily outnumbered, Arnold assembled his fleet in the lee of Valcour Island, hidden from the British as they sailed before the wind southward on the lake. They were past before they found the American ships, then had to turn and beat back to battle. The Americans fought stubbornly but vainly; after a day of battle they fled southward on the lake and were picked off one by one by the British ships. But, as it turned out, the losing battle was a winning campaign; the time required to build the British fleet and clear the lake delayed the British expedition until it was too late in the fall for them to continue southward, and they retreated to Canada, thus postponing the decisive campaign until Burgoyne renewed the attempt in the following year— with fatal results.

V

In contrast to Hopkins's personal fiasco, the American shipbuilders had produced designs for the thirteen authorized frigates of the Continental line that were successful beyond all expectations. The assignment of where the ships were to be built was a political matter—four to Pennsylvania, two each to Massachusetts, Rhode Island and New York, one each to Maryland, Connecticut, and New Hampshire. The contracts within these states were also let on a jobbery basis, but when things got down to the design level, the pride of craftsmanship, never long absent in colonial America, took a hand. In Philadelphia the firm of Wharton and Humphreys (mark that name, it will be around again) produced standard designs for the three types of frigates, and they were distributed to the various builders. The plans were on a large scale, each sheet being five feet or more long, and courier service was irregular. But the injunction was for extreme haste; before the official plans reached Massachusetts, Rhode Island, and New Hampshire, local builders had drawn their own on the basis of the specified size and armament. Also the individual contractors made some alterations.

But in every case they were animated by the same ideas—to produce a fast ship, a ship that would work well to windward, a ship not owing anything to any previous design, but conceived on purely empirical principles of how best to accomplish the job. All the designs were for ships somewhat larger, longer, and stronger than those of similar ships in other navies. There have been legends that some were copied from the best French or British models; they are not true. The new frigates differed from any others in hull form, sail plan and arrangements, and grew straight out of native American imagination. William Hackett's Massachusetts frigate, *Hancock,* 32, was pronounced the fastest and finest of her class in the world after the British captured her, and the French thought so too, after they took her from the British in the West Indies; they copied her. *Randolph,* 32, and *Virginia,* 28, of the official design, were nearly as good; after the latter was taken by the enemy, she did them wonderful service.

That was the trouble; all the Continental frigates that reached the sea did wonderful service—for the British. The two New York ships, *Congress,* 28, and *Montgomery,* 24, never reached blue water at all; they were burned at Poughkeepsie after the fall of New York City. Of the Pennsylvania vessels, *Washington,* 32, and *Effingham,* 28, were scuttled in the river when the British came to Philadelphia in 1777. *Delaware,* 24, came downstream to help in the defense, but her amateur crew ran her aground and she was raked into surrender by British field guns.

The end of the Baltimore ship, *Virginia,* 28, was even more illustrative; she went aground going down the bay, pounded, and lost her rudder. British sails appeared on the horizon; her captain, a politically important, squirish man named James Nicholson, had himself rowed ashore with his papers. The first lieutenant tried to get the ship warped inshore for defense, but the crew all cried that the majority should rule, broke into the liquor stores and were roaring drunk by time the British came to take the ship.

Hancock put out in May of 1777 under Washington's favorite, Manley, and in company with *Boston,* 24, cruised toward Halifax. Off the Grand Banks they found the British frigate *Fox,* 28, captured her after a short engagement and equipped her under the American flag, but after a month's cruising the three were sighted by the British two-decker frigate *Rainbow,* 44, with a brig in company. Now *Boston*'s captain was Hector McNeill, an older man than Manley, who resented the latter's seniority; instead of staying to fight as he might have done, he took advantage of a favorable breeze to bear away.

Manley, who before and later showed himself not the worst officer, seems to have lost his head this time, and tried to make his fine, fast cruiser still faster by altering her trim, which had the opposite effect. A two-day chase through mists and light airs brought a second British frigate on the scene, and both *Hancock* and *Fox* surrendered after only a token resistance. McNeill was court-martialed when he reached Boston and dismissed: Nicholson had been completely cleared in the loss of *Virginia*.

The only one of the Pennsylvania ships to get to sea was *Randolph*, 32. Her captain was Nicholas Biddle, and this was a political appointment, too, he being a member of the Philadelphia banking family. But he had been a mid in the Royal Navy, and he turned out to be one of the very best sea officers the colonies had. The ship put out early in 1777, made a successful cruise off the southern coast, taking several prizes, then a courier trip to France, and after a stop at Charleston to clean her bottom, sailed for the West Indies. There, on March 7, 1778, a large ship bore down from windward; she was within hail before being discovered as *Yarmouth*, 64, a small battleship, something like four times *Randolph*'s force. Biddle nevertheless stood valiantly up against her and they had a hot action for a quarter of an hour, in which the American did not come off worst and *Yarmouth* lost two of her topmasts. But as Biddle wore to get under her stern, *Randolph* suddenly blew up and that was the end of ship and captain.

The New Hampshire ship was *Raleigh*, 32, Captain Thomas Thompson; she put to sea in April, 1777, made a reasonably unsuccessful cruise, in which she was beaten off from a convoy by a British brig of half her strength, then sailed again for the West Indies, in company with the old *Alfred*. On March 9, 1778, they sighted two British ships and tried them in a test of sailing; *Alfred* fell off badly to leeward, was attacked by both Britishers and quickly forced to strike. Thompson's story was that *Raleigh* at first could not get around quickly enough to come down to her consort's help, and then he hardly dared close with two opponents, but it turned out they were only a 20-gun sloop-of-war and a 16-gun brig. When he got home he was universally blamed, and the court-martial which dismissed him was approved by everybody.

Honest John Barry, a Marylander of Irish ancestry, who had done well on a cruise with the 16-gun converted brig *Lexington,* was given *Raleigh,* but he had no better luck with her than the rest. Two days out of Boston, in September, 1778, he was sighted by a 50-gun two-decker and a sloop of 22, which hauled in chase. While the breeze held strong *Raleigh* pulled away, but after sixty hours light airs came in, the sloop gained and was soon close enough for cannon. Her second broadside brought down *Raleigh*'s main topmast, and as the two-decker now came pounding into range, Barry ran his ship ashore near Penobscot Bay and ordered her fired. Negligence or treachery, she was not; the British hauled her off and had another fine acquisition to their navy.

The Connecticut ship, *Trumbull,* 28, had infinite difficulty crossing the bar of the Connecticut River and did not make it until 1780. She made one cruise, fought a drawn battle with a heavy British letter-of-marque, and after a refit, put out again, when she fell in with H.M.S. *Iris,* formerly *Hancock,* and was captured after a sharp little battle. At this date she was the last of the original thirteen Continental frigates, for the other three had already found ways of losing their flags.

Warren, 32, carried the flag of Dudley Saltonstall as commander afloat of the expedition launched by Massachusetts state against British-occupied Penobscot Bay in the summer of 1779. He had in addition a Continental brig and a sloop, three state brigs, and four-teen sail of privateers taken into the state service—and he made a classic failure, dallying before a little fort for over a month, or until a British squadron appeared at the entrance to the bay, whereupon Saltonstall ran all his ships up the river and burned them, except one that the British captured. Five hundred Americans were lost; Salton-stall was court-martialed and dismissed from the Navy. *Boston,* 24, and *Providence,* 28, went to cruise in southern waters without conspicuous success and fell into the enemy's hands at the taking of Charleston in 1780.

This chapter of almost unalloyed disaster had hardly begun when five more frigates and three 74-gun battleships were authorized at the end of 1776, a year after the first program. Two of the frigates were barely begun at Norfolk when shortage of money and the fighting in Virginia brought them to a halt. One was laid down at Middletown, Connecticut, but the same financial trouble kept her from being completed. The fourth frigate, *Confederacy, 36,* was built at Norwich, Connecticut—almost as remarkable a vessel as *Hancock,* very fast and heavily armed. She had the usual luck—dismasted in a storm, re-rigged, and then taken off the Chesapeake capes by two British, without having accomplished anything but carry several packages of mail for the Continental Congress. The last of the frigates was *Alliance* of Massachusetts, the only one to survive the war, but her story and that of the single line of battleship to be built belong to a separate department.

The sum of the frigate story is that the effort to build a colonial navy from the keel up conspicuously failed under the pressure of the war; the physical and manpower resources were there, but no one knew how to bring them together.

VI

With the free-lances it was a different tale.

"The people is gone mad a-privateering"—the most obvious, the most profitable type of sea enterprise at such a time. It was not until March 2, 1776, that the Continental Congress authorized privateering in the name of the United Colonies and sent out blank commissions for it in such numbers that a thousand reached Massachusetts alone, while navy agents in France and the West Indies issued them to anyone who would take them. But even before this, even as early as the siege of Boston, the several states in their capacity as sovereign governments were putting out letters-of-marque and reprisal.

The "letter-of-marque" was a class of ship carrying such a document; the distinction between her and a privateer proper was theoretical and consisted in the fact that the former carried a hold full of goods bound for somewhere and intended to do some privateering on the side instead of making it her main business. This was an obvious convenience in the early days of the war, when there were no privateers except very slightly converted merchant vessels, all the way down to big whaleboats with oars and a row of swivels along the bulwarks. The letters-of-marque carried on most of the privateering in distant waters during the first two years of the war. Their captures were relatively few and the result of chance encounters, for they could make a good thing out of cargoes of American products (tobacco, rice, indigo) and were chiefly interested in carrying these goods to areas which lacked them because of the British blockade.

Closer in, along the shores of the continent, there was more pure privateering. Game was always plentiful, for British traffic never ceased. Quite aside from what surreptitious trade the Tory loyalists carried on, there was a continual major flow of movement in the Bay of Fundy, the Gulf of St. Lawrence and to the fishers, most of it necessarily in ships too small to be worth arming strongly and un-economic to convoy. Except for the brief interval between the evacuation of Boston in March, 1776, and the occupation of New York in July, the British always held a big seaport on the American coast, supporting it by supplies brought in from across the ocean.

Take a look at a sample case, which comes from 1780 and the diary of a Rhode Island general practitioner. Dr. Solomon Drowne, in straitened circumstances, felt himself obliged to sign on as surgeon aboard the small privateer sloop *Hope,* of six little guns and twenty men, fitting out at Providence. On October 3 she put to sea; during the next three days nearly all hands were violently seasick and strong winds blew, increasing to gale force by the 7th. The topmast was sent down, the guns snagged to the hold, the hatches nailed and a detail stood by with axes to cut away the mast if necessary. On the next day the weather moderated; Dr. Drowne offered prayers, and a large number of whales were observed playing around. *Hope* cruised up the traffic lanes northward and on the 11th sighted a sloop and a brig, but the former proved a New London privateer and the latter her prize. On the 14th a ship was sighted on the horizon, but approach showed her to be a ship of the line, and soon several more were in sight, firing signal guns. *Hope* sheered off southwestward along the Jersey coast, and next morning came up with a snow [2] sailing very heavy; the crew went to quarters and Dr. Drowne to the cabin, where he laid out his surgeon's instruments, but a few minutes later heard a huzza from the deck, indicating that the chase had struck. She proved to be out of Jamaica for New York with ten men and four 4-pounder guns, a big ship loaded with twenty hogsheads of sugar and enough rum to get the whole of Rhode Island drunk. "We hardly knew what to do with our prize," she was so large. The pris-

[2] A snow was a brig with an extra "jigger" mast close against the mainmast to carry the spanker, the shears for which interfere with the setting of the mainsail on a brig.

oners were taken aboard *Hope,* where loaded pistols were hung on the cabin in case of a rising and ten of *Hope*'s crew went aboard the snow. Both vessels bore for Martha's Vineyard through strong boisterous winds and snow, now most apprehensive of sighting any sail that might turn out to be a ship of force. The good doctor felt "qualmist" and sought to assuage his trouble with a draft of grog based on snow-water. On the night of the 18th, to the despair of all, they lost sight of the prize. However, she was in sight again by the next morning and by the 22nd, Sunday and a thick fog, they were passing up Providence River, firing 13-gun salutes. The capture and her cargo were worth over £20,000; the privateer captain was a rich man; Dr. Drowne was relieved of his financial embarrassments and he never went to sea again.

This is one of the few cases of detailed record, with a small but fast ship putting out to take many times her own value in a three-week cruise. The case *contra* is presented by the story of Andrew Sherburne, who entered as a ship's boy in the Continental sloop *Ranger,* 20, at the age of fourteen. She put into Charleston and was taken there when the harbor fell to the British in 1780; Sherburne escaped with most of the officers and went to Portsmouth, where the citizens had formed a fund to replace *Ranger,* which was their own ship, but they decided to fit her out as the privateer *Alexander. Alexander* cruised several weeks toward the St. Lawrence without taking a single prize. On returning to Portsmouth, Sherburne was accosted on the street by one of the officers of the new privateer *Greyhound,* then fitting out, and taken aboard the ship, shown round the cabin, told what a fine boy he was, and asked to sign. That night *Greyhound*'s officers went ashore to a tavern and gave a "jovial evening," with all seafaring men invited, and those sufficiently lubricated by liberal tots of rum signed on.

Sherburne allowed himself to be tempted. *Greyhound* put out early in 1781 and ran toward Halifax, off which port she encountered what appeared to be a big and valuable merchantman. It turned out to be a frigate, which held the privateer in close chase and would have taken her but for an opportune fog. *Greyhound* now steered toward the mouth of the St. Lawrence; numerous sails were sighted, but they all proved to be American privateers on the same errand as herself, and it was some weeks before they took a few miserable fishing shallops. Sherburne was placed aboard one of these with orders to take her into Salem, but they had not gone far before they were overhauled by a good-sized ship, which fired heavy swivels into them, then boarded with twenty men, against whom the five or six privateersmen could make no resistance. The captors were Newfoundlanders, in a great fury over Yankee depredations, all for killing their captives on the spot; it was with difficulty that their captain persuaded them to carry the prisoners alive to a town on the Newfoundland shore. There they were surrounded by a mob of a hundred, including a "lady of distinction," who asked after papers. Sherburne, who appears to have been the only literate in the group, handed over a copy of *Greyhound*'s commission, which the lady read aloud. When she reached the passage authorizing the privateer to "burn, sink, or destroy," the crowd became so agitated that it seemed the prisoners might be lynched, but the lady persuaded the mob to give them some indifferent food and lock them up in a fish house, which was done after the prisoners had been robbed of nearly everything they had, including their shoes and hose.

In the morning they were taken on a march overland, their feet being much cut, to a place named Morteer, where a gun was fired in honor of taking Yankee prisoners; they were then thrown into a guardhouse. This was May, 1781; it was September before a considerable group of captives set sail aboard a sloop-of-war for delivery to England, but the ship was wrecked off St. John's, and the people in her only attained safety after considerable hardships. Another sloop-of-war arrived to take the prisoners to England; her captain was an old British sea dog who had six men flogged a day, and he wished to force Sherburne and another boy into the British service. The counsel of his lieutenant prevailed; Sherburne was sent to Old Mill Prison, and it was the spring of 1782 before he was exchanged.

When he got home again things were so changed and so many people gone that he did not wish to stay and at once entered in the privateer *Scorpion*. She had bad luck too, being taken by a British frigate. Young Sherburne lived out the rest of the war amid the stinks and darks of the horrible prison ship *Jersey* in New York harbor, at the end having reached the age of seventeen without anything to show for his years but tales of misfortune and suffering.

These are the extremes, Drowne and Sherburne, rich in three weeks or three years of misery for no result at all; and they do not count the men cut in two by a cannon ball or those who died of typhus in prison. In between must be imagined all possible variations; the 12-gun sloop *Revenge* of Massachusetts, which took two ships, one laden with rum and sugar, one with French wines, then three brigs, one of which was abandoned to the prisoners because the privateersmen already had enough; *Warren* of Massachusetts, which took a ship with a cargo of gold-dust and ivory, and then was herself taken, so that her people had to wait till the end of the war to collect their money; *General Mifflin,* brig, which took two prizes and then fell in with a British privateer of 18, from which she had no profit but thirteen casualties, the pair abandoning each other as too tough for digestion.

Underneath and through it all there ran a developing complex of several patterns interlocking. One was the pattern of the ships: after the first rush the pulling longboats, coastal schooners, and warmed-over merchant craft, clearly no longer paid, in view of the gathering number and efficiency of British patrols. Something better was needed; and American shipbuilding began to flex its muscles and stretch, turning out new craft for the special purpose of privateering in the same empirical spirit that produced the Continental frigates. What were the requirements? Not for a fighting ship, though the increasing armament of British merchants and the number of their letters-of-marque brought it about that the average of the 136 privateers of 1776 carried slightly under 10 guns, while the average of the 449 privateers of 1781 was slightly over 15. The requirement was for sea-keeping qualities, ships that could make long voyages; and above all for speed to keep away from cruisers and overhaul anything else that floated. Inasmuch as it was possible to make a profit on a privateer with a single cruise and a single capture, it was worth while building especially for speed—and speed the builders got. It became possible to recognize an American privateer at a distance merely by her appearance. These privateers were mostly sloops, brigs, and ship-rigged vessels; the hour when the schooner's qualities for the work would be realized had not yet struck.

The pattern of strategy: in 1777 the number of privateers in commission and operating fell off by nearly half from 1776 as the British cruisers mopped up slow and inefficient ships. But by 1778 the French alliance was in force, and the conditions of the Seven Years'

War were reproduced with a change of accent. French fleets were on the ocean, forcing the British to concentrate their ships to meet this threat. At the same time the presence of French cruisers made dangerous the '76–'77 solution of scattering small British units for commerce protection. Not many of the French cruisers were off the American coasts, but there were plenty in the West Indies and in European waters. French bases were open to support operations. And the Royal Navy of France was in a period of renaissance which brought it to an efficiency greater than it had known since Louis XIV. The American privateers thus enjoyed the support of a powerful regular navy, and in strategic terms, acted as the light cruising vessels and raiders of that navy. Their numbers and effectiveness grew steadily; 115 in commission in 1778, 167 in 1779, 228 in 1780, 449 in 1781; and the captures piled up to a total of over 600 British ships by the end of the war.

The pattern of the men: in the beginning it was all seamen and watermen from the harbors. But as the war deepened and armies marched through the land, destroying normal activities, there became more and more Dr. Drownes, people who took up privateering to recover their fortunes or simply because there was little else to do. Clerks, farmers, lawyers, woodsmen went to sea, and with a leaven of professional seamen made very good practitioners of the privateering profession, for the basic techniques were simple and everyone of the age was somewhat a man of his hands. One William Whipple wrote from Portsmouth: "There is at this time five privateers fitting out here, which I suppose will take 400 men. These must be for the greater part Countrymen, for the Seamen are chiefly gone, and most of them in Halifax gaol." The same observer added: "No kind of business can so effectually introduce Luxury, Extravagance and every kind of Dissipation, that tend to the destruction of the morals of the people." That is, the privateersmen speedily became a hard lot, regardless of origin.

Finally, the pattern of the officers, most important of all in this essentially individualist economy and area of operation:

1—JONATHAN HARADEN. He was from Salem, long a seaman, who entered as a lieutenant in the Massachusetts state brig *Tyrannicide,* 14, in 1776; saw service in her through the middle of 1779, when she made several captures, two of them after sharp little combats that taught Haraden something of sea fighting. *Tyrannicide* was one of the ships burned up in Staltonstall's misbegotten Penobscot expedition that summer; Haraden returned to Salem and was quickly given command of the letter-of-marque *General Pickering,* 16, with a cargo of sugar for Bilbao, then a great resort of the privateers. Off the port they fell in by night with the British privateer *Golden Eagle,* 22; Haraden hailed her to say he was an American frigate of the largest class, and secured her surrender without a shot. Next morning and in full sight of the shore, a large ship was approaching; a British cruiser-privateer of no less than 42 guns. "I shan't run from her," said Haraden, and did not, maneuvering among the shoals at the entrance of the port so skillfully that he raked the Briton again and again, and eventually drove her in flight. When he landed he was carried through the streets on the shoulders of wildly enthusiastic Spaniards, for it was something of an event to see St. George's cross running away from a battle. On the return voyage Haraden found three armed merchantmen off Sandy Hook, two of 14 guns each, one of 12; and took them all by skillful maneuver. On the following cruise *General Pickering* fell in with a King's mail packet from the West Indies. They had a four-hour fight and Haraden, hauling off to repair damages, found he had but one more round of ammunition; but he closed in again, flying a red flag for "No quarter," and hailed to say he would send them to the bottom unless they surrendered in five minutes. Down came the British flag. In all he took ships carrying a total of 1,000 guns, and went on to live a long life, wealthy and respected.

2—LAMBERT WICKES. He was really an officer of the Continental Navy, but the British called him a pirate, and he operated as a corsair. In the spring of 1776, the Marine Committee, then the naval administrative body, gave him command of the brig *Reprisal,* 14, fitted out at Philadelphia and sent to the West Indies, the principal mission being to cover the shipments of munitions being bootlegged through from France and Spain. On the way he took three ships, the prize crews for which left him very shorthanded, so that when he fell in with the British brig-sloop *Shark,* 16, off Martinique, he only fired to damage his opponent aloft, then tacked away out of action. The next year *Reprisal* was sent to France with dispatches; Wickes captured several ships during the run and sent them in to French ports, which caused vigorous diplomatic exchanges between the British ambassador and His Most Christian Majesty's ministers. Wickes was the first captain to carry the new flag to Europe. After a refit, *Reprisal* cruised in Biscay and took five ships, one of them a 16-gun mail packet after a sharp fight. Wickes sold his prizes, used the money for another refit and to rearm his little cruiser and in July made a cruise quite around Ireland, during which he took sixteen ships and caused a great fluttering at Lloyds. On his way home at the end of summer, his ship went down in a storm off the Grand Banks of Newfoundland and the nascent navy lost one of the few officers who might have given it character.

3—GUSTAVUS CONYNGHAM. He was an American mariner of Irish birth, sent to Europe in 1777 by the Marine Committee to purchase munitions. The American commissioners to France bought a lugger at Dunkerque, commissioned her under the name of *Surprise* and placed him in command. Conyngham took two ships, but the British protests were so energetic that when he returned to port the French government took his commission away and threw him into prison. Franklin got him out, and he went back to Dunkerque, where a 10-gun cutter, *Revenge,* had been purchased and equipped with papers showing English ownership and a voyage to Norway as her purpose. The crew were mostly French; Conyngham cruised with his ship in the North Sea and all around England, taking so many prizes that the European print shops were full of ferocious-looking representations of him, bearing the caption: "Augustatus Kuningam, la terreur des Anglais." Cadiz was his port of call in 1778, where the British vessels in harbor were mortified to see *Revenge* exchange salutes with the Spanish admiral. Conyngham took several prizes among the Azores, then sailed for home by way of the West Indies. At Philadelphia his ship was sold out of service for lack of money to pay her crew, but immediately purchased by a group of merchants and fitted as a privateer, with Conyngham as captain. This was the end of his luck; two British frigates ran *Revenge* down among the islands and her captain was taken to England in irons as a pirate and thrown into Old Mill Prison. He escaped in November, 1779, but took no further part in the war.

4—JOSHUA BARNEY. The golden lad, the prince of privateers and adventurers, who became a shipmaster at 16. In 1777, aged eighteen, he was first officer of the brig *Andrew Doria,* 14, and was in her when she captured a British brig, of which he was made prize officer. This earned him an appointment as first lieutenant of the new frigate *Virginia,* but she was the ship that Nicholson ran aground in Chesapeake Bay, and which was delivered to the British by her anarchic crew, so Barney became a prisoner. He was released on parole, and just after word of an exchange came through in November, 1778, met on a street in Baltimore his old captain of *Andrew Doria* days, Isaiah Robinson, who was fitting out a fine new privateer named *General Mercer.* He offered Barney the first lieutenancy. The ship sailed for France in February, 1779, with a load of tobacco and twelve guns of almost as many calibers. On the way they encountered a heavy British letter-of-marque, which held them in action through most of a night, and at dawn came in to board over *General Mercer*'s stern, where the privateer had no guns. But Barney had chopped a hole in the counter during the night and placed a 3-pounder there. As the Britisher's bowsprit came in, her forecastle black with men, he fired the piece, loaded with stove lids, crowbars, and anything else that was iron. The would-be boarders shrieked and fled, down came the pursuer's headsail, and she was glad to get away. At Bordeaux the *General Mercer*'s tobacco was sold for enough to fit the ship with her proper armament of eighteen brass 6-pounders, and she took aboard a cargo of brandy and claret. On the way home she fought with and captured a British letter-of-marque which Barney brought into port as prize master, the proceeds of the voyage being sufficient for Captain Robinson to retire and for Barney to get married. On a trip from Philadelphia with his new wife, somebody robbed his chest of all the money he owned; therefore early in 1780 he accepted an appointment as lieutenant aboard the new Continental sloop-of-war *Saratoga,* 20. She was a stout ship with a good captain, James Young, who kept real man-o'-war discipline, and in the sea lane between the West Indies and Halifax captured a big letter-of-marque with a cargo of sugar and rum. Barney was sent aboard as prize officer with eight men, but before he got to port was run down by an English battleship and carried off to New York, prisoner for the second time. The local British admiral was kind to Barney, but before long that officer was replaced by another, who took a low view of American traitors, and shipped a batch of them to England in the hold of a ship, prac-

tically without food and so swimming in their own filth that they
had to be hoisted out with block and tackle to be taken to Old Mill
Prison. Here Barney recovered his health, and by his own adroitness
and with the help of money sent by Dr. Franklin, effected a sensational escape. He befriended a seasick lady aboard a ship for Ostend;
she turned out to be the mistress of the Emperor of Austria, who
smoothed Barney's way for a passage to Bilbao, where he joined the
Boston privateer *Cicero*, assisted in the taking of a couple of prizes,
and reached the colonies again in the winter of 1781. The Cabots of
Boston offered him command of a fine new privateer, but instead he
took a sleigh over the winter roads to Philadelphia to find a son he
had never seen. He was barely there before being offered another
command, mainly through the efforts of Robert Morris, the financier
of the Revolution, who had conceived a high opinion of this young
man.

In the coves along Delaware Bay numerous heavy pull-boats hung
out, called "refugee boats," manned by professed Tories, but operating rather for their own profit than out of loyalty to the Crown. They
made heavy going for merchant ships out of Philadelphia, being supported by an occasional British frigate or sloop in the mouth of the
bay. The merchants banded together, purchased a cargo ship named
Hyder Ally, armed her with sixteen 6-pounders, and she was Barney's
new command, to convoy thirteen of their ships to sea. He was ready in a
little over a week, eighteen days from reaching home; his marines were a
number of Bucks County backwoods riflemen. As he led his convoy
down the bay, the British had the frigate *Quebec*, 32, in the offing,
and sent on ahead the brig-sloop *General Monk*, of eighteen 9-pound-
ers, eighty-one pounds weight of metal broadside to *Hyder Ally's* forty-
eight, but Barney did not hesitate for all that, bearing boldly in. The ships
closed; the young captain said swiftly to his helmsman: "Follow my
next order by the rule of contrary," then shouted so as to be heard
aboard the enemy: "Hard a-port your helm!" *General Monk* ported
hers to keep abreast, but only succeeded in bringing her bowsprit
over *Hyder Ally's* side as the latter turned sharp in the other direction. Barney's ship raked the Englishman terribly and his marines
denuded her decks; in twenty-eight minutes the enemy surrendered.
The youthful captain crowned his work by hoisting British colors on
both and going upstream before the frigate could make up her mind

to interfere. *General Monk* was renamed *General Washington* and ran numerous errands for the Continental Congress till after the war. The Bucks County marines kept their organization and became famous during the Civil War as the "Pennsylvania Bucktails." Barney grew very rich, served in the French navy as a captain, and later commanded one of the most famous privateers of the War of 1812.

5—JOHN BARRY. Gilbert Stuart's portrait of him shows an amiable, cheerful man, somewhat stout, as might be expected of a shipping magnate. He had charge of fitting out the first Continental warships, *Alfred* and her consorts, and on March 14, 1776, received command of the *Lexington,* a brigantine armed with sixteen 4-pounders. In her he did well enough off the capes to receive appointment to the new frigate *Effingham,* but she was one of the vessels destroyed in the Delaware when the British came to Philadelphia, and Barry saw no more service, except in a barge raid down the river, until placed in command of *Raleigh,* 32, early in 1778. Her misfortune has already been told (see page 31); when Barry returned to Philadelphia after the loss of the ship, there was no Continental vessel for him and he was glad to become commodore of a group of letters-of-marque working to the West Indies. Two voyages were made with great profit from both cargo and the capture of British ships. He was considering another, when the Board of Admiralty, now the controlling body of the Navy, sent him to Boston to take charge of *Alliance,* 36, by all odds the finest of the Continental ships of war. Two whole months were spent in a court-martial of her former commander, a half-insane Frenchman named Pierre Landais, whom the American commissioners had picked up in France. Another month passed in trying unsuccessfully to recruit a crew. When *Alliance* sailed in February of 1781, she had little more than half a complement, including British, soldiers, jailbirds, and Indians. The mission was to carry John Laurens on an important embassy to France. *Alliance* had not been two days on the return voyage when one of the forecastle hands came aft to give information that the British and malcontents aboard were planning mutiny and the seizure of the ship. Barry had the named ringleaders aft and flogged them until they talked, and so on until twenty-five were punished. During the voyage two heavy British privateers were taken, but Barry had to neglect capturing a couple of merchant men he sighted because he simply did not have men enough for prize crews. Off Cape Sable he fell in with the British ship-sloop *Atalanta,* 16, and the brig-sloop *Trepassey,* 14, in weather almost a flat calm. The two Britons got out sweeps and worked within range of the frigate at a point where her guns would not bear, damaging her seriously and wounding Barry himself. But the breeze lifted, *Alliance* turned, her 12-pounders spoke out loudly, and down came the flags on both vessels.

After this the frigate made two more packet runs, carrying the Marquis de Lafayette to France and some money back to America, but spent most of her time in port, trying to gather a crew. In 1782 at New London, Barry had another mutiny to quell, when the crew set up an outcry for "Liberty and back allowances!" The accounts he submitted for expenses personally incurred as far back as the fitting out of *Lexington* were not even brought to audit until two years after the end of the war. He went into the East India trade.

VII

But the greatest of the individualist seamen, the one who did more than any other, was the mysterious John Paul Jones. John Adams visited this brave, vain, hot-tempered little Scotsman when he was stationed in France and recorded a shrewd Yankee appraisal. Noting that Jones had designed his own uniforms instead of following the design decreed by Congress, Adams went on: "Eccentricities and irregularities are to be expected from him—they are in his character, they are visible in his eyes. His voice is soft and still and small, his eye has keenness and wildness and softness in it."

Jones had been nominated the premier lieutenant on the list when the original roster of officers was prepared; was an immensely strong man physically, with very decided ideas of his own and no influence but that he gained by conduct. Although he operated as the king of the corsairs, Jones paradoxically never sailed in a private ship, and spent the best part of the Revolution in trying to make the Continental Navy into something like a regular service.

In May of 1776, Jones was appointed to the sloop *Providence* of Esek Hopkins's squadron; went to attack the Newfoundland fishers, which Congress had thought a job for a fleet, and singlehanded quite ruined those at Canso, in Nova Scotia, taking sixteen ships, of which half were sent in and the rest destroyed. A British frigate chased him; he outran her, impudently firing a single musket every time she delivered a broadside.

Arrived home, he was given command of *Alfred* and sent to the Cape Breton fisheries, where he did another heavy stroke of work, taking a whole fleet of prizes, including a big transport that held enough clothes for all Washington's army. But when he reached Boston he was greeted by an order to turn the ship over to one Elisha Hinman. This was part of as dirty a deal as was ever seen in American politics, which were as dirty during the Revolution as they ever would be. Congress had just passed a list establishing the relative rank of naval captains. James Nicholson, who lost *Virginia*, stood at the head of it and Jones, who had already done more than any other, was eighteenth. Most men would have resigned; this one was possessed of a high romantic ardor, an almost passionate sense of public duty, and he had the favor of Robert Morris, who by default had become a kind of general manager of the navy. Morris sent Jones to Portsmouth, where the new flushdeck sloop-of-war *Ranger,* 18, was building. The captain was to sail her to France, and there take command of one of the frigates which the American commissioners were procuring in Europe.

His lieutenants—as impossible and inexperienced a lot as could be conceived—were chosen by the local politicians. It is recorded in a diary of the voyage out that Jones had a dispute with one of them, ordered him under confinement to his cabin: "and as he was descending the ladder kicked him in the breech several times; in one-half an hour after, sent his servant to invite the lieutenant to come and dine with him." That was the way things were with the officers of *Ranger,* and the crew were a lot of sullen devils. Nor were matters better when France was reached, for one of the commissioners was Arthur Lee, whose character was founded in a combined malice and conceit so colossal as to be difficult to express in words. He hated Benjamin Franklin and Silas Deane, the other commissioners, and since Jones and Franklin hit it off at once, included the captain in his hatred. Someone in Lee's entourage leaked to the British that the fine new frigate *Indien,* building in a Dutch yard, was for the Americans. The British protested so vigorously that the ship was stopped.

Jones went up to Paris, where Franklin introduced him at court during the winter of 1777; got enough help to refit his ship and put to sea with her in February, 1778, dropping down to Quiberon Bay, where a French battle-fleet lay at anchor. There was a serious conference on protocol with Admiral Lamotte-Picquet; on February 14, the little *Ranger* ran down a line of booming French battleships, saluting each and by each being saluted—the first time for the Stars and Stripes, first recognition of the United States as an independent nation. It was not many days later that the ultimata began to flow and France was in the war.

The commander of a single small cruiser is hardly in a position to influence strategy, but John Paul Jones thought in terms of doing just that. He headed right up into the Irish Sea, with an idea he never ceased to express to anyone who would listen—that of attacking English commerce on its own doorstep and so drawing off forces that might be used against the rebellious colonists elsewhere. At Whitehaven in Scotland he landed a boat expedition with the purpose of burning the congregated ships in the harbor; two of his lieutenants were too frightened to go and the crew half mutinous, partly from fear, partly because this original Jones insisted on destroying his captures instead of sending them in to make prize money for all. He did succeed in spiking the guns at the harbor entrance and firing one ship, a proceeding that made a horrible row in England; then stood across to Carrickfergus on the Irish coast, where H.M.S. *Drake*, 20, lay at anchor. Jones's purpose was to sail in and cut her out, but his crew balked, the lieutenants backed them, and he had what amounted to a mutiny on his hands. *Drake* saved him considerable trouble by coming out to look for him, with a doubled crew of volunteers aboard; under Jones' iron will and skillful handling the semi-mutinous crew shot so hard and straight that *Drake* early became a wreck and a prize, with forty-two casualties.

Jones carried her into Brest and that was all he could do. The malign influence of Arthur Lee soared up like a cloud, the commissioners refused to pay the sailors, and the end of the story gave *Ranger* to Thomas Simpson, the most cowardly and incompetent of the lieutenants, who promptly lost her. The intrigues, cheats, and shiftings around the doomed court of Louis XVI as Jones tried to get another command form no real part of naval history, but his plan does. What he wanted was a raiding squadron that would strike a blow of real strategic effect. He proposed to lead it into the Channel approaches, capture one of the rich West India convoys, smash at Liverpool with a landing force, then while the pursuit gathered, double Scotland for another blow at the great shipping port of Leith, and bring matters to a climax by taking the annual convoy from the Baltic, which carried naval stores vital to Britain's sea power.

Even in its whittled-down stage this project came so near success that it is worth recording the process of diminution. First the landing force dropped out, no transports being available, which eliminated the descent on Liverpool. The only ship that could be found for Jones was an old East Indiaman with her timbers half rotten; she was named *Bon Homme Richard* in compliment to Franklin and converted into some kind of a frigate by putting six 18-pounders on her lower deck, twenty-eight 12s on the main deck and eight 9s on the forecastle and quarter-deck. In addition, he was given the splendid new frigate *Alliance,* but any advantage from that source was canceled by her captain, Pierre Landais—a man plausible and vivacious, but cowardly and utterly self-centered, who ended up by going insane. *Pallas,* 30, was a heavy privateer taken into the naval service, commanded by Denis Cottineau, a good man; *Cerf,* an 18-gun cutter, a very fine ship, and *Vengeance,* a 12-gun brigantine.

This was a respectable striking force, even if somewhat less than Jones had hoped or been promised, but his crew of 227 (he got a few more later) was an odd patchwork, contained only 79 Americans, the rest being English, Irish, Scottish, French, and Portuguese. The ominous personality of Landais lay like a dead weight on the whole, and before the little fleet even sailed the intriguers in the background imposed on it a form of agreement, which in effect placed all strategic decisions in the hands of a committee of captains. The French Minister of Marine added an instruction that any prizes taken after the sweep around Britain were to be sent into Texel, off the coast of Holland, whence the squadron was to convoy merchant ships to France. After various mischances the fleet sailed from Groix Roads on August 14, 1779, with the seeds of failure sprouting in its vitals.

A few prizes were taken off the coast of Ireland, but *Cerf* mistakenly fired on *Bon Homme Richard*'s longboat in a fog (causing its loss with the third lieutenant) and then deserted the squadron.

Landais would not hear of attacking the West India convoy and also sailed over the horizon, leaving Jones without the force to deal with this group and its escorts. *Alliance* somehow managed to find the squadron north of Scotland, but as the expedition pressed on toward Leith, she vanished once more. Off Leith, the captains of *Pallas* and little *Vengeance* thought the place altogether too formidable for attack. Jones had the two men aboard and talked till eleven at night, by which time he persuaded them, but when the argument was over and the marines loaded into boats for the descent, a gale of wind blew up, so severe that the men had to be taken aboard again.

Three of the four elements of the raiding plan had thus been knocked out. Jones pressed on toward the area where the Baltic convoy might reasonably be expected, and during a dark night sighted two ships, near which he lay to till dawn. They proved to be *Alliance* and *Pallas*. It was closing afternoon of the next day when no less than forty-one sail topped the horizon to the north-northeast—the Baltic convoy beyond a doubt. Jones made the signal to form line of battle, to which *Alliance* paid not the slightest attention, and headed toward them. The date was September 23, 1779, and they were off the cliffs of Flamborough Head, to which numerous citizens came out at the news of the ships maneuvering for battle. There had not been one in sight of English shores for a hundred years.

The convoy scattered for the coast at once; the escorts bore down toward the Americans. They were the 20-gun sloop-of-war *Countess of Scarborough,* and *Serapis,* 44 (under Captain Richard Pearson) a new, strong frigate with 18-pounders on her gundeck, something like three to two of the force of *Bon Homme Richard,* and a much better sailer. It was 7:15 in the evening when the two major ships came side by side and began firing, while *Pallas* paired off with *Countess of Scarborough* and *Alliance* lay off a mile distant, with Landais simply staring, oblivious of the pleas of his officers and crew to join action.

That fight has received an almost unlimited press; and it deserves every word. At the first fire, two of *Bon Homme Richard*'s 18-pounders burst, killing all their crews, and it was judged too dangerous to fire the rest. The survivors of the heavy battery went up to help Lieutenant Richard Dale, in charge of the 12-pounders above. Under Jones' orders he was directing his guns chiefly at *Serapis*' masts and rigging to cut down her maneuvering ability, but in the meanwhile the English ship's long 18s were tearing *Bon Homme Richard*'s guts out. One by one the 12-pounders fell silent, crews killed, pieces dismounted. The old Indiaman had taken so many shot on the waterline that she was filling, beside being on fire in more than one place. But on the upper deck, the fire of a file of steady French marines cut down everyone in sight, and when *Serapis* jabbed her bowsprit over *Bon Homme Richard*'s quarter, Jones himself leaped up with a rope and lashed her fast.

It is said that he cried: "I've got the son of a whore!" and he very likely did. The ships swung bow to stern and stern to bow, so locked that the crews of *Serapis'* guns had to run their rammers into the holes they had made in the American. *Bon Homme Richard* had been so cut through that many of their shot went in and out without touching, and the last of Jones' 12-pounders went, leaving him with only the 9-pounders mounted above. At this moment *Alliance* made her appearance through the smoke and flame. She came right down toward the struggling ships—and poured one broadside, then another into *Bon Homme Richard,* killing some fourteen men, while people shouted, screamed, and tried to make signals. The master-at-arms released two hundred British prisoners from the hold, but Jones shot one and with Lieutenant Dale's help persuaded the others their only hope of survival was to man the pumps and keep the ship from sinking.

The gunner came aft to haul down the colors, but they had already been shot away. The carpenter on the forecastle cried to the English for quarter and someone hailed from *Serapis* to ask Jones whether he had struck.

"Struck, sir? I have not yet begun to fight!" Jones replied in a watchword for the ages.

He had not, either. His French marines kept shooting people down on *Serapis'* upper deck, her tops were cleared out, and an American seaman inched along the mainyard to begin dropping grenades toward the British ship's main hatch. The third one popped in, on the gundeck it set fire to rows of cartridges lined up ready for the guns, there was a frightful running explosion that killed more than twenty men and disabled the main battery. Captain Pearson called for boarders, but could do nothing against the musketry that dominated the weather decks, and at 10:30 struck his flag. They made him a baronet for his valiant defense against a far weaker ship; when Jones heard of it he said he hoped to fight Pearson again and get him into the House of Lords. *Countess of Scarborough* had already surrendered to *Pallas*.

VIII

The outcome of that heroic duel was anticlimax and disappointment. *Bon Homme Richard* was too shattered and too badly afire to be saved; she sank at dawn and Jones put out in the captured and badly battered frigate, ultimately to reach Texel. Diplomatic action from Britain clipped his wings for a long time, and court intrigues in France did the rest by depriving him of his prize. He ultimately reached America aboard a small supply ship, and the fame of his great exploit having become what it was, Congress voted him the command of the line-of-battleship *America,* building at Portsmouth, and sent him to superintend her completion. She was not quite ready when a French battleship was wrecked on the bar in Boston harbor, and Congress both expressed its gratitude to France and relieved itself of the need for finding money and men to equip *America* by presenting her to Louis XVI.

So John Paul Jones passed out of the story, leaving a heritage of indomitable courage and presence of mind which has never been erased. The qualities were there all right, and they were of immense inspirational value; but in the establishment of a regular naval service they were not the most essential things. The real contribution made by John Paul Jones was in the domain of strategy—how to strike with an inferior, an amateur, raiding force where it really hurt and had an effect on the war; as in the raid on the fisheries; *Ranger's* trip to the Irish Sea; and the plan for the squadron around England, not making prizes for personal profit, but doing something to change the war. Nobody wanted that contribution at the time and Jones remained a solitary and misunderstood figure, while the Continental Navy came to a miserable end, borne down under the weight of administrative officers and captains alike concerned with self-aggrandizement and profits.

The tiny Continental Navy faded away before the overwhelming numbers of the British blockading squadrons, but for anyone who cared to see it was plain that sea power was the vital ingredient in the achievement of American independence. Through most of the war, the British had moved their troops up and down the coast at will by sea. When Cornwallis retreated to the peninsula at Yorktown, the sea road to safety was closed to him. The British fleet that had sailed to his rescue was met by a French force off the entrance to Chesapeake Bay. Nobody "won" the battle that followed in terms of captured and sunken ships—but the British were unable to enter the Chesapeake and Cornwallis was abandoned. The siege of Yorktown and American freedom were won by the ships of our allies. To some Americans, at least, it was obvious that to keep that freedom we needed ships—a Navy—of our own.

★ ★ ★ ★ ★

2

The Second Birth

APPARENTLY it was obvious to no one of political standing, since for several years the new nation had no navy at all. In some ways this was perhaps fortunate for at least the defects of the Continental service were granted no opportunity to become bred in the bone. During those fifteen years there happened two things of the greatest importance. One was that England and Revolutionary France embarked on the series of wars that was to last for more than two decades. Every nation of Europe became involved and their ships lawful prize to one party or the other; but America remained neutral. The farming areas began to produce a surplus of food just at the time when European food production declined under the weight of the war, and at the same time the European navigation laws became obsolete because the sugar growers of the West Indies simply had to move their product in American ships if they wanted to move it at all. American seaborne trade had become important before the Revolution; now at the turn of the century it became of global significance, at least the second largest in the world; and it was no longer carried on in furtive little schooners that scuttled among the islands on their smuggling missions, but in ships of every class, which made Naples and Copenhagen and Canton their ports of call.

The second great alteration was that the colonies had united under a central government with taxing powers and George Washington at its head. As early as 1791 that government began to consider a naval force for the protection of its growing commerce, not at this date so much because of the restrictions imposed by the warring powers— who benefited as much as they suffered from having Americans in the carrying trade, and were only anxious to have that trade drawn into their own orbit—as because of the Barbaries.

Who were the Barbaries? The four states of the North African coast, Morocco, Algiers, Tunis, Tripoli, which for more than two centuries had lived by piracy. The smaller nations paid them tribute to let shipping alone; the great commercial sea powers, England, France, Holland, paid subsidies to keep the Barbary powers in operation as a checking factor which imposed on neutrals' commerce the same handicaps they themselves suffered from the wars. When the bey or dey of one of the Barbary powers decided he wanted money, he declared war on one of the small nations by having its consul's flagpole cut down, and sent out his corsairs to take ships. The crews were hustled into slave-pens and set to work hauling stones under the lash, with an iron ring around the ankle and a daily ration of three loaves of black bread and some vinegar. Those who survived might be ransomed later; the captured ships were sold at a handsome profit. The negotiation of a new treaty of peace had to be paid for with an additional honorarium.

In 1792, the U.S. Senate approved a payment of $100,000 annually to Algiers, Tunis, and Tripoli, with $40,000 ransom for the American slaves then held. The next year, when the general sea war in Europe broke out, American ships began to penetrate the Mediterranean in numbers, and in spite of the payments to the Barbary states, no less than eleven were taken by the Algerines. This sent Washington to Congress with a recommendation for a naval force as the only means for dealing with these bandits. But it was an economy-minded Congress, dominated by such ideas as that a navy was a menace to liberty, and that a navy would probably involve us in complications with Britain. When a bill authorizing six frigates passed early in 1794, it carried a proviso that if a peace, any peace, should be made with Algiers, construction would stop. The peace was made, and the frigates held on their building ways. It is worth noting that while the appropriation for the six ships was just under $700,000, the Algerine treaty cost over a million in tribute, including the donation of a 36-gun ship to enable the pirates to capture more Christian slaves. But no navy; dangerous to liberty. The forces at sea were to be under the direction of the Secretary of War.

There the matter hung until 1797. By this date unescorted British ships had grown quite scarce on the seas, and it was hard for French privateers to make a living, especially in the West Indies, where it was estimated that one hundred fifty of them were operating. The French government topped a series of decrees regulating neutral commerce with one that any ship carrying goods to an enemy country was subject to confiscation. A group of American sea captains signed a petition to the Secretary of State listing twenty-seven ships so taken and plundered, and these were by no means all. John Adams was President now; he sent three commissioners to negotiate with the French government. But that government had become the Directory, the most corrupt of all the series that grew out of the French Revolution; it met the commissioners with a flat demand for money, 32,000,000 Dutch florins as a loan, and 1,200,000 gold livres as a present.

The payment of tribute to the Barbaries was something that could be swept under a rug; everyone else was doing it. But with a major and supposedly civilized power like France, it was a different matter, especially in view of the sums involved; and the insolence of the French privateersmen who came to American ports to spend the money they had taken from American ships did not help matters. The whole country thrilled at the news of how C. C. Pinckney banged his fist on the table, crying: "Millions for defense, but not a cent for tribute!" [1] And on a wave of shouting and Adams black cockades in the streets the United States Navy was abruptly born, to the lilting strains of the new march song: "Hail, Columbia."

II

Some merchant ships were purchased and armed, as during the Revolution; some revenue cutters were taken into naval service; the shipping men of Philadelphia, New York, Salem, and Boston, hard hit by the French, contributed to build gift ships from their cities. But the heart of the new navy was in the six Washington frigates, and they were something to talk about. When the first President got his authorization to build them, he turned to Joshua Humphreys, a Philadelphia Quaker who had been the junior partner in the firm of Wharton & Humphreys, when they laid down the basic design for the

---

[1] As a matter of historical record, it was not Pinckney who said it, but he received the credit. What Pinckney said when the demand came up was: "No, and no again. Not a penny."

Continental ships. This Humphreys had ideas of his own, which through a long line of succession have profoundly influenced the building of every American warship.

"As our navy for a considerable time will be inferior in numbers," he reported to Washington, "we are to consider what size ships will be most formidable and be an overmatch for those of the enemy; such frigates as in blowing weather would be an overmatch for double-deck ships and in light winds to evade coming to action. Frigates will be the first object, and none ought to be built less than 150-foot keel, to carry 30 24-pounders on the gundeck. Ships of this construction have everything in their favor, their great length gives them an advantage of sailing, which is an object of the first magnitude."

It was a concept so enormous as to be fantastic, so grand as to be grandiose. Since the Revolution, the ordinary heavy cruiser of European practice had grown from the 32-gun 12-pounder ship to the 36, with about twenty-four long 18s on the main deck, 125 feet length of keel. The 24-pounder was exclusively a battleship gun; to put such pieces on a vessel of frigate construction would obviously make her hog and strain, leave her clumsy and unmaneuverable; and the length proposed by Humphreys was twenty feet greater than that of any existing frigate, almost exactly that of *America,* the battleship Paul Jones never got to command. Humphreys proposed to meet the difficulty about structure by using enormous beams and bracing; the difficulty about clumsiness by sweeping up the mainmast one hundred eighty feet from the deck, and finally by trimming the hull to the fish-like lines of those Chesapeake Bay schooners, the Baltimore clippers. Washington said yes: and so built, so arranged, the frigate *United States,* 44, slid down the ways on May 10, 1797, first ship of the United States Navy, followed in no great space of time by *Constellation,* 38 (a smaller version), *Constitution,* 44, *President,* 44, *Congress,* 38, *Chesapeake,* 38.

They excited general derision, especially from British sea-captains. But there was one thing that did not excite derision, and that was Mr. Adams' method of recruiting his crews. He considered the British practice of forcibly impressing sailors from the merchant marine as degrading to free men, and in the Revolution he had had close experience of how a volunteer system failed under the superior appeal of privateering. His solution was to make the Navy so attractive that no seaman in his right mind could afford to overlook such an opportunity. It was laid down that there would be prize money for all, at a fixed rate per ton and gun of the captures, and double if the enemy were of superior force. Wages were set at $15 to $17 per month and found, $7 more than merchantmen were paid, and above the best rates for skilled mechanics ashore. Adams wanted young men to grow up with the service: all captains were instructed to take in as many boys as possible. Sailors were invited aboard to view the roomy quarters in the enormous new frigates and to have a meal from a ration bill set so high that the American seaman got more in two days than a British sailor did in a week—better food, too.

In an age when food preservation did not go beyond salt meat in casks and bread baked rock-hard, it was solid diet: Sunday, one and one-half pounds of beef and one-half pound of rice; Monday, one pound of pork, one-half pint of peas, and four ounces of cheese; Tuesday, one and one-half pounds of beef and one pound of potatoes; Wednesday, one-half pint of rice, two ounces of butter, and six ounces of molasses; Thursday, one pound of pork and one-half pint of peas; Friday, one pound salt fish, one pound of potatoes, and two ounces of butter; Saturday, one pound of pork, one-half pint of peas, four ounces of cheese. In addition, every man received a pound of bread and either a half pint of spirits—usually rum—or a quart of beer per day.

Under such conditions, the captains of the new Navy had no trouble whatever filling up their complements; they could pick and choose among the world-girdling seamen.

The officers also were a somewhat different lot than those of the Revolution. Pay was better: a captain drew $75 a month plus six rations a day figured at 28 cents each. Lieutenants made $50 and three rations, surgeons about the same; warrants $20 plus two rations. The officers' uniform remained blue, but epaulets were used for rank, the buttons were brass, and the breeches and facings were buff.

President Adams had to pay a certain amount of deference to patronage to keep his hold on Congress, but he set his flinty blue New England nose against jobbery as a principle; it appeared mostly on the lowest levels, where young sprigs could be taken in as midshipmen or very junior lieutenants and later trained. The higher officers were appointed on merit, or supposed merit. John Barry became head of the service, with *United States* under his command. Samuel Nicholson of Maryland, a political appointment, ranked second, but proved incompetent and after one cruise was sent ashore and never served again. Then came Silas Talbot, an army officer who had run a cutting-out expedition during the Revolution and later commanded a successful privateer; followed by Richard Dale, Jones' lieutenant in his great battle, who was the first captain of the new Navy to go to sea, being commander of the East Indiaman *Ganges,* which arrived at Philadelphia early in 1798 and was promptly armed and commissioned.

But the real prize drawn by the nascent Navy was in its fifth ranking captain, Thomas Truxtun, a sea-squire, a man of substance from Jamaica, Long Island, who had commanded two highly successful privateers during the Revolution. He was also a famous squire of dames, and so addicted to the pleasures of the table that he was bothered by gout, against which, in the custom of the age, he took peach brandy as a specific. Beneath this he was an intellectual of the first order who kept a large library, chiefly on naval subjects, read it most thoroughly and meditated deeply. He received command of *Constellation,* and even before putting to sea, drew up a long series of letters to his officers and petty officers laying down the duties of each in the most minute manner, which letters would be the foundation of definitive navy regulations.

These instructions were clearly not enough. The frigate had not been long at sea when discipline began slackening off in minor ways, in the old privateering fashion. A water cask sprang a leak; Truxtun snapped at the occasion to show how things would go by putting the crew on four and a half pints of water a day. He expected grumbling and threats of mutiny and he got them. After they had mounted for three days he had all hands piped to the waist, read the articles of war, then told them that he knew all about their mutinous intentions and who were concerned, he had had no one flogged since the ship went into commission, but would not hesitate to do so. A marine with a cutlass was stationed at the scuttlebutt to split the head of the first man who took more than his share. Three weeks later, as orders began to be executed with satisfactory snap, Truxtun returned the water ration to normal without a word.

The officers were checked sharply, too. Truxtun's method with them was less spectacular, but more useful in understanding what he accomplished. He wrote them letters and the letters have been preserved:

To Lieutenant William Cowper from Captain Thomas Truxtun,
Sir, Had I exercised my Authority, and arrested in all Cases
where many would not have Hesitated a Moment, the *Constellation* must 'ere now, have exhibited for the Out set of our Navy,
a sad spectacle indeed. But Sir, I have cast a Veil over so many
Improprieties and Neglects from Delicacy to Gentlemen's Char-
acters that patience and temper in me is now nearly exhausted.—
As I know full well that it is much easier to make a deep Wound
than to heal a small one, I have believed that a little Reflection
would induce you to appreciate the Measure I have taken to
make your duty plain, and easy. I have hitherto been disappointed, I can no longer continue disobeyed. If I am, Recourse
must be had to an Alternative, by no Means pleasant to me, or
honorable to you.

When the ship pulled in from an uneventful cruise off the eastern
coast in July 1798, two of the lieutenants liked this close treatment
so little that they resigned. Truxtun was quite willing to see them go,
but one of the mids who also wanted to leave was an eighteen-year-old
named David Porter, who seemed to have the makings, and him the
captain invited for dinner and a glass of sherry in the cabin, asking
him what concerned him. The young man gulped and murmured
something about not being able to bear such tyranny.

Truxtun's face wreathed in an expansive smile. "Why, you young
dog!" he shouted, "Don't you know that every time I swear at you,
you go up another round on the ladder of promotion? You shall never
leave the Navy if I can help it." Porter stayed, and it was well that he
stayed; and on that ship with her taut discipline and the daily exercises
at the guns, little practiced in other navies, there slowly grew such a
spirit that one of her lieutenants could write home: "With these officers and men I should feel happy to go alongside the best 50-gun ship
of the conquering French Republic."

Yet it must be remembered that this was one ship and one captain
only, and what was going on aboard *Constellation* was hidden from
all eyes but those of the new Secretary of the Navy, Benjamin Stoddert, who handled the official correspondence. Aboard the others it
was different: John Barry's *United States* was run more like a business
enterprise; on Moses Brown's *Merrimac*, 24, there were daily prayer

meetings; Daniel McNeill's *Portsmouth,* 24, was something of a mad-house, the captain full of inexplicable caprices. Transfers from ship to ship were rare, and although the officers were supposed to be part of a permanent establishment, there was still in them much of the old free-lance spirit, as evidenced by Richard Dale, fourth ranking captain, securing a furlough to command a big merchantman for China and taking no further part in the war. Put it this way: the new Navy had as yet no stamp or character of its own, was as much a collection of individual ships as that of the Revolution, differing from that earlier unhappy service chiefly in having better financial backing and not being borne down by the crushing weight of the British marine. By the middle of 1798 it was also out from under the wing of the War Department, which at first had been put in charge of both Army and Navy. In April the Navy Department was established with Stoddert as its first Secretary.

It had nevertheless yielded fairly impressive results in terms of its reason for establishment by the end of 1798. The total cost of the navy to that date was $2,500,000; the fall in insurance rates alone was $8,500,000. French privateers had been driven from American waters; Adams and Stoddert decided to go hunt them where they lived and set up two cruising squadrons for the West Indies. One was under Barry, with two of the 44s and several lesser ships, to work down the Windward Islands from St. Christopher to Barbados, with a base furnished by the British at Dominica; the second, under Truxtun, with *Constellation,* a corvette and two brigs, to cover the islands between St. Christopher and Puerto Rico. It can be said in anticipation that these squadrons did their job; in the next two years they laid by the heels no less than eighty-five sail of French privateers, and made the West Indies nearly as safe for shipping as Chesapeake Bay. But this was only a matter for congratulation in counting-houses and made no headlines; the really operative events of the war began on the morning of February 9, 1799, five leagues off the island of Nevis.

III

A brilliant Caribbean day with a strong breeze; *Constellation* sighted a large ship southward and bore down toward her. She was easily recognized as the French frigate *Insurgente,* 40, reputed the fastest sailing frigate in the world. But the ship the British had laughed at, walked right up on her, and when *Insurgente* tried to put on more sail, she lost a spar and they were side to side. With balls whistling through his rigging Truxtun held his fire till every gun bore; then let the Frenchman have the entire broadside, and the divisions fired at will. One of *Insurgente*'s shots damaged the American frigate's fore-topmast; young David Porter, kept in the navy by Truxtun, lowered the yard in its slings without orders and saved the mast. Meanwhile, *Insurgente* was being hit very hard below, half the guns in her starboard battery dismounted, her braces and headsail cut away, so that she slowed, *Constellation* gained, and swung under her bow for one, two, three, four raking broadsides that made a wreck of the French ship. Truxtun turned down her other side, and before the enemy could change batteries, gave her two more broadsides, turned under *Insurgente*'s stern, and her flag came down a little over an hour after the first gun.

The figure-chasers came around later to point out that *Constellation* outmatched her opponent by something like four to three in weight of broadside metal, but the chief reaction at the time was— how the Hell did that happen? For the French ship had lost seventy men, while *Contellation*'s casualties were but three, and Truxtun had picked *Insurgente* to pieces with an accuracy and dispatch that the best ship in the world might have envied. In the taverns where seafaring men met, in the grog-shops where sailors with "Constellation" broidered round their hats tossed off their rum, there were conversations about this, of which there is no precise record. But there was an inevitable if not easily definable seepage of ideas, and after the *Insurgente* battle, a Navy not quite two years old began to believe in itself and to take on the aspects of a professional service. Or maybe something more; the British Lords in Admiralty discouraged the use of powder and shot on anything but enemies, but John Adams, in the same spirit that made him raise sailors' wages, approved bills for unlimited practice without a murmur.

Then Truxtun did it again.

It was almost a year later, and he was Commodore (by courtesy) Truxtun now, in charge of the cruising station set up to watch Guadeloupe, a great haunt of privateers. On February 1 a large ship was sighted, standing downwind across the Caribbean; Truxtun squared away his yards in a chase which went on all night and all the next day until late in the evening, the enemy being made out as a frigate of the heaviest type. She was in fact *Vengeance,* 52, stronger than *Constellation* by five to three, and her captain only avoided battle because he had a cargo of money aboard. It was night when the American frigate's speed brought her alongside and they began shooting at each other. The dingdong battle continued for four hours, and on *Constellation* they could tell they were hitting for there were cries through the smoke and the Frenchman's fire fell off. At this point *Vengeance*'s mizzentopmast went and she flew up into the wind. Truxtun ordered his own ship to be eased off to save wounded spars, for the enemy had fired high and there was much damage aloft. Too late; *Constellation*'s mainmast pitched out, taking with it Midshipman Jarvis, in charge of the top, who refused to abandon his post of duty when told he ought to go.

Vengeance got away, then, but reached Curaçao with only the stumps of her fore- and mainmasts standing, bulwarks beaten in, eight feet of water in the hold, and one hundred fifty casualties in a crew of four hundred. She had struck twice during the night and the last desperate turn toward the wind had been an effort to make the Americans understand she was giving up. Only luck deprived Truxtun of his second prize, and when the news seeped through, Congress expressed the proud elation that was sweeping the country by voting the Commodore a gold medal and declared the death of Jarvis a subject of national regret. The new Navy had a hero and a leader, and by the good fortune that sometimes comes to nations, of all the captains he was the one most capable of giving the service a stamp of quality.

There were also the young men. By the summer of 1799, captains' reports from the Caribbean showed a need for small warships that could work through shallow drafts and varying airs. Benjamin Stoddert, who had developed rapidly into a very good employer of experts, commissioned the Navy agent at Baltimore to have built two schooners of the clipper model of that city—*Enterprise* and *Experiment*—12 guns each. They were ready before the end of the year, and at once became great favorites with the young lieutenants, for they were each a junior officer's command.

Experiment was the first in action, when a calm came down on her and a convoy of four merchantmen in the Bight of Léogane, off the

Haitian coast. Against this little group there emerged from the shore ten big barges, with 4-pounders and swivels, manned by forty to seventy men each, of the kind called "picaroons," pirates of that coast, who had no mercy for any man. The schooner's crew was but seventy strong, and Lieutenant William Maley, commanding, thought it would be better to surrender, but young David Porter, who had moved up another round of the ladder of promotion to be first lieutenant, cried it should not be so, and having the ship turned over to him, warped round on her sweeps and double-shotted his guns with grape.

As the barges came in, *Experiment* gave them so heavy and rapid a fire that they were forced to pull out again; but only to lie under the lee of the land while the killed and wounded were taken out and re-inforcements joined them. Now there were twelve of the barges; they came down on *Experiment* in three divisions of four barges each, one for her bows, one division on each side, with red "No quarter" flags at their mastheads, the picaroons shrieking and yelling. This was a very desperate bout, the barges trying to get to board, the schooner using her guns and musketry from the decks. It lasted three hours; two of the barges were sunk and the others driven off with many oars missing beat. The calm held and when two of the merchants drifted out of range of *Experiment*'s guns, they had to be abandoned by their people and were taken. But Porter was considered to have done better than well and Maley was allowed quietly to resign the service.

Enterprise worked down among the lower islands under a bold lieutenant named John Shaw, and had several adventures, taking a couple of small privateers before she fell in with *Aigle,* 10, tacked like lightning under her stern for a raking broadside, then ran under the Frenchman's lee and carried her by boarding, an action in which skill and valor were equally mingled. This was in July, 1800; on the 23rd of that month *Enterprise* fell in with the heavy privateer brig *Flambeau,* 12, and took her after a hard fight of three-quarters of an hour, the force of the Frenchman being such that Secretary Stoddert awarded the schooner's crew double prize money. All told, *Enterprise* took eighteen ships with a total of forty-two guns and three hundred prisoners, killed and wounded sixty-one of the enemy—no poor record for a ship of 12 guns and seventy men.

But in 1800 the nascent Navy encountered two disasters. A convention settled matters with France, and the elections brought into power the Democratic-Republican party, replacing John Adams with Thomas Jefferson.

IV

Thomas Jefferson was one of our greatest men, but the very adherence to principle that made him so, often led him into strange alleys of thought. "We are running navigation mad," he wrote during the campaign that brought him to the presidency, "and commerce and Navy mad, which is worst of all." Not that he wanted altogether to abolish the Navy; he considered it "the only form of force a republic should possess or exert," and merely wished to keep it within what he considered reasonable bounds. The line of argument was pretty subtle for the anti-Federalist politicians who formed his administration, and they had on hand a bill for the reduction of the service to a peacetime establishment, passed by the lame duck Congress on the day before the 1801 inauguration.

It was administered with a rigor that shook the young Navy to its core. All the ships were sold but five light frigates and eight heavy ones, plus little *Enterprise,* which had made such a name for herself. A plan of Stoddert's for the construction of six line-of-battleships and as many sloops-of-war was quietly forgotten. The number of officers was so drastically cut that only nine of the twenty-eight captains remained on the active list, preference being given to those not known to harbor Federalist opinions. The scale of pay was heavily trimmed also; it was no longer possible to outbid the merchant marine for men.

The shock was one that could have destroyed an insecurely rooted service. It was kept from doing so by the fact that in May, 1801, two months after Jefferson had taken office, the Pasha of Tripoli decided that a war with the United States was what he most needed, and cut down the consul's flagpole, demanding a payment of $250,000 to set it up again. Among Jefferson's assortment of ideas was one that no compromise with these barbarians was possible. "Tribute or war is the usual alternative of these Barbary States," he had written, back in Washington's administration. "Why not build a Navy and decide on war? We cannot begin in a better cause or against a better foe." When the Tripolitans themselves declared war, he overrode party doctrine to equip a squadron and sent it to the Mediterranean—the heavy frigates *President*, 44, *Philadelphia*, 38, the light frigate *Essex*, 32, and little *Enterprise*. The over-all commander was Richard Dale, back from his trip to China and in service again. By July, 1801, the ships were off Gibraltar, began convoying American merchantmen through the Mediterranean and setting up a rather languid blockade of Tripoli. The only event was that *Enterprise* fell in with a 14-gun corsair, shot her all to pieces with twenty dead and thirty wounded and sent her home with a single spar and an old sail, having no authority to take prizes. Back in Tripoli, the commander of the corsair, one Mohammed Sous, was ridden through the streets backward on a jackass and then bastinadoed to show what the Tripolitans thought of anyone who gave up to an American.

The enlistment of most of Dale's men was running out (under the new establishment they were recruited for a definite period, not the cruise—a system that later led to a mutiny aboard *Constitution* at Malta in 1805, when time-expired men feared they would be held in the Mediterranean). A new squadron was prepared for the next year, to be commanded by Truxtun. But when the man who had done so much for the early Navy found that he must personally command his flagship as well as direct the squadron, he turned touchy and resigned the service, so Captain Richard V. Morris was appointed.

Morris went to his station complete with his wife (and maid) and small son, Mrs. Morris having obtained the Secretary of the Navy's permission on her own. She was pregnant and in due course was put ashore at Malta, where she gave birth to a fine son. She was by no means the only woman to accompany the squadron, and some of her sisters on the lower decks were not so particular where they were confined. The wife of the captain of the forecastle on the *Constitution* bore a son in the boatswain's storeroom, and had a merry christening party in the midshipmen's quarters, while the wives of the boatswain, carpenter, and marine corporal, who were not invited, got drunk out of spite in a little party of their own.

Perhaps approaching fatherhood kept Commodore Morris' mind distracted from his command; whatever the reason, he was a failure. He could not seem to keep up any blockade of Tripoli, particularly with regard to small inshore craft, which went to and fro unmolested. In fact, he could not even keep control of his own captains; one of them, Daniel McNeill, kidnaped a French band from Marseille, then

sailed for home without orders. When an explosion took place aboard
Morris' flagship, he ordered the boats hoisted out; only the good conduct of his lieutenants saved the ship. That is, the whole naval service
of the United States was in the state one might expect of the new navy
of a minor power, a here-and-there service—and now its best leader
was gone. When Morris came home he was dismissed for incompe-
tence, and Jefferson and his Navy Secretary determined on an entirely new deal for the summer of 1803.

They fitted out *Enterprise,* two new 16-gun brigs and two new
schooners, built for close inshore work, the type that would damage
the Tripolitans most. To command the squadron they went down to
the tenth man on the list of captains and appointed Edward Preble.
He was a lonely, frosty-faced individual from Maine, in his late forties,
who had been a lieutenant on a Massachusetts state ship during the
Revolution, and during the French war had taken *Essex,* 32, on a
protracted convoy job to the East Indies, and thus missed contact with
most of the other officers of the young service. He was chosen mainly
for this reason; Jefferson and Secretary Robert Smith believing that
jealousies among the other captains were responsible for the unsatis-
factory performance thus far. He also suffered frightfully from stomach
ulcers and had a high temper. Beside the five small ships they gave
him *Philadelphia,* 38, and *Constitution,* 44, with a group of officers
of whom the eldest was his junior by fifteen years, the average by twenty.
"Nothing but a pack of boys!" he cried when he saw the list—a phrase
which was to be called up later.

It is utterly improbable that either President or Secretary knew
what they were getting. They had appointed the man who would make
the United States naval service.

Preble kept a taut ship, even tauter than Truxtun, and there seems
to have been no little grumbling about the old man on the voyage
out—at least until one midnight off Gibraltar, when a heavy ship became visible close alongside, and there were hails from both, each
seeking to learn the other's identity without disclosing her own. Preble
lost patience: "I now hail for the last time," he shouted. "If you do
not answer I'll fire a shot."

"If you do, I'll answer with a broadside."

"I should like to see you try that!" bellowed Preble. "I now hail
for an answer; what ship is that?"

"This is His Britannic Majesty's ship *Donegal,* 84, Sir Richard Strachan. Send a boat aboard."

"This is the U.S. frigate *Constitution,* 44, Captain Edward Preble, and I'll be damned if I'll send a boat aboard any ship. Blow up your matches, boys!"

Well, the Englishman sent the boat and he turned out to be a 32-gun frigate, but his force was not the point. What they talked about along the berth deck and in the wardroom was how the old man faced him down, quite willing to exchange broadsides with a three-decker in the process. Whatever impression this left was not in the least hurt by the fact that when *Constitution* arrived at Gibraltar, it was to find that Morocco was turning nasty, and one of its cruisers had captured an American ship. Preble sent *Philadelphia* up the Mediterranean to watch Tripoli until he arrived and sailed for the Moroccan capital of Tangier with his whole squadron, pulling into harbor with decks cleared for action and guns double-shotted. The Sultan expressed himself as much pleased that the United States had sent so fine a fleet to visit him and re-ratified the existing treaties without additional demands. But when *Constitution* reached Gibraltar again, there was a dreadful piece of news—*Philadelphia* had been captured by the Tripolitans.

It was an accident, and William Bainbridge, who commanded the frigate was never blamed for it. She ran on an uncharted reef outside the harbor, was heeled over by the outgoing tide until no gun would bear, and taken by gunboats that came forth. All the same this cut away a good two-fifths of Preble's force and added that much to the enemy. The winter gales were coming on, when ships were not supposed to keep the open Mediterranean, it would be a good four months before the news could go home and any sort of help arrive. The shadow of utter failure loomed over the campaign.

What Preble did was sail for Tripoli. He dared not risk his one remaining frigate off that coast in the storm season, so he kept her at Syracuse most of the time, and with the five little ships began a close blockade, shifting his pennant from one to another. It was a savage winter; there was ice in Venice that year, and storms so violent that on many days the American flag was the only one at sea, but at sea it stayed, and the corn traffic on which Tripoli mainly depended for food was utterly cut off.

There were some fairly hot numbers among the young lieutenants who were the "boys" of Preble's squadron. Stephen Decatur, for instance: In a Spanish harbor the year before his gig had been fired on by a guarda-costa, whereupon he next morning had himself rowed to the ship, and finding the captain not aboard, left word that Lieutenant Decatur of the U.S. Navy pronounced him a cowardly scoundrel and would cut his ears off when next they met.

But however hot these ardent young men blew, they found Preble ahead of them, taking whatever ship he was aboard in closer than they dared, on station though the worst weather. It would be worth a good deal to have record of the conversations that went on aboard as men and officers realized what kind of leader they had, but even without that record there is evidence of the feeling in the fleet.

In January, a ketch was captured and the old Commodore proposed nothing less than to send her into the harbor through the heavy batteries along its shores to cut out *Philadelphia*. The Mediterranean rig of the vessel offered some chance of slipping in without drawing too much fire. She was renamed *Intrepid* and Decatur was appointed to command the desperate venture. When word of it went through the squadron every man aboard *Enterprise* volunteered and nearly every man aboard *Constitution,* the only other ship then off the pirate stronghold. Decatur picked eighty-four and coached them carefully— they were to use no firearms; they would have to burn the frigate, since her foremast was down and yards on deck, no chance of getting her out alive. On February 7, 1804, *Intrepid* came in sight of the port, but a gale blew up and they had to beat back and forth before it for nine days, with the provisions "decayed and offensive," and the people sleeping on planks placed across casks of explosives and combustibles, in utmost squalor, but with no loss of spirit.

On the night of the 16th there was a fine new moon and a light breeze. *Intrepid* drifted into the harbor, guided by a Sicilian pilot named Salvator Catalano, who jabbered at the pirates in their own barbarous tongue as the frigate was approached, with all hands below hatches. Just as the ships touched, the Tripolitan watch saw the hatches rise and yelled: "Americano!" But it was too late, the boarders swarmed over the bulwarks and through the gunports with a hearty cheer, drove the Tripolitans overboard or cut them down, and began passing in the fire materials. *Philadelphia* was all ablaze in a matter of minutes, but now *Intrepid* had to work down the harbor in the brilliant light of the fire, with all the guns in the castles banging. They missed; not a man was hurt as Decatur beat out after what Lord Nelson called "the most bold and daring act of the age."

When the little ketch reached Syracuse all the ships in harbor manned yards and cheered her in, and Congress voted American citizenship to Catalano, with a gold sword and a full captain's commission to Decatur. But Preble was not satisfied; he had only reduced the odds against him and somewhat annoyed the Pasha by his winter blockade. He wanted to hurt; and as spring came on he borrowed six gunboats and two mortar craft from the King of the Two Sicilies and fitted them for service, enlisting ninety-six Neapolitan gunners to fill out his exiguous crews. It took some time to get things ready, for the twenty-five-ton gunboats were unstable and almost totally unseaworthy, could work in nothing but the finest weather; but at the end of July the Commodore was off Tripoli harbor, preparing to attack the place.

The relative forces must be borne in mind, also the fact no one had dared attack the Barbary powers at home since the age of Charles V. The castle batteries held one hundred fifteen guns and were manned by not less than twenty-five thousand men. The Tripolitans had five ships afloat, beside nineteen gunboats of a model much superior to those under the American flag. Preble had *Constitution,* and six little ships, including a brig taken from the enemy and refitted as a cruiser. "I expect we shall be hurt very much," he wrote, and went in, with Decatur and Lieutenant Richard Somers leading the gunboats. It is also to be noted that for many years the Turks had been famous as vicious hand-to-hand fighters, who accomplished their objectives by boarding.

The date was August 3, fine and clear; *Constitution* and the smaller ships moved in under the guns of the castle and exchanged fire with it, so hot and quick that the pirates were driven from their guns. At the break of the reefs Decatur's gunboats led the way; his own ship clashed side with one of the Tripolitans, leaped across the bulwarks leading his men and incredibly carried the enemy by boarding. Word came to him that his brother had been treacherously killed by a Turk aboard another gunboat after its spoken surrender; he followed up and took that one too, in a fierce action in which he was borne to the deck by a giant enemy whom he killed by firing a pistol through his own pocket. Lieutenant John Trippe took a third gunboat, also by boarding; from that day forth the Tripolitans would no longer engage Americans in close action.

But Preble kept after them. All that month he was in and shooting at their buildings on every day the weather allowed. *Intrepid* was sent into the harbor under Lieutenant Somers by night, loaded with explosives to blow up the massed gunboats, but something went wrong, there was a vast explosion in the harbor and the ketch was lost with all hands. The guns kept on; the Pasha hid in a dungeon; a letter from the French consul reported that the Tripolitans had become very gloomy and savage, their town was being knocked to pieces, and they sent out an offer to forego future tribute and release the *Philadelphia* prisoners for a mere $500 ransom apiece. The terms might have come down still further, but on September 10 there arrived a reinforcement squadron of four frigates, all their captains senior to Preble, who was thus superseded, and the negotiation of peace was turned over to the diplomats.

On the way home *Constitution* put into Gibraltar with one of the brigs, and Admiral Lord Nelson watched them from the quarter-deck of his three-decker battleship. He remarked: "In the handling of those trans-Atlantic ships there is a nucleus of trouble for the Navy of Great Britain." Just a year previous Napoleon had flung down his pen after signing the Louisiana Purchase and remarked: "I have this day given Britain a maritime rival who will sooner or later humble her pride."

Neither Nelson or Napoleon knew how soon.

V

The story of Preble's campaign is in the lieutenants and midshipmen who, like Porter, had achieved some ideal of service before the campaign began, or were too young to have felt other calls. There was no prize money in the Barbary War; as a motive it had to be replaced by something else, and under Preble that something became new and fierce—a feeling of emulation and a desire for glory. Those young men were proud and ardent. They fought duels—though not with each other, one of Preble's proudest boasts being that the squadron had not had a single duel or court-martial under his command. They looked on sea service under the United States flag not as a source of profit, but as something well beyond profit. The Navy had become a career; in the three years between Jefferson's inauguration and Preble's return from Tripoli sixty-three officers resigned the service, but in the next eight years, only twenty-six, in spite of some highly discouraging circumstances. The young men got to calling themselves "Preble's boys" as a title of honor, and an excellent way to get yourself knocked down was to speak disparagingly of the old man.

Truxtun supplied much of the technical equipment that lay in the background, the how-to-do-it. The young men could look to him and imitate; but Preble was in closer command, and it was he who brought out the spirit. He constantly dealt with odds and, against all odds, won; it is no disparagement of John Paul Jones to say that while the Continental captain conquered through indomitable will and personal courage, Preble's method went beyond, for to the will he added skill and cool discipline. *Constitution* was not "very much hurt" in those duels with the batteries; she got a 24-pounder shot through her mainmast and one man wounded, but the Tripolitans had many dead, and the lesson that the best defense is a stout offense was not lost.

The only trouble was that no one outside the Navy knew what this meant at the time. Preble himself gradually sickened and he died in 1807. The Administration, with a President who had an abiding interest in gadgets and a theory that naval defense meant coastal defense, developed a fantastic program for doing the whole business by means of gunboats, like those Decatur had led through the reefs off Tripoli. One hundred seventy-eight of them were built, using up all the timber that Benjamin Stoddert had accumulated for battleships. They so rocked to the recoil of their guns that they could only fire once in half an hour. Most of them never left the wharves where they were built. But by 1812 they had become the effective Navy in the eyes of the government.

★　　★　　★　　★　　★

3

A Sound of Wings

BY AT LEAST the date of the American trouble with France, it had become almost impossible for the Royal Navy to meet its personnel requirements. Only compulsion could make most men take up the dog's life of the British sailor, and compulsion was usually supplied in the form of impressment, sweeping up unwary seamen in port and stopping merchant ships at sea, forcibly inducting into the service as many of her people as the captain of a warship thought he needed. It early became evident that the acknowledgment of the independence of the United States did not place on any man's brow a mark by which he could be recognized as an American; and what was more, the British government rejected any process by which one of its subjects could become American through naturalization. It thus early became the practice for British cruisers short of men to halt and search American merchantmen as well as British. The sailor who could not positively prove he was American-born was automatically assumed to be subject to impressment and carried off to the stinking hold of a British battleship. "Having no documents to prove his American citizenship, this man is refused to be discharged by their lordships," was the most common of all replies to protests through the State Department.

It was a bitter, burning, continuous wrong, which grew worse as the years progressed and the pinch for seamen became tighter, and few of the men taken by the British ever returned. When he moved from the office of Secretary of State to the presidency in 1809, James Madison had submitted to the Admiralty the cases of more than two thousand impressed American seamen, and three years later there were

herited the Jeffersonian idea of coastal defense, and in view of the fact
that England had over six hundred warships at sea, the acknowledged
best in the world, proposed to lay all the ships up for harbor defense,
with the batteries on one side arranged to sweep channels, those on
the other removed to supply forts. At the time of the declaration of
war two of the captains were in Washington in time to hear of this
plan—William Bainbridge and Charles Stewart, both members of the
Preble's boys' club. They went round to see President Madison and
pleaded that for the honor of the flag the U.S. Navy should be allowed
to fight.

"Eight times out of ten," said Bainbridge, "with equal force we can
hardly fail; our men are better men, better disciplined. Our guns are
sighted, which is an improvement of our own the English know nothing of. While we fire cannon with as sure an aim as musketry, striking
twice out of every three shot, they must fire at random, without sight
of their object or regard for the undulations of the sea. We may be
captured and probably shall be, even after taking prizes from them,
because their numbers are much greater than ours."

There was a little more argument; after a time Madison sighed and
said: "You will give us victories, then, you think?"

"We do," said Stewart, "and not upon irrational premises."

"Which victories," Madison said, "will give us ships; for with victories Congress will supply them faster than they can be lost."

The President had a strong argument with his Cabinet the next day
and took the unusual step (for Madison) of overruling it and de-
creeing that the Navy ships should try at least one cruise apiece before
being laid up.

Commodore John Rodgers, who had been Truxtun's first lieutenant
in *Constellation,* therefore put out of New York with three of the
heavy frigates and a sloop-of-war on June 21, 1812, his main objective
being a big British convoy from Jamaica. He missed it; and in a long
chase failed to take a British frigate, mainly because one of the four
chase guns on his flagship blew up. His cruise therefore confirmed
the unfavorable opinion Washington had of the Navy, which in the
main was not far from that of the *Times* of London:—"a handful of
fir-built frigates manned by bastards and outlaws," doubting whether
they would be much use to the Royal Navy after having been captured during the first weeks of the war.

Washington completely failed to realize that Rodgers' cruise had had a genuine strategic effect; it forced the British Halifax squadron to remain concentrated as a unit, and thus covered the home-coming of a cloud of American merchantmen, who raced for their ports at the news of war. What the capital heard of was the failure to take the British frigate or the Jamaica convoy; and the next news was that *Constitution,* 44, had barely escaped the Halifax squadron after three days of agonizing chase through calms and light airs. She put into Boston; the orders that went up were that she was to stay there, a logical decision, since the verdict of the Revolution that American ships could not compete with British seemed confirmed.

The captain of *Constitution* was Isaac Hull, son of a Connecticut militia captain who went on whale boat cruises against the British in Long Island Sound during the Revolution. Short, beefy, Hull was no scholar, but a thorough seaman and a highly competent officer. He was acutely conscious of the state of mind in government circles, having begun his cruise from Chesapeake Bay. Borrowing money from a private citizen, he supplied his ship as rapidly as possible, and on August 2 sailed without orders, something for which he certainly could have been court-martialed; then compounded his fault by cruising up toward Halifax, looking for trouble. On the afternoon of August 19 he found it; the British frigate *Guerrière,* 38, was visible on the horizon, and shortened sail as *Constitution* came down.

It is worth-while reviewing the background; the miserable background of the Continental Navy, the fact that in fourteen years of war and more than two hundred combats, no British ship had yielded to an enemy of anything like equal force; the fact that the American Navy was universally regarded as a kind of privateering service, unwilling or unable to fight. Isaac Hull thought differently. He was one of Preble's boys, and had trained his crew in the sharp school of that old man, with daily gunnery drills, and his bastards and outlaws were Maryland men and New Englanders, not a few of whom had personally known impressment and had a bone to pick.

Constitution bore down—"rather too boldly for an American," the British captain remarked, as he maneuvered for a raking fire. He missed; *Constitution* turned as sharply as her opponent and kept sliding in on the lee beam. *Guerrière's* after guns were fired one by one;

on *Constitution*'s quarter-deck Lieutenant Morris asked anxiously: "Shall we open fire?"

"Not yet, sir, not yet," said Hull, pacing back and forth. There were more shots from the Briton; a man was wounded and another killed. "Not yet, sir," said Hull, but as they drew abreast, fifty yards apart, he leaped in the air and fairly screamed: "Now boys, pour it into them!" His tight breeches split from waist to knee and every gun in the battery went off together.

On *Guerrière* they felt "a terrible crash, the frigate reeled and trembled as though she had felt the shock of an earthquake. The next minute the cockpit was full of wounded." There was a second exchange of broadsides. *Guerrière*'s mizzenmast came down and dragged her around. *Constitution* forged ahead, swung under the bows of the British ship and raked her frightfully, with the gunners shouting: "Hull her, boys!" *Guerrière* went to pieces, her mainyard came down, then the foremast, dragging the mainmast after it. As *Constitution* moved off to repair what little damage she had, her opponent was a hulk, and the red cross of St. George came down for the first time in over a decade. The British frigate was too wrecked to save; Hull burned her and put back to Boston.

He arrived at a crucial moment. News had just come of the surrender of Detroit to the British, the campaign on the Niagara frontier was a failure, while the Indians had taken Fort Dearborn, which is now Chicago; but here was *Constitution* with a battle flag captured from the mistress of the seas. It was later computed that she was the heavier ship by the ratio of 10 to 7; but this does not alter the fact that the British Navy never before made such computations, or the other one that *Guerrière* had twenty-three killed and fifty-six wounded against fourteen casualties in the American frigate. The country went wild with delight; Hull was saluted with artillery when he landed, the whole crew was played through Boston streets by a band; New York raised a subscription to buy swords for Hull and all his officers; Baltimore fired salutes all day long and hung the streets with flags; the South Carolina legislature met in special session to pass resolutions of delight.

Essex, 32, was out on cruise at the time. She had not done so badly herself, tempting the British sloop-of-war *Alert,* 20, alongside by disguising herself as a merchantman, and crushing her into surrender with a single broadside. But even aboard *Essex* they failed to understand when they came up the Delaware and people turned all along the banks to cheer the flag in. Nothing like it had ever happened.

The next news was of the loss of a ship, but even in loss, victory. U.S.S. *Wasp,* 18, five days out from the coast, was caught by a hurricane that damaged her spars severely, then fell in with the slightly heavier H.M.S. brig-sloop *Frolic,* 20. There was a wild, heaving sea; Captain Jacob Jones, one of Preble's boys, ordered *Wasp*'s crew to fire on the dip, and they did so with such effect that much of the British sloop's top-hamper came down, and in spite of her own injuries, *Wasp* got across her bows in a raking position. Jones ordered another broadside, but a seaman named Jack Lang, who had been impressed in His Majesty's Navy, leaped on the enemy bowsprit with a cutlass in hand to fight his personal quarrel with England, and as the rest of the crew followed with a cheer, they found only three wounded officers on *Frolic*'s deck. She had ninety casualties in a crew of one hundred seven, so murderous had been the American gunnery, and the fact that a British line-of-battleship appeared to take both contestants before repairs could be made could not conceal Jones' triumph or the fact that *Frolic* was so battered that she had to be condemned.

Guerrière, Alert, Frolic: a ball was held in Washington to celebrate these improbable victories, with the British battle flags on the wall. At the height of the celebration there was a flurry at the door, and young Lieutenant Hamilton, son of Secretary of the Navy Paul Hamilton, marched down a wildly applauding hall to present dispatches and lay still another British battle flag at the feet of Dolly Madison.

It had belonged to H.M.S. *Macedonian,* 38, a new, strong frigate which on October 25 found *United States,* 44—known affectionately as the "Old Wagon"—broad off the Canary Islands. The captain of *United States* was Stephen Decatur, of Tripoli fame; no man more beloved in the service. "God bless him, he has a soul to save," said the sailors as he passed, and touched their caps. When he sighted the American frigate, Captain Carden of *Macedonian,* a strict disciplinarian known as a heavy flogger, thought he was dealing with *Essex.* Now that ship was armed throughout with 32-pound carronades, lightweight guns very effective at short range but possessing no carry; Carden determined to fight it out at a distance. This was his mistake; *United States* had long 24s on the gundeck, and probably no ship that ever put to sea had been more carefully drilled to fire by the numbers. There is an account from a boy then aboard the British frigate:

It was like some tremendous thunderstorm, whose deafening roar is attended by incessant streaks of lightning, carrying death in every flash; only, in our case, the scene was rendered more terrible by the torrents of blood. The cries of the wounded men rang through the *Macedonian*. The boys belonging to the guns next to mine were wounded early and I had to spring with all my might to keep three or four guns supplied with cartridges. I saw two of these lads fall; one was struck in the leg by a large shot. The other had a grape-shot through his ancle (sic). A man named Aldrich had one of his hands cut away by a shot and the same moment another tore him open; he was thrown overboard. One of the officers was struck by a canister shot near the heart and never spoke again. Mr. Hope, our first lieutenant, was wounded. So terrible had been the work of destruction around us that that part of the ship was afterward called "the slaughter house." Not only were the men being killed but several of the guns were now disabled.

Seeing that he was going to lose this long-range game, Captain Carden clapped on all his sails and charged in to try to win by boarding. It was no good; *United States* curved off, picking the British frigate to pieces with accurate shooting and within an hour from the first gun, the latter surrendered. "I am undone," said the British captain when he was brought aboard; "what will they do to me?" For he had not heard of *Guerrière,* and thought he was the first British captain ever to give up to these degenerate colonials. He had one hundred five casualties against twelve American.

As his flag was borne triumphantly down the hall in Washington, Navy Secretary Hamilton cried: "Never forget that it is to Captains Bainbridge and Stewart that you really owe these victories!" But at that very hour Bainbridge was below the equator, doing something he would infinitely have preferred to any ball. On December 29, he sighted the British frigate *Java,* 38, off the coast of Brazil, and stood out to avoid neutral waters. *Essex,* which was to join him for a squadron cruise in the south, had not come; *Hornet,* 18, had stayed at São Salvador to watch a British sloop in the harbor.

Captain Lambert of *Java* had no hesitation in accepting battle; he was taking a 38 into action with an American 44, but British captains were as little used as ever to counting such contemptible odds, and his ship was a French-built, exceptionally heavy 38, with a crew and a half, since she was taking out a draft of sailors to India. The difference in force was somewhat less than 10 to 9; a brief trial of speed in the bright sunny weather showed the Briton the faster ship. She closed in from windward, trying to gain a raking position, was foiled by Bainbridge's quick maneuvering, and they ran side by side, firing broadsides into the smoke. A shot carried away *Constitution*'s wheel and drove a copper bolt into Bainbridge's thigh, and as *Java* gained a little by her superior speed, she tried to come around under *Constitution*'s bows for a rake.

The effort failed disastrously. *Java* had been hit so hard below that she hung on the turn; *Constitution* got around first and twice raked her frightfully. Aboard the British ship lieutenants were screaming and beating men over the head; they turned her somehow and brought her down with her bowsprit jabbing across *Constitution*'s quarter, with the bugles calling "Boarders!" and Captain Lambert ran forward to lead a try at winning hand-to-hand. It melted under a terrific fire of musketry from the American tops, Lambert himself was killed, the British frigate's bowsprit was shot away, and the *Constitution* jerked clear, the foremast followed. For a few minutes more they were side by side, but now everything had begun to go aboard *Java,* her people's cheers were mingled with swearing and sobs, her guns were firing raggedly, she could do nothing to stop the dreadful accurate volley of the long 24s and her mizzenmast came down. Bainbridge stood off a little to make things right about some damaged ropes; then came standing grandly back, as *Java*'s last mast pitched out and she surrendered, with forty-eight killed and one hundred two wounded against American casualties of twenty-four.

"Good God, can such things be?" asked the *Times* of London, which had spoken of bastards and outlaws, and there was a wild rush of indignation and anguish, which can only be offset against what happened on the American side of the Atlantic as the news of this series of victories flowed in. Gold medals, officers' swords, and ceremonial dinners came to every seaport; the bookshop windows were filled with ballads and prints. Congress shook off the gunboat dream

to order the building of four ships-of-the-line, six more of the incompara-
ble 44-gun frigates, and six heavy sloops-of-war. At the time nobody
thought of analyzing it down to the ships designed by Humphreys,
crews trained as they had been by Truxtun, and led as they had been
by Preble. It was thought of as just something wonderful that had
happened.

Then the blockade came down.

III

The extent of that blockade and what it did to the United States have
received no little attention from people qualified to investigate that sort
of thing. It closed in tight early in 1813 and as Britain had strangled
Napoleon's naval effort by this date, she could well afford the ninety-
seven ships currently employed—eleven battleships, thirty-four frigates,
the rest sloops-of-war and smaller. In the interval since the Revolution,
the United States had become less a group of islands than before, but
the main traffic movement was still by water, carried on in larger
ships than in the previous period, with more dependence on overseas
commerce, and it was more subject to interruption. The whole economic life of the country was so hard hit by the blockade as to be
practically paralyzed. Flour, which came mainly from the Chesapeake
Bay region, went to over four times its pre-war price in Boston. It
took nearly two months for a wagon train loaded with drygoods to
reach Charleston from Philadelphia. The main financial resource of
the government was customs duties; they practically ceased, and the
administration was at once in financial difficulties.

Moreover, as a secondary result of the blockade, the British at
least succeeded in reversing the verdict in a frigate action. While
Constitution was off to keep her date with *Java* she left behind the
sloop *Hornet,* 18, Captain James Lawrence (another of Preble's
boys). He was driven from his position by the appearance of a British
battleship and made for the West Indies. On February 24, 1813, he
found H.M.S. *Peacock,* 18, off Demerara under a tropical twilight.
They passed on opposite tacks, firing as the guns bore; then *Hornet*
came around and closed in again, firing so rapidly and accurately that
Peacock hauled down her flag twenty minutes after the fight began,
then sank before they could get all the men out of her.

For this victory Lawrence was promoted to *Chesapeake,* 38, then fitting out at Boston. Her crew was completely new, having never been together before, but on May 20 Lawrence dropped down into the outer roadstead, being under peremptory orders to go to sea at once. A British frigate was visible on the horizon and had sent in a challenge to battle. Lawrence never received it, but he put out for her anyway.

The enemy ship turned out to be *Shannon,* 38, commanded by Philip B. V. Broke. He had had her for ten years and was an anomaly in the Royal Navy of his day, in that he insisted on target practice, both with the large guns and the small. Lawrence tried to swing down the windward side of this experienced frigate, give her a couple of broadsides, then round her bows for a rake. But everything went wrong; *Shannon*'s fire was more accurate than any Britisher's had a right to be; the wind caused smoke to cover the British decks, but left *Chesapeake* clear to the fire from *Shannon*'s tops. Three of the American lieutenants were killed and Lawrence himself mortally wounded. He was carried below, saying: "Don't give up the ship!" In a matter of minutes *Chesapeake*'s jib sheet was shot away, she came sharply into the wind, was taken aback, and drifted with her stern to the British cruiser. Broke raked her twice, then swinging his cutlass, led his crew across the bulwarks. The resistance of the leaderless Americans was fierce, but disorganized; in fifteen minutes *Chesapeake* was a captured ship.

The fact that Broke was made a baronet and *Shannon*'s victory has always since been regarded as one of the finest in British naval history shows how far opinion had changed about those American frigates. It is to be noted that *Chesapeake* inflicted more damage on her opponent than any of the three captured British frigates did on theirs. But the facts remain that she had been taken; practically all the small American brigs were easily mopped up by superior force and the remaining American frigates held closely in port. The old prescription of British seapower—overwhelmingly applying superior force—could not (it seemed) be reversed even by such a band as Preble's boys and the men they trained.

The only spark of light in 1813 came from Lake Erie. In a naval sense it was considered an adjunct of Lake Ontario. As soon as war was declared there began on the latter body of water a building race between Commodore Isaac Chauncey of the Americans and Commodore Sir James Lucas Yeo of the British, two men who were peas out of a pod for temperament. Both men were great builders and organizers, but utterly unwilling to fight unless they had a clear superiority. The result was a series of naval skirmishes that decided absolutely nothing and blockades that ended as soon as the blockaded squadron built a new and bigger ship. The service on the lakes was not altogether unpopular; word early got around the seafaring communities that although there was no prize money to speak of, cruises were short, and instead of salt horse on the table, it was more likely to be fresh beef, venison, or wild turkey, since it was easier to get supplies locally than to bring them in. The building campaign reached its absurd climax toward the close of the war, when each side had 58-gun two-deckers afloat and was building 110-gun line-of-battleships, heavier than any they had on the ocean.

The situation on Erie was this: Detroit and all the troops that held it had been surrendered to the British at the very outbreak of the war, and the whole northwest was gone, down to inside the Ohio line, where General William Henry Harrison maintained a difficult defensive against the British and their Indian allies. News of the disaster was presently brought to President Madison by one Daniel Dobbin, a lake trader who had escaped from Detroit. He pointed out that everything in the northwest depended upon the control of Erie. Troops in quantity for a campaign and their supplies could be moved only by water. Madison gave Dobbin $2,000 and sent him to Presque Isle to build a fleet and regain the vital lake.

Somewhat later Captain Oliver Hazard Perry was sent up to take operational command. He reached Presque Isle after a trip through snowy winter roads to find things in a terrible state. Dobbin had started work on two fine 20-gun brigs, but the shipwrights were on strike and deserting through the woods toward Pittsburgh, principally because the few storekeepers were profiteering so outrageously; there was not a cable, anchor, or cannon within a hundred miles; there were not even enough tools, and no land protection at all for the shipyard. Dobbin had fitted out three little schooners with a gun apiece as gunboats, but they would not be much use. Against this, quite accurate information from the British side said that over at Malden they had all ready for sail as soon as the ice went out a fine

ship of 17 guns, two brigs of 13 and 10, a schooner of 3 and a sloop
of 1, added to which there was being built another ship-rigged corvette
of 20.

A good part of the necessary iron and stores had been sent along
the snow trails to Buffalo, and there loaded aboard five more schooner-
gunboats, one captured from the British by Lieutenant J. D. Elliott.
But at Buffalo they must stay, for the British had batteries at Fort
Erie across the river, and could prevent anything moving out against
the current. Perry solved his first difficulty by persuading Pennsylvania state to send five hundred militia to protect his base; not much use
as troops, but legally allowing him to declare Presque Isle a military
reservation and to bring food prices into line by order. The solution
of getting his guns had to wait till May, when the British fleet was
already ramping up and down the lake. At this point, for the only
time in the war on Ontario, Chauncey developed both naval superiority and willingness to co-operate with the army authorities. He
brought his fleet to the western end of the lake and the main British
fort there was stormed in a fight in which the main load was carried
by Perry and the marines.

Next day Fort Erie was evacuated and Perry, though burning with
a fever, began to take his supply ships up—a risky operation, for
there was no wind, the ships had to be dragged alongshore by oxen
and men pulling ropes, and there was always the danger that the
British would come over the horizon and shoot them all to pieces.
Perry's daring and will paid off; the last of the laden schooners slid
over the bar into Presque Isle Bay just as the enemy sails appeared
on the rim.

Perry was quite literally not out of the woods yet; by mid-July the
two brigs, named *Lawrence* and *Niagara,* were rigged and ready,
while General Harrison from the west was crying for naval help,
but there were simply no crews. Perry wrote desperate appeals to
Chauncey, through whom men must come: "For God's sake and
yours and mine, send me men and officers." But Chauncey clung in-
flexibly to the superior importance of his own squadron, and it was
not until July 23 that a draft of seventy arrived, "blacks, soldiers and
boys who had never been aboard a ship." At the same time there came a
missive from Harrison; the British were besieging Fort Meigs on the
Maumee, and Ohio was likely to follow the rest of the northwest

down the drain unless he had naval command of the lake. Perry enlisted some frontiersmen and put up his sails.

But at the bar *Lawrence* stuck fast. Her stores were taken out, then her guns, and finally all the ballast; no use. At this point Perry bethought himself of a device he had seen in Holland. Huge boxes, called "camels," were brought up to the ship's sides, filled with water, spars run across them through the ports, and then they were pumped out. The first try failed. Perry kept his people at it through seventy-two hours of day and night labor, with men dropping from exhaustion, and on the morning of August 4 *Lawrence* skimmed across the bar. At this precise moment the sails on the British squadron showed white in the sunlight.

It must not be supposed that young Commodore R. H. Barclay was without difficulties of the same order as those that beset Perry. He too had trouble getting crews and supplies and so much trouble in obtaining guns that although most of his pieces were long guns of considerable range, none were anywhere near as heavy as the 32-pound carronades with which he knew *Lawrence* to be armed. Her ports were housed as he approached, and there in line with her were Perry's eight schooners, anchored off the bar and ready. His own big new ship *Detroit* had not yet joined and he could see only that he would be faced with the unappetizing business of attacking a squadron probably heavier than his own in a position where any disabled ship must be lost. He sailed away, therefore, and missed his chance of making the northwest a part of Canada.

Now Perry got *Niagara* also over the bar and beat down to Sandusky, leaving behind two of his schooners, for which there were not enough men. General Harrison loaned him some soldiers to help handle his artillery, and as marines to fight from the tops one hundred Kentucky buckskins, the famous "long rifles" of the frontier; Perry bore for Malden.

The British forces everywhere west of lower Lake Erie had to get all their supplies by water, and were terribly short of flour. Barclay had the choice of advising the military command to abandon the west and retreat to the shore of Lake Ontario—or fighting Perry. Though he feared himself overmatched, being a British sea dog he chose to fight. On the morning of September 10 off Put in Bay, both fleets formed line, *Lawrence* behind two of the schooners on the

American side, *Niagara* leading the remaining schooners in a second division; on the British side *Lady Prevost,* 13, the strong *Detroit,* 20, followed by *Hunter,* 10, *Queen Charlotte,* 17, and two schooners. The wind was light from the American side; Perry bore down at an angle, but as he came in was hit so accurately by the British long guns that he had to make sail to close, while Elliott in *Niagara* failed to imitate him and the wind began to fall. The consequence was that the American flagship found herself involved with a semicircle of the four most powerful British vessels in a dreadful battle in which she gradually melted. The surgeons' mates and ships' boys were summoned to handle cannon; there was a call for some of the wounded to help pull a rope.

Perry's ship was thus crushed; but not Perry's spirit. He launched a boat, and, wrapping himself in the big blue flag embroidered with Lawrence's "Don't Give Up the Ship" which had been made for the occasion, was rowed to the *Niagara.* Whether Elliott had held back from petulance (for he was a petulant man), misunderstanding, or physical inability to close, became unimportant. Perry said shortly: "Get out of this ship and bring up the schooners;" he himself took the quarter-deck of *Niagara* and bore down to break the British line. Their ships had already taken a bad beating from *Lawrence*'s heavy short guns and most especially from the buckskin marines who had killed nearly every officer on the British decks. As the completely fresh brig broke through on them, firing double-shotted broadsides in both directions, they had no real defense. One by one the flags came down, and Perry could return to his shattered *Lawrence* to write the celebrated dispatch saying: "We have met the enemy and they are ours." Lake Erie was American and the northwest always would be.

IV

At the outbreak of the war it was much as it had been during the Revolution. Everybody wanted to go privateering and nearly everybody in the seaport towns did, including all sorts of butcher boys and bums. The ships in which they put to sea were also those of the early days of the Revolution—coasters and commercial craft, carrying one or two guns, desirous only of taking enough of a vessel to pay expenses. The fate of these early warmed-over commercial vessels was also that of their Revolutionary counterparts; they were quickly cleared out by the smallest type of British cruiser.

But it became evident that this war was not in the least like the Revolution—in several ways. One was that, at least after 1777, the French Navy was in the background of the colonies; the British could not establish a close blockade anywhere along the American coast, and commercial voyages could be made very successfully, especially if one carried a letter-of-marque in case anything British were met. This time the blockade was clamped down tight and there was no French Navy in the wings; commercial voyaging was impossible unless it was under the Swedish or Portuguese flags, as some vessels were. A seaman could enlist in the navy, then go for a privateer or set out inland and hoe corn.

Certainly many of them went for privateers; but soon British battle flags began to be shown through the streets, and all the taverns burst out with signs reading: "Free grog for Navy sailors!" Congress voted $50,000 prize money for the capture of *Guerrière,* and $25,000 for *Frolic.* Even without the human desire for glory, the most obvious self-interest told any seafaring man that the money he could make from the capture of a British 38-gun frigate was vastly above what he could gain anywhere else. Not to mention that the cruisers also took their share of merchant shipping; *Constitution* captured nine on one cruise, most of which were profitably sent in.

This does not mean that Navy captains found it always easy to get crews. Some thirty or forty of the men who followed Lawrence to defeat aboard *Chesapeake* were Portuguese who spoke little English. But it is worth noting that even in defeat, with most of the officers shot down early, this "inexperienced" crew did a lot of damage to one of the best British frigates on the list. In the pool of American sailormen there had developed a group of individuals who had made one or more cruises in a Navy warship and had received the kind of training that Preble's boys gave them. They were ready to take their stations at guns or ropes with only the most general direction. The captain of *Constitution* on her last wartime cruise said his men could have fought the ship without any officers at all.

This leaven worked down through the men of a merchant marine that necessarily went armed during the Franco-English wars and the prevalence of pirates, and who, if not made of better basic material than the men of the Revolution, knew a great deal more about defending themselves. Nor should it be overlooked that many of these men had been in the Royal Navy; that is, had been pressed. A note of almost passionate resentment over that infliction runs through the whole war, as was expressed by Jack Lang. Such men were damned well interested in prize money, but quite as much interested in knocking somebody's block off. When an officer with a flag and a drummer boy marched through the streets, shouting: "Come one, come all!" and led the way to a tavern where the skipper of a privateer was taking names, such men only asked how fast she was and how well armed.

And she was fast and well armed; the British saw to that. When they cleaned out the small craft and hastily converted merchant ships, it became evident that only one thing provided safety for a privateer, and that was speed. But if you built for speed and made everything else secondary, the speed was likely to exceed previous records; and the builders of the privateers had behind them that wonderful Baltimore clipper hull model, probably the best ever devised for a sailing ship, which yacht makers of today find it hard to equal. The result was that late in 1813 there began to emerge from the yards those Yankee topsail schooners which were the fastest, most beautiful, and certainly the deadliest sea-raiders the world has seen. By the end of the year the merchants of Jamaica protested that their island was under actual blockade; they could get commerce neither in nor out. Admiral Sir John Borlase Warren, in command of the American station, was informed by the Lords of Admiralty that he had over a hundred warships, surely enough to take care of a small power like the United States, and he himself voyaged on a frigate to the West Indies to inspect the situation. The trip was a nightmare; there was not a day when he was out of sight of some American privateer, and if he chased her, she vanished.

And not only vanished; went somewhere else to do harm. In 1813, the year when the U.S. Navy seemed effectively beaten down, the privateer *Yankee* of Providence took seven ships off Ireland and came back with nearly a million dollars in her hold. *Scourge* of New York and *Rattlesnake* of Philadelphia shot into the North Sea and quite ruined the Baltic trade for the year. *America* of Salem, built and armed like a sloop-of-war, cruised off Land's End and took everything she met, including the mail packets. *Lion* of Baltimore captured $400,000 in

was quite ruined in the Pacific. Twelve-year-old David Farragut, son of a Revolutionary captain, learned his trade on this cruise when he was given independent command of a prize. Eventually, however, a British frigate and a heavy sloop found *Essex* at Valparaiso early in 1814, and they glowered at each other for some weeks before the American lost her maintopmast in a gust. Now a captain at the Washington Navy Yard named Tingey had thought to improve *Essex* by replacing her lighter maindeck guns with heavy carronades, and the trouble with carronades was that they would not shoot to any distance. In the neutral harbor the British captain calmly posted himself at a range where *Essex* could not reach him and shot at her till she surrendered.

Thus by March of 1814 the U.S. Navy had apparently reached the stage of the Continental Navy in 1778 or 1779. It was bottled up and, in spite of a few short cruises by the heavy ships, was being ground down and destroyed by the infinite numbers of the British sea forces. The judgment seemed confirmed in February when *Frolic*, 20, the first of the new sloops-of-war, put to sea and was promptly run down and taken by a British frigate after a long chase in which she threw over her guns in the effort to escape.

But on a blowing March night Captain Lewis Warrington put out of New York in *Peacock*, 20, and things changed within a week. Warrington was one of Preble's boys, a pale, cold Virginian who insisted on personally examining every man who wished to ship aboard. Before he had been at sea for five hours, he realized that designer William Doughty, one of old Humphreys' assistants, had given him just about the fastest warship in the world. He headed down toward the West Indies, and off the coast of Spanish Florida on April 27 encountered the brig-sloop *Epervier*, 18, the latter having aboard a cargo of money which the merchants had not dared place on a commercial vessel for fear of privateers. The two came toward each other from opposite directions; at the first exchange of broadsides *Peacock* lost a spar, but *Epervier* was dreadfully mauled, and as they ran off side by side, was hit again and again. The British captain called for boarders, but his bold tars cried: "She's too heavy for us!" and threw down their weapons. Warrington carried his prize into Charleston and took his own ship out for a cruise in the mouth of the English Channel.

Two days after *Peacock* took *Epervier* a gale blew across Portsmouth, New Hampshire, and on the wings of it there rode through the blockade the new *Wasp*, 20, commanded by still another of Preble's boys, Johnston Blakeley. Now the British had a real problem, for *Wasp* also made into the English Channel. In the lips of it she took twelve ships, and back-breaking work this raiding was, for the people had to stand double watches, and when a capture was made there was always boat work, the search of the prize and transportation out of her of anything of value, with guards for prisoners. On June 28 a sail was made out to windward, coming down fast. She was H.M.S. *Reindeer,* 18, a brig-sloop of a good deal less force than *Wasp,* but commanded by Captain William Manners, who yielded nothing even to the famous Broke in the care with which he trained his crew or the courage with which he led them. The ships had a violent gunnery duel, side by side, the fiercest of the war, and *Wasp*'s heavy metal gave her the best of it. Manners closed in, and although badly wounded, hauled himself into the rigging to try fortune by boarding. He was shot through the head; the British boarders were cut down at the bulwarks, and *Wasp*'s men swept across like a storm to clear *Reindeer* from end to end.

Now Blakeley took his ship to French Lorient for a refit and put out again for the Channel, where he took three more ships, one of them in full view of a British battleship that could not catch him. On the evening of September 1 he sighted three ships near the latitude of the Azores, some little distance apart. They were all warships and clearly of *Wasp*'s own class; Blakeley clapped on sail and bore down on the nearest. At 9:30 *Wasp* was alongside H.M.S. *Avon,* firing across the dark heaving water at the line of foam along the enemy's keel. The other two British ships closed toward the scene, firing signal guns and letting off blue flares. Before they got there *Wasp*'s New Hampshire farmers had reduced *Avon* to such a state that she sank before midnight.

After this *Wasp* headed down into the Atlantic, took four more ships and then disappeared, never heard from again. But this was not the point; the point was that *Wasp* and *Peacock* (which also took fourteen ships in the Channel that summer) had introduced major defects into the whole British system of protecting commerce. The operations of the strong, fast privateers that began to come out late in 1813 showed that it was no longer adequate merely to put some armament aboard merchant ships, as against the French. The Admiralty had adopted the device of placing valuable vessels under the escort of the 18-gun brig-sloops, which were an overmatch for nearly all privateers. But now the United States was out with a class of light cruisers that not only gutted convoys but destroyed their escorts, too. This was reinforced by a piece of news that did not reach England till after the end of the war. The British had sent to the South Atlantic the brig-sloop *Penguin*, 18, a new ship specially equipped and with an extra-heavy crew, to take care of the large privateer *Young Wasp*, which had been doing much damage among the Indiamen. Instead she met *Hornet*, 18, was dismantled and reduced to surrender in fifteen minutes.

Moreover, these light cruisers had taught the privateers a trick or two. During the Revolution, in the early days of 1812, the invariable technique was to put a prize crew aboard the capture and send her into port; she represented valuable property. But the British blockade of the American coast had become so close and the actions of neutrals in dealing with prizes were so uncertain, that unless a ship were a very fine vessel indeed, with a bulky and expensive cargo, it was not worth while trying to send her in. The privateers began to adopt the Navy method of taking out everything worth while and burning her. Lord Eldon pointed out that under such circumstances the war could go on forever; the Americans were supplying themselves with new resources out of their captures.

VI

Now that Napoleon was down, the British plan for 1814 was to throw utterly coercive forces onto the little republic of the west. A great expedition against Louisiana was prepared; another to the Chesapeake Bay area for an attack on Washington, which was duly burned when its militia defenders ran away, and another on Baltimore, the great harbor of those irritating privateers. The latter produced nothing but repulse, the death of the general in charge, and the writing of "Star-Spangled Banner." There was also to be a main effort in the north, and the Duke of Wellington, fresh from his great triumphs in Spain, was invited to head it. His lordship was disinclined to leave London, but gladly looked over the documents, and offered advice. Sir George Prevost was the British army commander in Canada; the "Iron Duke" believed him fully competent, and adequately supplied with resources for an invasion of the northern states, but since the only means of transport in that wild region was by water, it was absolutely essential to have naval victories on the lakes. Erie had become hopeless, being under complete American control since Perry's battle, and the building race on Ontario promised no early conclusion. The only route that offered a fair prospect was up the Richelieu River to Lake Champlain, the line taken by Burgoyne during the Revolution, when he failed precisely because he lost his good naval communications. Accordingly Captain George Downie, R.N., was sent out with a staff of naval constructors and crews of naval sailors to make a fleet that would sweep the Americans from the lake.

Downie worked fast; by the early days of September he had ready a heavy frigate, *Confiance,* 37, with long 24-pounders on her gun-deck, backed by the brig *Linnet,* 16, a pair of sloops, *Chubb* and *Finch,* 11 each, captured from the Americans in the river during the previous year, and twelve big galley-gunboats, mostly armed with two heavy guns apiece. On September 7, in spite of the fact that Downie said his fleet was not ready, Prevost took up his march along the shores of Lake Champlain, the squadron following.

The army commander had a good case for hurry. The Americans had to be beaten from the lake before October, as it was impossible for him to conduct a winter campaign through the Adirondacks, and his intelligence department, which was very good, told him that the enemy was weaker now than it was likely to be again. Ashore the Americans had only two thousand men in the trenches behind the little river at Plattsburg where they had elected to make their stand. On the lake there was a squadron hardly two-thirds the strength of Downie's—corvette *Saratoga,* 26, brig *Eagle,* 20, schooner *Ticonderoga,* 17, sloop *Preble,* 7, and ten galley-gunboats, individually inferior to the British type. Mechanically *Confiance* alone was a match for the lot, and the American ships had been put together in as much haste and were as little ready for action as the British, but their commander was Thomas Macdonough, still another of Preble's boys. If the marines of the little fleet were largely borrowed soldiers, the men along the gundecks were more of those Yankee seamen who had followed Hull and Bainbridge and seen the red cross flag come down.

They waited at anchor in Plattsburg Bay on September 11, with *Eagle* at the head of the line, followed by *Saratoga, Ticonderoga,* and *Preble,* the galleys scattered along the gaps, the line being so placed that Downie could get around its head only by passing every ship against a headwind, and round its tail not at all, because of a shoal. Downie did not try to turn the line; he brought *Chubb* and *Linnet* ahead into the way to beat *Eagle,* his own big *Confiance* to knock out *Saratoga,* while *Finch* and the gunboats took care of the rear of the American line.

Coming in, the British accepted an angular raking fire that did some damage, but when *Confiance* rounded to, she laid 40 of *Saratoga*'s men on the deck with her first broadside. Some of her guns bore on *Eagle,* which also had *Chubb* and *Linnet* to deal with; the American brig's cables were shot away, she came head to wind where she could not fire, and had to sheet home topsails and run down the line to help *Saratoga* against *Confiance;* whereupon *Linnet* swung round into a raking position on the American flagship.

Meanwhile several of the minor pieces were moved off the board. *Chubb* lost her bowsprit and mainboom, and with nothing that could carry sail, drifted through the American line and was taken. At the southern end *Finch* tried to lead the twelve British gunboats in against *Ticonderoga* for boarding, and had they reached her side, they must have taken her, for they had fifty men apiece and she only a few more than one hundred. But she shot back with resolution and accuracy, despite the fact that her guns had no locks, and young Midshipman Hiram Paulding had to fire them with pistol flashes. *Finch* was utterly crushed by two broadsides, drifted onto an island and was captured. The gunboats drove the little *Preble* out of line, and five times charged *Ticonderoga,* once getting within a boat-hook length, but she gave them cannister and bags of shot so fiercely that they drew out shattered, barely able to man the oars.

At the main whorl of battle *Confiance* and *Saratoga* were pounding each other with cannon balls across a quarter-mile of water, each raked by one of the enemy's lighter ships. But after that first crushing broadside the English frigate did not do so well. Downie was killed, so were all his lieutenants but one, and no one noticed that quoins on the guns gradually loosened, sending their shot higher and higher, while *Saratoga*'s fire, though much weaker, came so low and straight that the guns on *Confiance*'s unengaged side had to be run out to keep her from foundering from waterline wounds. Macdonough himself was aiming cannon, but one by one the pieces were crippled and at last the final piece leaped from its carriage and down a hatch.

All Preble's boys had imagination, and Macdonough proved it by having foreseen exactly such an emergency. He had arranged his anchors so that by hauling in on his lines with the capstan, the ship would swing around at her mooring. Now the crew were set to winching the ship around; she slowly turned, and one by one the guns of an entirely fresh battery began to open on *Confiance*. That frigate's masts were shattered, her sails in rags, she could not move or shoot, and down came her flag. *Saratoga* wound further around to fire on *Linnet,* which stood it for a while, but she was sinking, her gundeck awash, and she surrendered too. For the second time in the war and in history an entire British fleet had been captured. Sir George Prevost started his retreat to Canada the next morning.

Peace was actually signed at Ghent on December 24, 1814, and when the British papers found that it did not include a single concession from the United States or an inch of territory, they were extremely indignant. They took the view, very reasonably according to the European system of thinking, that a nation whose Capitol had been burned, whose President put to flight, and whose Administration was in a state of near-collapse, should acknowledge defeat by giving up something material. But as the news from overseas began to come in, the press fell silent or shifted round to the Duke of Wellington's point of view, who told the peace commissioners roundly: "You have no right to demand anything."

For behind the barred doors of the blockade the U.S. Navy was not only still alive, but growing stronger than ever, and with the aid of the privateers, more than ever able to hurt. It was true that the British captured the frigate *President,* 44; she tried to get through the blockade of New York on the night of January 14, 1815, under Decatur, caught on the bar, pounded for so long that her sailing qualities were badly cut down, and was taken in a running fight by four British frigates. But the same month saw *Hornet* get to sea, with *Peacock* on a second cruise that was as destructive as the first. *Con-*

stitution also broke into the Atlantic, having seized a gale to run through a blockading squadron of three frigates as though they were not there. Her captain was now Charles Stewart, the same who helped Bainbridge appeal to Madison to let the warships loose, and her crew has been described as "picked men," which they certainly were. They picked themselves; everybody wanted to serve in "Old Ironsides," and this was the crew Stewart described as being capable of fighting the ship without any officers at all.

The big frigate ran to the Bay of Biscay and down the coast of Portugal, clearing out British merchant ships, then turned toward the islands of the mid-Atlantic. Burning merchantmen was dull work; in February the lieutenants sent a delegation to Stewart to beg to be led to battle; they wanted to prove that they really were aboard the finest warship in the world. "Be content," said the captain. "I promise you that before two suns have set you will be in action with the enemy and it will not be with a single ship." That second sun was almost setting on February 20 when the weird promise was made good; for out ahead there were sails on the horizon and they belonged to H.M.S. *Cyane,* 32, a light frigate of two decks, and *Levant,* 20, a heavy sloop-of-war.

Of all the combats of the War of 1812 this was one of the most remarkable. A big moon came out to watch as the firing began; under it the smoke piled into a tower, and Stewart peering aloft, saw the yards of *Cyane* swing as she tried to get across his stern for a rake. Instantly the topmen were up, the sails flung back flat against the mast; *Constitution* backed down hard, and before *Cyane* could get across her stern, raked the Britisher heavily. Ahead *Levant* was now also turning, trying for a bow rake; Stewart's swift ship-handlers sheeted home, the big frigate bounded forward and raked *Levant* also. Once again *Cyane* tried to turn for a rake; *Constitution* turned faster and crushed her, then ran *Levant* down. Both ships had struck by nine o'clock in the evening, and the news that came to London was not only that they had failed to keep *Constitution* in port, but she had taken two British warships in a single action.

This was followed by the tidings that the expedition to Louisiana had met defeat with appalling losses before New Orleans. The victory belonged to Andrew Jackson, the riflemen of the woods, and the Creoles and reformed pirates who followed him; but here also the Navy and the privateers had a part. The Navy furnished many of the artillerists along his lines who so dismayingly beat the British during the bombardment phase, and one single privateer delayed the whole expedition by three weeks, which were invaluable to Jackson.

That key event took place at Horta in the Azores, where the British battleship *Plantagenet*, 74, the frigate *Rota*, 38, and the sloop *Carnation*, 18, put in for water, while carrying all the artillery and some of the men for the Louisiana expedition. Lying inshore they sighted the privateer *General Armstrong*, 14, of New York, whose guns including a Long Tom on a pivot, commanded by Captain Samuel C. Reid who was later to invent lightships and the arrangement of the American flag, which up to his time had its stars in a circle. She had some ninety men. The harbor was neutral, but this is something that never discouraged British seamen; about eight o'clock in the evening four of *Carnation*'s boats pulled toward the privateer. Reid hailed them to keep off and when they answered by coming on, fired into them. The privateer's shooting was better than they had bargained on; they were presently pulling out again, crying quarter.

Captain Lloyd, in charge of the British squadron, now became very angry. He sent a note to the Portuguese governor, demanding that the privateer be given up to him, and in the meanwhile prepared to make sure of her by hoisting out the barges and longboats of his warships to the number of twelve, each carrying a boat carronade, and altogether not far short of four hundred men.

The news had spread through the town; fires were lighted along the shore and people came out to the rooftops as the British rushed in at midnight, firing their boat carronades and shouting: "No quarter!" Reid handled the Long Tom himself and hit them hard with it, but they came on through the storm and the blaze from the broadside guns and laid *General Armstrong* aboard, bow and stern and beam.

In the dark and fitful firelight there was a terrific struggle of pistol and pike and cutlass as the British strove to reach the deck, and once Reid had to lead the afterguard forward to clear the forecastle, which had almost been taken. "No quarter!" the British had shouted, and the Americans gave them none. "They fought more like bloodthirsty savages than anything else. They rushed into the boats sword in hand and put every soul in them to death." Two of the barges were captured, others drifted ashore full of dead and the survivors limped away. The attack on that one little privateer cost England more than any frigate battle of the war; one hundred seventy-three according to Lloyd's own admission, who did not overstate matters and who forbade his officers to write home about it.

He now threatened to treat Horta as an enemy town, so Reid scuttled his ship and took to the hills with his men, and Lloyd was rid of the annoying ship. All the same he had to lay over for three weeks while his depleted crews and officer lists were refilled. *General Armstrong*'s figurehead was saved; it stood for many years in front of the American consulate, called "O Santo Americano" by the local people, and annually decorated by them with flowers on the anniversary of Reid's great fight.

★ ★ ★ ★ ★

4

The Navy and the New World

THE UNITED STATES NAVY, which entered the war unregarded even in its own country, thus emerged from it as pound for pound the most formidable fighting service in the world. And it was a growing Navy. The need for battleships to challenge squadrons blockading our ports had been recognized, and while peace slowed the building program, the decade after the War of 1812 saw the United States Navy acquire its first ships-of-the-line—the earliest being the *Columbus* of 1816.

At the same time the structure of the Navy Department itself—which up to now had consisted almost entirely of the Secretary and a handful of clerks, was expanded by organizing a Board of Naval Commissioners composed of three senior officers of the Navy. The function of these professional administrators was at first uncertain; but eventually it led to a division of duties, with the Commissioners handling supplies and construction while the Secretary controlled ship movements, personnel, and appointments. The Commissioners organized the work of the navy yards effectively, but as the years passed and the war in which they had earned their experience faded into history they became a highly conservative brake upon the Navy, clinging to the tried and known, hostile to innovation such as steam and shell guns.

Essentially the Navy was a service of officers—Preble's boys and the lieutenants and midshipmen they had trained. There was little continuity below their level, and there did not seem to be any need for it. When a ship was put into commission, a popular captain could always count on finding enough of the type of men who had managed *Constitution*'s long 24s and defended the deck of *General Armstrong* to make up at least a strong cadre for his crew, and as the basic techniques were simple and the cruises relatively long, these men quickly trained the rest. A few old petty officers made a career of the service; the rest signed on for two years or more to see far lands and have a tale to tell, very much as the fledgling seamen since before the Revolution.

And there were far lands to see, tales to be told. The close of the War of 1812 brought something like an explosion of the American merchant marine, manned by people who had learned their business in the privateers. The coast of China, the South Atlantic, the Mediterranean became suddenly interesting; the shores of northern Europe, the West Indies, and the Grand Banks always had been. Moreover, and although there were still some restrictions such as port dues, it was no longer really necessary to smuggle; the old monopolies had been abolished and the ships of the new merchant marine could be built big and go ahead boldly in the world that followed the Napoleonic wars. The privateer *Chasseur,* become a peaceful trader, made a passage to China that stood for many years as a speed record for that run.

The new world was not an entirely peaceful world, but now that the Navy had shown what it could do, there was a noticeable difference in temper since the days when we paid tribute to the Barbary powers. Just after the outbreak of the War of 1812, Algiers, the strongest of the Barbary states, captured an American ship and enslaved the crew. The moment the news from Ghent arrived, Congress declared war and sent Decatur to the Mediterranean with three frigates, two sloops-of-war, and five light Baltimore clippers. Inside Gibraltar the squadron sighted the Algerine flagship, a heavy frigate, ran her down and reduced her to a wreck in twenty minutes. Two days later a pirate sloop-of-war was run ashore and blown up. Decatur went on to Algiers itself, where he made the Dey of Algiers the amazing proposal that he should sign a new treaty, not only abolishing tribute, but paying an indemnity for the enslaved crew. Such a thing had never been heard of before in the history of Barbary, and threatened the whole base of its economy. The Dey squalled and tried to temporize, but Decatur told

THE NAVY AND THE NEW WORLD

him that every Algerine ship in the Mediterranean would pay for it, and as the sails of some of them appeared off the mouth of the harbor and *Constellation* got under way to intercept, the barbarian signed. It is probable that he meant to wriggle out of his agreement, according to established Barbary practice, but Decatur had hardly left his port before Bainbridge arrived with one of the new American battleships, two more heavy frigates and a trail of Baltimore clippers, merely for a social call.

The two squadrons visited Tunis and Tripoli and collected indemnities there, too, and this was the real end of the North African piracies, for if a small power like the United States could thus set them at defiance, they were no further use in restraining neutral commerce. The English and Dutch sent down a powerful combined fleet which nearly blew Algiers apart.

In view of the uncertain temper of the Barbaries and certain other Mediterranean matters that needed clearing up, it was decided to set up a regular "cruise"—the ships usually out for two years or more and making various harbors, but normally employing Port Mahon as a base. It was a much prized assignment for both officers and seamen. Drills at sea with guns and sails had been so thoroughly built into the structure of the service ever since the days of Truxtun that they were a matter of habit, a part of life. But there was more time in harbor on these Mediterranean cruises, and the ports had a lot to offer— Marseille, Naples, Syracuse, Cartagena, with an occasional trip to the Levant. Many of the songs of American sailormen reflect the gay mood of the period:

> I lost my hat at Cape de Gat,
> And where do you think I found it?
> Behind a stone at Port Mahon,
> With three pretty girls around it.

Curiously, officers' dress became more informal about this time: they had been given permission to replace knee-breeches with trousers, and they had a tendency to stand watches in frock coats and high silk hats. For the men, however, uniforms became more and more standardized. Purchases by naval agents in the 1820s included blue cloth jackets and trousers, duck frocks, flannel shirts and drawers, duck trousers, pea jackets, red vests, and black silk handkerchiefs.

These were probably kept for full dress occasions, the rest of the time seamen wore pretty much what they pleased until the 1841 Naval Uniform Regulations set the first definite rules for enlisted uniforms:

> The outside clothing of the petty officers, seamen, and ordinary seamen, landsmen and boys, for muster, shall consist of blue woolen frocks, with white linen or duck collars and cuffs, or blue cloth jacket and trousers, blue vests where vests are worn, black hat, black handkerchief and shoes, when the weather is cold: when the weather is warm, it shall consist of white frocks and trousers, and black or white hats as the commander may direct, having regard to the convenience and comfort of the crew, black handkerchiefs and shoes. The collars and breasts of the frocks to be lined or faced with blue cotton cloth, stitched with white thread or cotton.

During those years there was a considerable amount of seepage of foreign elements into the service as men's time expired, and they were replaced by Italians, French, Greeks, and most especially English, enlisted on station. This was of no particular importance at the time, since the supply of able seamen trained in the booming clipper trade was practically unlimited, but it set a precedent that rose up later.

The Mediterranean was not the only cruise. A considerable number of ships had to be kept in commission off West Africa against the slave trade. During all the early years of the century there was endemic warfare with the pirates of the Caribbean, and a graceless service it was against them. The Latin Americans of the South American coast were in revolt, but the islands remained faithful to Spain. Both the new republics and Spanish governors issued privateering commissions to men who would pay off shares, and none of them particularly cared what flags the ships they took bore. The only answer was a continual naval patrol. It began with a pair of frigates and three or four sloops, but they were too heavy for close inshore work, yellow fever cut the crews to pieces, and the American law courts usually released captured men for lack of evidence.

Things were not notably improved until David Porter was sent out in 1823 with a squadron of light-draft schooners and heavy barges, plus a little New York ferryboat, the *Sea Gull*. The Navy's first steamship to see active duty, she was assigned to tow other craft into the inlets in pursuit of the picaroons. Porter established a base at Pensa-cola, and kept out of the Caribbean during the fever season; also he discovered that the British had a patrol of their own, and made a zoning agreement with them. Oddly enough, the captured pirates were always taken in the British zone and could therefore be taken to Jamaica and hanged.

But Porter got into trouble over the "Foxardo affair," very famous in its day, when one of his lieutenants landed at the town of that name in Puerto Rico to recover some goods lost to pirates, and was jailed by the local alcaide, who later released him with a warning about coming back. Porter sent the lieutenant back with two hundred sailors and got an apology, but Washington was playing up to Spain just then and suspended the Commodore for the "insult," whereupon he re-signed the service. This produced no appreciable easement for the buccaneers and their shoreside backers; instead of Porter there came to the West Indies command Lewis Warrington, who had been skipper of *Peacock* during the war, and he never reported taking any prisoners because he never took any. Under his administration West Indian piracy withered on the vine.

Meanwhile, in the Pacific the sloop-of-war *Ontario*, 16, was ex-ploring the utterly unknown waters on the west coast of North Amer-ica. In 1818, her captain nailed a lead plate to a tree at the mouth of the Columbia River and claimed possession of all the lands that fed it for the United States—something not without effect on the diplo-macy of later years. On the way out she had an adventure typical of the Navy of those days, when she put into Callao for water. It was still in Spanish hands at the time and North Americans were unloved because of their sympathy with the South American revolutionaries. The water-boat's crew was set on with stones, then with sword and pistol. James Biddle, captain of the sloop, sent in a note asking for explanations, and when it was not answered, sent in another, saying he would start shooting in twenty minutes. He was clearing for action when a shore-boat pulled out with the offending soldiers in irons and a letter from the governor asking they be flogged, then otherwise punished as the Americans wished and returned for court-martial. Biddle let them off; he had what he wanted, which was respect for the flag.

Indeed, the concept of making the American flag respected dominates the whole of the long period after the War of 1812. It turned naval captains into armed diplomats. Under the guns of the frigate *Congress,* Captain J. D. Henley gained from the Chinese the right for American ships to buy provisions in their ports in 1820, and under more guns Biddle negotiated a trade treaty with that power in 1845. Captain Geisinger of *Peacock,* 18, won a trade treaty with Siam in 1833. Sometimes the guns had to be put to use. In 1831 an American trading ship was set upon by the Malays of Quallah Battoo in Sumatra and most of her crew murdered; the frigate *Potomac,* 44, presently appeared, sent ashore a powerful landing party which killed one hundred fifty of the offenders, including their sultan, and burned the town. The same treatment was meted out to natives in the Fijis, who assassinated an American sailor in 1835, and in 1839 the frigate *Columbia,* 44, had to make a second visit to Sumatra, where the natives of Mukkee had killed a trading captain and plundered his ship. The usual corrective was applied.

There is in existence the journal of a seaman on that voyage and it has a good deal to say, both directly and by implication, about what concerned men of the class and profession at the time. The journalist treats the fight with the Sumatrans *en passant,* as merely a matter to fill out the record. He is deeply concerned with the religion of the people of Ceylon, the use of the taliput tree, the physical appearance of Arabians, and thoughts of melancholy on a death at sea. (He read Byron and quoted him to other members of the crew.) Meetings with various ships and the exchange of news that always took place on such occasions are carefully recorded; so is an occasional flogging.

Columbia's cruise, which lasted from May, 1838, to June, 1840, was one of a pair of special exploring expeditions; she did a good deal of charting in the Indian Ocean. The other expedition, under Lieutenant Charles Wilkes, was for the South Pacific, with two sloops-of-war, one brig, and two small schooners. Wilkes set up a base at Sydney, Australia, discovered the Antarctic continent and ran for nearly a thousand miles along its coast, then turned north and surveyed one hundred fifty-four islands (some of his surveys were still being used in World War II) before exploring the Pacific Coast from Puget Sound to the Sacramento River. He came home in 1842, after nearly four years at sea, with one of the largest budgets of information ever produced by a single expedition.

Much of the data brought back by these expeditions was put to good use by the Navy's Depot of Charts and Instruments, later to become the Hydrographic Office. Under leadership of Lieutenant Matthew Fontaine Maury, an outstanding officer who had come ashore because of an injury that had lamed him, the Depot began compiling reports on weather, currents, and tides all over the world. Culled from the logs of merchantmen and warships and assembled on charts, this information showed the clipper masters what routes to sail for the fastest passages: the average voyage from New York to California was cut by forty-seven days and American shipowners saved—thanks to Maury and the Navy—some $2,000,000 a year. Maury made storm and rain charts, trade wind charts, temperature charts, climaxing his work with his famous *Physical Geography of the Sea,* a milestone in oceanography.

Not all reports on far places were scientific. The men of the cruising Navy found unadvertised fringe benefits. A gunner aboard the sloop-of-war *Cyane* has left a vivid picture of shore leave at Honolulu in the early '40s:

. . . Whilst inquiring the customs and manners of the Natives, I suffered myself to become the victim of the Seducing wiles of the beautiful Maria Hilia. She was a beautiful creature—a being of more than earthly mould. She was moulded with exquisite taste, and about 14 years of age—a putapaa or virgin. In a fit of passion I purchased her from her father. . . . With a flute I lounged of afternoons in her savage boudoir and drank in the mild accents of her silvery voice. Upon my arrival at the Hut my coat and vest were taken and hung carefully up. The Father took my boots to clean. The Sisters sat by me with fans to fan me to delicious slumbers. The younger brother held a calabash for me to spit in; the older brought fruit, segars, or whatever I asked for. By playing upon the flute and listening to them upon the same instrument, & hearing them sing, I passed the afternoons and evenings like a King . . .[1]

But life in the Navy had a darker side as well. In 1843, the old frigate *United States* picked up a stranded 24-year-old whaleman at

[1] *Journal of a Cruise to the Pacific Ocean, 1842–44,* edited by Charles R. Anderson, copyright 1937 by Duke University Press.

Hawaii who signed on for the voyage home. Number 572 on the muster roll was a quiet young fellow, but he was probably the most gifted literary man ever to wear Navy blue. Some years after he got home, late ordinary seaman Herman Melville, USN, sat down and wrote a book on his fourteen months in the Navy. "White-Jacket" told not only of his life aboard the U.S.S. *Neversink* but pointed up what he felt were abuses in the service, particularly flogging. Flogging had been limited for years to twelve lashes, but official records show that one hundred sixty-three floggings occurred during Melville's enlistment, mostly for drunkenness or liquor smuggling.

Melville's book came out just as a bill was introduced into Congress to abolish the lash and undoubtedly played a part in arousing public support for the measure. The bill passed amid loud complaints from conservative officers that discipline at sea could not be maintained without the threat of flogging. Naval leadership answered the challenge, however, and proved the die-hards wrong.

II

The flogging controversy was one evidence of the strains that appeared in the service as inevitable change had to be faced. For one thing, the old Board of Naval Commissioners had not been very satisfactory administratively, while they had aroused the distrust of Congress by attempting to control departmental policy. In 1842 they were replaced by a series of bureaus, each headed by a single officer reporting to the Secretary, a system that with many modifications has survived to the present. Almost simultaneously a new branch of the service was created, an Engineer Corps, not yet regular officers, charged with handling the new steamships that were appearing on the Navy's lists. For many changes were technical, connected with the slow coming of steam and the more rapid acceptance of the new shell-firing guns. Robert Fulton built the first steam warship during the War of 1812, a craft with a catamaran hull enclosing a paddle wheel, intended as a harbor defense ship and blockade-breaker. The war was over before she was finished, and nobody wanted the freak. She lay at Brooklyn dock as a receiving ship until an accidental explosion destroyed her in 1829. The little *Sea Gull,* the fighting ferryboat, was not retained after the West Indian operations. Another *Fulton* was built in 1830, along much the same lines as the first, and had very little influence.

At this point there entered the picture one of the dominant figures of the Navy during the first half of the nineteenth century, Matthew Calbraith Perry, "the cast-iron commodore," younger brother of the victor of Lake Erie. He had done a tour of duty in Europe, where he witnessed the experiments of the French Colonel Henri Paixhans with shell-firing artillery, and furnished such detailed and enthusiastic reports that when he returned the second *Fulton* was equipped with these guns and he was appointed to command her. He took the ship down to Sandy Hook and embarked on a series of firings that convinced everyone in the Navy of the value of the new guns; soon all the frigates and heavy sloops were mounting two or more on their upper decks.

The transfer to steam was not so easily achieved. Old-line sailors were disgusted with the dirty business, and in the early days of steam they had some arguments on their side. Coal consumption was high, which meant that much of a fighting ship had to be given up to bunkers and even then there was only enough for a few days' steaming. The paddle wheels took up much of the broadside space normally used for guns, cut off light and air, making midships unsuitable for quarters, and were easily crippled by a single shot. The engines themselves were balky and unreliable and equally vulnerable to damage. Boilers exploded or could be blown apart by gunfire, dooming the black gang to death by scalding.

Yet it was imperative that the Navy learn to use this kind of ship that could maneuver in battle independent of the direction or strength of the wind—and Perry saw it. Finally he was driven to the expedient of using his family influence (of which he had a great deal) to get the best civilian engineers organized into their special corps, like the medical branch.

He also used his influence with friends in Congress to push through an appropriation for two paddle-wheel, ocean-going cruisers, *Mississippi* and *Missouri,* a third larger than *Constitution,* but carrying only 10 guns each, shell-firers of the largest type. Getting the appropriations through required a certain amount of give and take, and part of the support for the idea came from Robert F. Stockton, one of the few naval officers who ever got mixed up in politics. He had a steamship project of his own, the result of meeting in London a Swedish engineer named John Ericsson, who showed him the drawings for a ship driven by a screw propeller under her stern, which would get rid of the vulnerable paddle wheels and permit the engine to be placed below the waterline, where they would be in less danger from shot. The screw propeller had been tried before without success; Ericsson explained that this was because previous makers had not calculated the pitch and size of the propellers correctly. Backed by Stockton, Ericsson built a 70-foot ship on his own design, which crossed the Atlantic with great success.

Stockton brought Ericsson to the United States, where the engineer designed the screw sloop *Princeton,* of 10 heavy guns, like those of the paddle-wheelers. Of course Stockton himself received command; he brought the ship up the Potomac in February, 1844, and the Cabinet and a party of Congressmen went aboard. On the quarter-deck and forecastle *Princeton* mounted two huge guns, one designed by Ericsson, the other by Stockton himself; and when the Stockton gun was fired it blew up, killing the Secretaries of State and Navy and some of the Congressmen. Stockton wanted Ericsson to testify that there was nothing fundamentally wrong with the design of his gun, but the engineer refused, saying that there was everything wrong with it and he had told Stockton so in highly specific terms. Stockton thereupon saw to it that Ericsson's bill for engineering services on *Princeton* was refused payment and the Swede declared he would never again do anything for the U.S. Navy.

This was one of the developing strains; but a more acute one was in the field of personnel. At the bottom of it lay an invincible prejudice of the age against anything that smacked of aristocracy. It led to repeated calls on Congress for the abolition of West Point, on the ground that it was training a "caste" of officers, and with regard to the Navy, it kept the officer list small and rigorously held the highest rank to that of captain. In addition there was no retirement system, and Preble's boys, who had fought the War of 1812, were an exceptionally long-lived group. In the 1840s four of them still held as many of the major squadron commands. The result was almost complete stagnation of promotions; between 1816 and 1826 only one lieutenant moved up to captain. This bore with peculiar weight upon the lower officer ranks, the midshipmen coming up for lieutenancies, during the '30s and '40s. Midshipmen thirty years old were quite ordinary, and there was at least one "passed midshipman" waiting for rank as a lieutenant at the age of fifty.

The midshipman was not quite an officer, and the only instruction he received was from the professors of mathematics attached to each of the larger ships—a system haphazard at the best. Increasingly, the junior lieutenants of those years showed the effects of their long association with the lower deck. Boredom, an exaggerated sense of personal honor, and the bad example of some of their seniors of the war generation led not infrequently to duels on the beach; sometimes with comic but sometimes with tragic results. When one squadron commander required his midshipmen to sign a pledge not to duel, some resigned the service in disgust at this infringement of their "personal liberty."

Not only were the mids rough and given to heavy drinking, but they lacked initiative and were unwilling to accept responsibility. This was felt particularly by Matthew Perry in relation to the new engineering branch; it was his theory that officers of the line and engineers should be interchangeable, for which there was no chance whatever in the existing state of training. Perry's solution was a series of training cruises, during which instruction should be thorough, and which should include not only young midshipmen newly appointed, but also a class of apprentice seamen, getting preliminary training for petty officer and technical ratings.

The first such ship, the brig *Somers,* 10, put out in 1842 on a cruise to Africa, under Alexander Slidell Mackenzie, a relative of Perry's. He was certainly not an ideal choice for the billet. Among the mids he had aboard was one Philip Spencer, son of the Secretary of War, a juvenile delinquent with a thoroughly bad record. On the way back from Africa, a purser's mate came to the cabin to tell Mackenzie that Spencer had tried to get him to join a mutiny which was to seize the ship, kill her officers and sail her to the Spanish Main as a pirate. Mackenzie had Spencer arrested and his locker searched; it contained papers that seemed to Mackenzie to be fairly definite proof that something very serious and dangerous was cooking. Next day the crew began to behave badly—stamping, shouting and gathering in groups. Mackenzie had two more men ironed—Bosun's Mate Cromwell and Seaman Small, who were listed as Spencer's main assistants—and when the demonstrations did not cease, the captain ordered a court of inquiry which decided that Spencer, Cromwell, and Small should be hanged from the yardarm.

They were swung off, and when the brig reached home there was a terrific scandal and a controversy still not completely resolved. A board exonerated Mackenzie. But just at this point James K. Polk came to the presidency, it was practically certain that there would be a war with Mexico, maybe one with Britain in addition, and perfectly obvious that the Navy needed overhauling. Polk appointed George Bancroft, the historian, as his naval Secretary, and Bancroft proceeded to organize a naval school by subterfuge, since he never could get the authorization through Congress. The money for the professors of mathematics was earmarked "for instruction." Bancroft borrowed an old fort at Annapolis from the Army, dismissed most of the professors and sent the few who could really teach to that town, with a lieutenant to give training in steam and gunnery. As fast as the ships came in from cruise, midshipmen were sent there to be taught. The school opened on October 10, 1845, with a classroom in a shed and exactly three students.

Its early days were hectic, with mids who had been pretty much uncontrolled on foreign cruises. But Bancroft stuck with it, he was backed by Polk, and a new generation of officers began to filter into the service. From now on it was not enough for a naval officer to be a brave seaman and a gentleman: he had to be professionally educated for his career.

III

Mexico had no Navy, and the active service of ours in the war that broke out in 1846 was limited to a series of landings on the California coast, which had a good deal to do with the rapid conquest of that area, and blockade and inshore work along the Gulf of Mexico. Under Commodore John D. Sloat and later Commodore Robert F. Stockton, the Pacific squadron landed sailors and marines to seize the California ports and co-operate with the American forces ashore. In the Gulf, Commodore David Conner and his second in command, Commodore Matthew C. Perry, battled weather, climate, and the problems of maintaining a blockading fleet nine hundred miles from the nearest base. The chief result of the early part of the war was to demonstrate the utter inadequacy of the Navy Department organization to handle any such problem. Pensacola was at the opposite end of the Gulf, and it was so poorly supplied that it took thirty days to bake enough ship's biscuit to supply the flagship for three months. The Mexican coast is lashed by violent onshore winds and its harbors beset with bars. There were few ships of light draft available, and these all sailing craft that could not keep station against the gales. When small steamers arrived there was no coal for them, and they had to anchor helplessly in sight of the shore.

In the face of these obstacles, Matthew Perry made a name for himself first as second-in-command and then as commodore of the Gulf Squadron. The American squadrons not only conducted what was in effect a series of commando raids along the coast, but also co-operated in large scale combined operations with the Army—a foretaste of what was to be the Navy's major function in the Civil War. When it was decided to land an Army at Vera Cruz to march inland to Mexico City, the Navy put the troops ashore under their guns, then provided heavy fire support from the harbor in the siege of the city that followed. After the fall of Vera Cruz, Perry captured a number of coastal towns with a special landing force of sailors and marines, climaxing his operations with the seizure of Tabasco, seventy miles up a river. Steamers towed up boatloads of marines, successfully passed batteries along the banks, breached obstructions in the channel, landed them far inland. The outcome of the war was decided in battles ashore, but the Navy demonstrated once again the immense advantage that control of the sea provides an invading force.

Perry's successful operations led to his appointment a few years later to command a naval squadron assigned to open up Japan. Not a casual act of imperialism, this project was rooted in the interests of the northern whalers and the trading ships that visited Chinese ports. Currents and storms not infrequently cast these vessels on the coast of Japan. That nation had sealed itself off from the world, allowing no contact for more than two centuries except through the single Dutch ship that was permitted to visit Nagasaki once a year, and throwing the visitors of disaster into prison to be shipped out by this vessel, minus their possessions. Practically every nation of Europe had tried to persuade the Japanese that they really did not live on an island in the sky, but without the slightest success.

Perry spent nearly two years in preparation for his effort to break this barrier, first carefully studying every document of previous visitors to Japan—whether Dutch, Spanish, Portuguese, English, or Russian—to form some idea of the psychology and institutions of this people. He personally hand picked the crews of the two steam frigates and two sloops that were to make the expedition, for he had worked it out that the leading danger to such an enterprise would flow from acts of inadvertent discourtesy, and he wanted to be certain that everything was under the firmest control of the high command. Every sort of scientist and artist wanted to go; he refused all but those who would enlist in the Navy, so he could hold them tight. President Fillmore gave him a letter to the Emperor of Japan, which was installed in an elaborately carved box, together with a package of gifts to illustrate the products of Western civilization.

The fleet went first to Hong Kong, then to the Bonins, where Perry persuaded the natives to let him set up an advance base, then sailed for Japan, anchoring in Yedo Bay on July 8, 1853, with his ships cleared for action, obviously strong enough to beat off any attack. They were instantly surrounded by a cloud of picket-boats which came to warn the foreigners away, including an officer who spoke Dutch. He asked to see the Commodore; Perry sent a gunner's mate, who said that "the Lord of the Forbidden Interior" was of such exalted rank that he could not think of talking to anyone in a boat.

The Japanese said: "We have the vice-governor of Uraga aboard. He is of very high rank."

The petty officer: "Why did you not bring the governor?"

"He is forbidden to board ships. Will the Lord of the Forbidden Interior send an officer of low enough rank to talk to the vice-governor?"

Perry sent a junior lieutenant, who told them that the expedition had a letter from the Mikado of America to the Emperor of Japan, which must be delivered in person. The vice-governor said it should be sent through the Dutch agency at Nagasaki. The lieutenant (under instructions) replied that they were mere merchants, of insufficient dignity for such a matter. The vice-governor was impressed by this reasoning, but asked to see the letter; the lieutenant replied that if an officer of adequate rank appeared he could see a copy; the original was for the eyes of the Emperor alone.

The vice-governor retired. Next day a gilded barge brought the governor who, as a great concession, was received by Captain Buchanan of the flagship, said he did not believe there was any letter, and was shown the carved, inlaid gold box, but not allowed to peek. The letter must be carried by Perry in person to the Emperor in person. The Commodore sent word that if necessary he would land with an armed party and deliver his message or die.

The governor was charmed; these were the first barbarians seen in Japan who understood rank and responsibility. He accepted a glass of liquor and asked for three days for consultation, at the end of which he reported that a very exalted personage was coming down to receive the letter, and a special house would be built at Nagasaki for the ceremony. Perry said no, not Nagasaki, and the Japanese finally admitted that the Lord of the Forbidden Interior was a functionary too important to consort with the low-caste Dutch, while the Commodore agreed to deliver the letter to the Prince of Idzu, an official of alpine dignity, third ranking individual in Japan. He would come back six months later for an answer. And all the while the ships were cleared for action and the men at battle stations.

In February, 1854, Perry was back, with all the vessels that could be collected from the Eastern squadron—three steam frigates, four sloops —and commissioners sat down to talk matters over. There were three weeks of these discussions, but the result was now inevitable; by acceptance of the letter under Perry's terms, the Japanese had admitted the Americans as equal in dignity, and they could not do less than grant the request for contact without losing face. Two ports were opened to American commerce and the shell of the hermit empire was cracked. It was the outstanding achievement of the long course of naval diplomacy.

★　　★　　★　　★　　★

5

New Beginning Under Pressure

IN THE MEXICAN WAR, West Point brilliantly justified its existence; the young officers from the Military Academy carried the load, although the high command was mostly composed of political appointees of a rather low degree of competence. At the outbreak of the Civil War few of the Annapolis men had risen above very junior lieutenants, and all the higher offices were in the hands of old captains, settled in their ways. Promotion by seniority had clogged the officer lists to such an extent that there had been produced a whole body of routine men without initiative. Although in 1855 a special personnel board—of which the moving spirit was Captain Samuel Du Pont—had summarily dismissed or retired more than two hundred senior officers in an attempt to speed promotion and raise the standard of the corps, many of these had been restored to active duty by political pull.

Now when open civil war broke out, about one-third of the officers went South with their states. Among them was Maury, the brilliant oceanographer, and notable senior officers such as Franklin Buchanan and Commodore Josiah Tattnall, who had won a niche in history by proclaiming "Blood is thicker than water!" when he took the American China Squadron to the aid of harassed Britishers in 1859. On the other hand many prominent Southern officers stayed by the flag. Farragut, the most outstanding Union naval commander in the war and our first admiral, was Tennessee-born and had close ties to Virginia by marriage. The famous naval family of Porters was divided; and so were such lesser-known families as the Draytons and the Parkers.

Among the ratings, Union feeling was strong and the Navy entered the war better prepared. There was a strong body of career petty officers, bosuns, gunners, quartermasters, and an even stronger group of available seamen, for the 1850s were the age when the American clipper ships, with their fine lines and towering clouds of sail, had captured nearly half the carrying trade of the world.

Materially, the service was less ready for war than at the date of the struggle with Mexico. There were five heavy screw frigates, built in the '50s, some of the most powerful warships in the world, but all were out of commission and one of them, *Merrimac,* was burned to the waterline when Virginia seceded and Norfolk Navy Yard fell to the Confederates. Behind these were seven strong first-class screw sloops and eight smaller second-class screw sloops, plus four paddle-wheelers. It was thus a Navy that in appearance had fully accepted steam; but this appearance was illusory. The old officers still regarded steam and the engineers with unconcealed dislike, and the Department kept as many of the older sailing frigates and sloops on its various cruising stations as it possibly could, because they were less expensive to operate than steamships. The character of Isaac Toucey, President Buchanan's Secretary of the Navy, also played a part in the unreadiness; he was most completely a "dough-face," a Southern appeaser, unwilling to do anything that might drive the slave states nearer the secession they had already decided upon, and he scattered the Navy to the ends of the earth to make it clear that no aggressive action was intended, not even summoning a single ship home after the hectic December which began with South Carolina passing her ordinance of secession.

The result was that when Lincoln proclaimed the blockade of three thousand miles of Southern coast on April 19, 1861, there were exactly three ships in commission in home waters to enforce this blockade. Jefferson Davis somewhat eased the situation for the North by proclaiming an embargo on cotton, with the idea that the European powers who wanted it would be forced by economic pressure to break the blockade. Things were still more eased by the fact that the cotton-shipping season was in the late winter and all but one-seventh of the

1860 crop had already gone out at the date of the embargo. There was thus granted to the Federal government a certain amount of time to make good its boast.

This time was well spent by Gideon Welles, the Connecticut editor and politician whom Lincoln appointed his Secretary of the Navy. With his long beard he looked like a slow-witted farmer, but his rustic exterior concealed a sharp intelligence. He was a man who understood naval administration—he had once been a bureau chief in the Navy Department—and how to handle political contacts on a strictly moral basis of New England principle. In the beginning he and his advisors believed that an adequate blockade would be established if warships were stationed off the leading cotton ports—Wilmington, North Carolina; Charleston; Savannah; Pensacola; Mobile; Galveston; and the entrances to the Mississippi. By July each of these places had at least one warship in the offing, but it was at once evident to Welles that he would not have ships enough even for such a limited operation. What was worse, he would still be short of blockaders after all the vessels abroad came winging home. The Secretary at once launched a buying program in all of the Northern ports to obtain commercial ships that would be able to carry guns. These were considered to be adequate in view of the fact that the blockade-runners were not armed at all and shell-firing guns could cripple any of them with a shot.

In addition, and without even waiting for Congressional authorization, Welles began a huge building program. He had laid down twenty "90-day gunboats," so called from the speed of their construction, quite fast and handy vessels with one big gun and a pair of howitzers. Under a neglected authorization of 1858 for six second-class screw sloops, he built fourteen rapidly.

It was June, 1861, before any of the purchased ships arrived off Southern ports, and then there were only two. But by this date it was already evident that merely placing a ship off each harbor would nowhere near make an effective blockade. There was a very large coastal traffic, as there had been since before the Revolution, and it was important to the Union to put a stop to it if possible. Much of the Confederate coast was protected by barren islands leaving long sounds and inlets between island and mainland—a system of inland waterways very accessible to light-draft vessels. Nearly all the Southern harbors under blockade had subsidiary side entrances to these inlets, so that they both harbored coastal traffic and aided blockade runners to slip in.

Thus, from the beginning, the blockade was by compulsion different from any previously undertaken; closer, intended to interrupt small traffic as well as large, ships constantly called on to duel the batteries the Confederates set up along the shore and in the estuaries of the great rivers. As this pattern became apparent, every kind of vessel was snapped up by the purchasing program; sailing ships and fast steamers for cruising off the coast. (It is worth noting that the side-wheelers were generally faster than the screws; and one of the finest and fastest of the blockade-runners, *Circassian,* was taken by an armed walking-beam ferryboat off the Bahamas far to the east.) Tugs were bought for the inlets and curious craft from New York and Boston harbors, one hundred thirty-seven all told by the end of 1861. The available guns were nearly all in the larger sizes, such as 8- or 9-inch smooth-bores, mostly produced through the energy of Commander John A. Dahlgren of the Washington Navy Yard. But this was all right in view of the fact that few of the ships could carry more than one or two in any case.

The ferryboats turned out a great success because of their ability to reverse direction without turning round. Before the year was out Welles had authorized the construction of twelve naval adaptations—the "double-enders," with a rudder at each terminal and independently revolving paddle wheels. Among all the ships built for the Navy during the period these were among the oddest.

To supply officers for this expanded fleet, the regular service was not only greatly enlarged, but thousands of volunteer officers commissioned—largely from the merchant marine and commercial steamers—the first step toward a regular system of naval reserves. The volunteers did valuable duty but they included men of a wide range of capacities. Some of the oddest were in the engineer corps: engineers were in such short supply that almost anyone with a recommendation could get commissioned there. One ship went to sea with the Chief—a regular—ill: His four assistant engineers were a semi-literate fireman, promoted for bravery in battle; a New Hampshire schoolmaster whose only acquaintance with engines was a picture in a textbook; his favorite pupil; and an ex-skipper of a tugboat. Another Navy ship suddenly appeared going full speed astern into New York harbor, from which she had sailed shortly before: the engines had gone into reverse and none of her volunteer engineers could get her going ahead again. But taken as a whole, the volunteers were invaluable, most of them learned their jobs rapidly, and the Navy could not have carried out its job without them.

II

One of the first acts of the new Confederate government was to authorize privateering, and this was, in fact, the proximate reason for Lincoln's blockade proclamation. Small Confederate vessels immediately began working out of the Carolina sounds, Wilmington, and the mouths of the Mississippi, doing no little damage to seagoing traffic. It was evident from the start that armed sailing ships were nearly useless in stopping this business. On the other hand, maintaining steamers off the Southern ports involved long trips northward for refueling.

There was a man named Gustavus Vasa Fox, who had been an officer in the Navy for eighteen years before retiring to go into the textile business. He came forward with a plan for the relief of Fort Sumter during the Buchanan administration, and as soon as Lincoln became President, Fox was appointed to carry out his scheme. It failed—Fox thought because at the last moment Secretary of State Seward detached his most powerful naval unit to go to Pensacola on an errand of the Secretary's own devising. Fox returned to Washington in high dudgeon, and as he was a close connection of the influential political family, the Blairs, one of whom was in the Cabinet, something had to be done to placate him. Lincoln had Welles make Fox chief clerk of the Navy Department (he was legislated in as Assistant Secretary in December, 1861), and never was a piece of political jobbery better rewarded. Fox had everything Welles lacked —burning energy, a vast assortment of new ideas, intimate acquaintance with nearly every shipping man in the North and first-hand experience with the Navy afloat.

At the beginning of the war he appointed a board to consider effecting a lodgment on the Southern coast, both to acquire a convenient coaling station and to discourage privateers. It was a rather remarkable committee, including captains S. F. Du Pont and Charles Davis of the Navy, Major Barnard of the Army Engineers, and Professor Alexander Bache of the Coast Survey; the two latter knew the ground intimately, and the two former were as well informed as any men in America on naval strategy. They reported that neither Charleston nor Wilmington could be taken with the forces available, but Port Royal, on the South Carolina coast between Charleston and Savannah, probably could, and it could be held, since it was on a complex of islands with a good, deep harbor inside. It was reported, however, to be well fortified, and with the Bull Run fiasco fresh in the public mind it was felt that the Union could not risk the possibility of a naval defeat as well. It was therefore decided to try first for an easier objective. The choice fell on Hatteras Inlet, the entrance to the North Carolina sounds, where the Confederates had erected two small forts.

The expedition sailed from Fortress Monroe on August 26, 1861. It was composed of the big screw frigates *Minnesota* and *Wabash,* the paddle-wheeler *Susquehanna,* and the sailing sloop *Cumberland,* the best-armed of her class, in addition to two smaller vessels and a landing force of eight hundred troops. It was under the command of Flag Officer Silas H. Stringham. The troops were set ashore on a sand-spit below one of the forts and accomplished nothing; but when the big frigates moved in and began shelling, there came to light an important fact of strategy—that it is easier to move heavy guns by water than overland. The squadron outranged the forts and it had far greater fire power; there was no damage or casualties in the fleet and after a day and a half of bombardment the white flags came out ashore.

It was the first clean Union victory of the war, but when it was not followed up by a sharp offensive into the sounds the papers criticized Stringham and he resigned active command. This made practically obligatory the appointment of Du Pont to the command for the far more ambitious Port Royal project, since he knew more about the coast than anyone else.

Du Pont, tall, handsome, courtly, from the family of Delaware powdermakers, was a highly intelligent officer with the ability to inspire great devotion among his junior officers. The Department gave him *Wabash* and *Susquehanna,* with four of the new 90-day gunboats, four pre-war gunboats, six purchased steamers, and a landing force of thirteen thousand troops. A terrific gale off Cape Hatteras destroyed two of the transports and all the special landing equipment, and when Du Pont reached Port Royal early on November 7, he decided to go in with the ships alone. The batteries of the Confederate forts on both sides of the entrance were heavy, but not as heavy as the ships' guns. Du Pont maneuvered his battle line in long, slow ovals which gave his artillery maximum accuracy and the guns ashore the minimum. He was chiefly worried about the gunboat *Pocahontas,* commanded by Percival Drayton, a South Carolinan whose brother was in charge of one of the forts; she had not appeared since the gale, and Drayton might be hanging back. But just as the ships started their second oval *Pocahantas* came down under full head of steam, and having no place in the line, drove right in to engage muzzle to muzzle. What were left of the Confederates fled, and Port Royal and its fine harbor were taken.

The effect was a dreadful shock to the Confederacy, whose engineers had pronounced the Port Royal forts as strong as it was possible to build anywhere along the coast. Du Pont was encouraged to further efforts. As soon as the hurricane season was over in March of 1862 he sent an expedition which took Fernandina in northern Florida, then successively St. Augustine, St. John's, and St. Mary's. This practically knocked Florida out of the war, for inland communications there were poor and few. It had another effect, slow to appear. The Florida salt mills supplied most of the material with which the hams and bacon of the South were cured. Through all the rest of the war Federal inshore gunboats were engaged in sending landing parties to burn these mills, and no little part of the food shortage that afflicted the Confederacy was due to the Navy's Florida salt blockade.

Du Pont's seacoast landings also made it possible to set up a blockade new in history, one in which the blockading ships not only hung off the coast, but also penetrated the inland rivers and sounds. No view of the destruction of the Rebellion is complete that does not recognize the vital importance of the fact that after Du Pont's operations, the Confederacy's windows on the Atlantic were limited to Charleston, Wilmington, and Savannah. The blockade was no easy duty. All sorts of accidents befell the Union ships. They were ambushed by flying batteries of field artillery, they were sniped at by sharpshooters, ran aground, or were driven ashore in storms. Their men sweltered in summer, shivered in winter, and nearly expired from

monotony the year 'round. But they held the whole Atlantic coast in
a grip of iron.

III

The river navy was even more of an improvisation than that on the
ocean, because there was no fund of experience to say what a warship
for river service should be like. The Confederates built theirs by placing heavy inner bulwarks in towboats and packet steamers and filling
the spaces between them and the sides with highly compressed cotton,
fitting the bow with an iron ram. The Union had better luck in the
design phase. Early in the war there came to Washington the famous
engineer and salvage operator James B. Eads, with a plan for iron-
plated gunboats to control the western rivers. These waters were technically under Army jurisdiction and Simon Cameron, the Secretary
of War, asserted his authority; but he assented to a naval commander
going west to see about this business. The naval commander was John
Rodgers of a distinguished Navy family, who had no experience in
rivers at all and only the most limited acquaintance with steamships.
He refused to have anything to do with Eads' plans, but he bought
three river ships at Cincinnati, thickly plated them with timber, and
managed to get some heavy guns aboard by drawing on the lake
naval stations.

But Eads, like Fox, was closely allied with the Blairs, and the end
of it was that he got a contract to build seven gunboats to a basic
design of his own, considerably modified by naval constructor Pook.
They became known as "Pook Turtles," and were the first ironclads
in the United States and the first in action, armored only around the
bows and abreast the engines; square-ended, with their heaviest firepower ahead, where they had three 8-inch guns apiece. Certainly they
were not the most perfect ships in the world, built of green timber
and with furnaces so close to the deck that it had to be sanded and
watered constantly to prevent fires, but they were better than anything
the Confederates had.

The squadron commander was Flag Officer Andrew H. Foote, an
old schoolfellow of Welles, a devout Christian and firm temperance
man, something in the Stonewall Jackson strain, who had flung landing parties ashore at the Chinese coast a few years before to capture

four forts that failed to apologize for firing on his ships. His officers were very junior lieutenants and the crews mostly rivermen, with a few army artillerists. In September, 1861, Brigadier-General U. S. Grant, then in command at Cairo, Illinois, was directed to make a gesture toward the great Confederate fortress at Columbus, Kentucky, on the Mississippi River. On meeting Foote he approved him at once —in some ways they were the same breed of cat—but the General entertained no high opinion of the help gunboats could give. When he landed across the river at Belmont, Missouri, opposite Columbus, the Confederates launched highly superior forces across to the south of him to make a counterattack; whereupon *Lexington* and *Tyler,* two of Rodgers' wooden gunboats, covered Grant's retreat so effectively that he conceived a new idea of shipborne heavy guns. After the ice went out of the rivers in 1862, Grant accordingly consulted Foote with regard to combined operations.

Now the Confederate defense system in the West was quite reasonably based on holding key points on the river lines. Most heavy traffic still had to travel by water, and while an army could maintain itself briefly at a distance from the rivers, no solid operation could be contemplated without water-borne logistic support. With the reluctant approval of General Henry W. Halleck, the Union area commander, Grant moved against Fort Henry on the Tennessee River early in February. On the 5th, Union troops landed to take the Fort from the rear, while Foote moved against its face with four ironclads and three wooden gunboats. It was strictly no contest; one of the gunboats was disabled, but Fort Henry was a water-level work, that could not stand the pounding from the 8-inchers, and in a couple of hours had only two guns left in operation. When the army arrived the place had already surrendered to the navy.

Grant immediately marched overland for an attack on Fort Donelson on the Cumberland River, while four of the ironclads and two wooden gunboats moved against its river face, attacking on February 14. This was an altogether different proposition than Henry, a terraced work reaching up high bluffs, whose plunging shot fell on the unarmored upper decks of the ships and put all the ironclads out of action. Donelson had to be taken from the land side, and the naval operation could be called a failure.

But when Grant moved up the Tennessee to Pittsburg Landing and was violently attacked at Shiloh on the morning of April 6, it was the gunfire of two of the wooden ships that saved his sensitive left flank and stopped the Confederate drive. All night the gunboats fired into the rebel lines, a heavy shell a minute, and when the Union forces were ready to counterattack in the morning, it was on that flank that the enemy gave way.

There were thus established the conditions of this peculiar inland naval war. The ships could not attack batteries on high ground with any chance of success, but where the ground was low their big guns invariably carried everything right away before them. There was no fortress in the Confederacy to which cannon could be carried fast enough to meet the menace from the water.

This was emphasized on the same day that Grant's counterattack won the Battle of Shiloh. The Rebels' big Columbus fortress had been abandoned as outflanked by the loss of Henry and Donelson, but the Confederates had another river plug at Island No. 10, where the Mississippi swings a perfect S-curve at the Kentucky-Tennessee line. The island was low-lying; its communications were via the Tennessee shore opposite, where a narrow strip of dry ground follows the bank. There were batteries along this ground, with strong forts opposite the island. Union General John Pope came down against the place on the Missouri side of the river and his engineers succeeded in cutting a canal through a spit of land opposite the island. This was adequate for moving troops safely down river from the fortified island, but they still could not cross in the face of the batteries on the Tennessee side. Direct bombardment of Island No. 10 by Union mortar-boats—they carried a single heavy mortar apiece, with a kind of coop built around it, the mortar men going out on deck when the gun was fired—produced no particular effect, and Pope wanted an ironclad below the fort to take out those batteries.

Foote explained to him that if Eads' ships suffered any damage to their machinery they would drift helplessly down under the batteries—and at Donelson, all the ironclads had received disabling mechanical injuries. A council of officers was nevertheless held at which Commander Henry Walke of the gunboat *Carondelet* volunteered to try running the batteries.

He piled cordwood around her boilers, covered the upper deck with all the hardware he could find and lashed a huge hay-barge to her port side; then on the moonless night of April 4, with a thunder-storm just breaking, set out on his perilous adventure. Nearly oppo-site the forts the soot in his smokestacks caught fire and two tall pillars of flame revealed his position to the enemy, but in the dark, lightning, and pouring rain she was an elusive target for gunners suddenly called from sleep to their pieces. On the bow, Seaman Charles Wilson stood in water to his waist, casting the lead; he saved the ship by keeping her from going aground. By midnight *Carondelet* was tying up at the bank where Pope's troops lay and firing minute guns in token of success; two days later she moved downstream, knocking out the light Confederate batteries on the Tennessee side, while Pope's men crossed behind her, and Island No. 10 surrendered, April 7 with seven thousand prisoners.

The river was now clear as far as Fort Pillow, but General Halleck called in Pope's force for a drive from Pittsburg Landing against the Confederate rail center of Corinth, and without land troops to sup-port, there came a pause in operations on the upper Mississippi.

IV

Stephen R. Mallory, the Confederate Secretary of the Navy, had been head of the U.S. Senate Naval Committee. He had ample officers from the old Navy list who had gone with their states on secession, but no ships at all except a few gunboats improvised from commercial craft on the Mississippi and in the sounds of the Carolinas, and he faced the problem of the Union blockade. To him the most logical solution was that conceived during the War of 1812—building a few ships so powerful that they could smash through any blockade. Dur-ing the Crimean War of the 1850s, the French had employed "float-ing batteries" plated with iron armor against the Russian forts. They proved highly successful and this success was followed by the con-struction in France and England of frigates with iron plating along their sides.

Confederate agents abroad were instructed to buy a few of these monsters, which would be just the thing for breaking a blockade com-posed entirely of wooden ships. The naval rivalry between France and England gave this plan no chance of success, however, and Mallory early realized that if he wanted an ironclad he would have to build his own. In his department were two lieutenants from the old Navy, J. M. Brooke and J. C. Porter, both of whom had been conducting experiments with guns fired at iron plates over wooden backing. The ship design that resulted was worked out between them; it called for the raising of the frigate *Merrimac* at Norfolk, which had been burned down to her berth deck when the Confederates took the yard. Atop the center of this deck Brooke and Porter built a sloping-sided, round-ended citadel, plated with four inches of iron and armed with six 9-inch smoothbores and four heavy rifles. The ends were flush with the water, and the prow held an iron tooth of a ram.

They named her *Virginia,* and she became the prototype of all the ironclads built for the Confederacy; highly original ships, never imitated anywhere else and owing most of their characteristics to the fact that they were intended to operate in landlocked waters, not go to sea. Two were laid down to be built from the keel up at Memphis, one at Charleston, and one at New Orleans before the end of 1861; others came later.

Word of the work on *Virginia* reached the North early in August. When the bill for an increase of the U.S. Navy was passed, Gustavus Fox had added to it an appropriation for the construction of three ironclads, and invited plans and bids. A board was appointed to consider proposals, including the intellectual C. H. Davis, who had been part of the committee on Atlantic strategy. Fourteen plans were submitted. The committee had no difficulty in accepting one from the Philadelphia firm of Merrick for a gigantic frigate with a heavily plated box-battery amidships, which ultimately became *New Ironsides,* a ship which fired more shots and took more hits than any other in the history of the Navy to her date—and throughout never had her plating penetrated.

Most of the remaining designs had obvious impossible defects, but one from Asa Bushnell of Connecticut hung on the edge of doubt; it called for a rather small vessel with upper sides curving sharply inward, these sides consisting of iron plates over a system of rails, between which were courses of thick oak. The board questioned whether the hull would carry the weight of metal proposed, and Bushnell took his model to New York to have it checked by the best marine engineer he knew, that same John Ericsson who invented the screw propeller and swore he would never have anything more to do with the Navy.

Ericsson, whose peculiar genius was mathematical calculation, rapidly checked Bushnell's figures and demonstrated that his ship would float, but shook his head over the design of the vessel, and went to a pile of papers, from which he produced a dusty box containing a model. It showed a hull shaped rather like a flattened football, with a round tower projecting from it. The engineer explained that this hull would be nearly flush with the water and armored; the tower was an armored turret, which could turn on a pivot, holding two heavy guns. The ship would be very hard to hit and any part of her that could be hit would be immune to shot.

Bushnell was so impressed that in spite of Ericsson's unwillingness to deal with the navy he borrowed the model and laid it before Secretary Welles, who was spending a few weeks in Hartford. Welles, also impressed, took Bushnell and model to Washington, where the project was submitted to Lincoln, who remarked: "There seems to be something in this, as the girl said when she put her leg in the stocking."

The members of the "Ironclad Board" were not as easy to convince and the naval constructors to whom the project was submitted still more dubious; they did not think the thing would float. Bushnell rushed back to New York, and by working on Ericsson's reasonable vanity about the accuracy of his calculations, persuaded him to come to Washington, where he dazzled the board and the constructors with figures. They gave him a contract for his peculiar ship, surrounding it with some of the most onerous conditions ever placed on an inventor, and he began letting out sub-contracts all over the Northeastern states for the parts he needed.

This was the genesis of *Monitor,* one of the most remarkable warships ever built; she contained over forty inventions entitled to basic patents. It is worth noting that when she put out for her trials at the end of February, 1862, no one aboard knew how to work any of the strange devices Ericsson had installed, although the crew was a picked lot, personally chosen by Lieutenant John L. Worden from volunteers aboard the receiving ship at Brooklyn. The trial was a dreadful failure; the ventilating system did not work well, neither did the device for turning the turret, and the rudder would not work at all. *Monitor* put back sadly; Ericsson rushed through the ship with his mechanics, making alterations everywhere.

There was need for hurry; the Confederates got their ironclad ready first and brought her down into Hampton Roads on the afternoon of March 8, under command of Flag Officer Franklin Buchanan, who in a brighter day had had much to do with the success of the Naval Academy. At anchor in the Roads lay the sailing sloop *Cumberland* and the sailing frigate *Congress,* blockading the James. (No one has ever been able to say why two sailing vessels at anchor in a river with their sails furled made a valid blockade.) Outside the bar were two of the big steam frigates, *Minnesota* and *Roanoke,* with the sailing frigate *St. Lawrence.*

Virginia made for *Cumberland* first because she had an exceptionally powerful battery; took station under her bows and poured in a raking fire that killed or wounded one-tenth of the ship's crew. Then the Confederate ironclad backed off to drive her ram into the side of the sloop, making a deep hole. For a few minutes *Cumberland*'s guns bore; the crew were brave and well trained as any men, and in the face of their losses they fired back, but without the slightest effect. The sloop slid to the bottom with one-third of her crew, her flag still flying.

Virginia next turned toward *Congress,* which had slipped her cable and moved into shallow water. From a distance and position where the frigate could not bring a single cannon to bear, a deliberate, accurate fire was opened by *Virginia* and continued until, with her skipper, Lieutenant Joseph Smith, and one hundred twenty men killed or wounded, the ship afire in several places, *Congress* hauled down her flag. It was now near evening; *Minnesota* had entered the Roads to help and was hard aground, but she could wait till the next day. *Virginia* steamed back to Norfolk.

There was wild excitement when the news of that day's work spread through the North, and preparations were made for harbor defense all along the coast. But next morning when the conquering ironclad came out to finish her job, there stood between her and the stranded *Minnesota,* a low, fantastic shape, "like a cheesebox on a raft." It was *Monitor,* which slid through the glare of burning *Congress* during the night, after as wild a voyage as any crew ever made. Off the Delaware, accompanied by a tug, she ran into a storm; water washed down her smokepipes and hawse-holes and caused the bands that actuated the ventilators to break. The engine room filled with gas;

the men in it had to be taken to the top of the turret to be revived. The engines went out; she was kept afloat by hand pumps and bailing. But after a mad forty-eight hours during which no one slept and hardly anyone had anything to eat, there she was, the hope of the Union.

As *Virginia* ponderously approached, the little fellow headed straight toward her. The Confederate ship swung and fired a broadside; most of the shot flew right over, while those that did hit spun away in a shower of sparks. Then *Monitor*'s turret revolved rapidly, and two 11″ shot hit *Virginia*'s armor with such an impact that though they did not come through, the iron was broken and every man on that side of the ship was dashed to the deck. One of the most famous naval battles of history lasted for nearly four hours after that. It has often been called a draw because neither ship was seriously damaged, and the major casualty was Lieutenant Worden, who had powder driven into his eyes when a shell struck the lookout of his pilothouse. But *Virginia* lost her smokestack, cutting her speed to practically nil, and though *Monitor*'s shot did not come through, they jammed a couple of port shutters and started the armor in several places so that there were many wounded by splinters. Twice the Confederate ironclad tried to ram; the little *Monitor* was altogether too nimble and well protected; and *Virginia* could not get at *Minnesota* without finding her opponent in the way. In the end the Confederate ship steamed back to Norfolk, never to emerge again, for the operations of the Union army soon placed that city in such peril that the ship was blown up at her dock.

Monitor came back to her berth beside *Minnesota* with the crew of the frigate cheering her till they were hoarse; Lincoln sat beside Worden's bedside with tears in his eyes; and twenty more monitors were ordered on the spot.

V

The Confederate naval commander at New Orleans was G. N. Hollins, whom Mallory sent out with instructions to emit raiders against Union commerce and to build a big ironclad. Hollins was a man of energy, and before the blockade of the Mississippi had more than one ship in it, he did shake loose the cruiser *Sumter*, Captain

Raphael Semmes, which immediately made her presence felt by destroying clipper ships all through the Caribbean and down the coast of South America.

Another intended raider, *McRae,* proved too slow for ocean work; Hollins made her one of the ships of a river squadron, armored with cotton bales and timber in the usual Confederate fashion. He also had a strange vessel named *Manassas,* converted from a powerful tug, with turtleback armor down to the waterline, a single gun in the bows and a strong ram. She had been built as a privateer by a group of speculators, but like *McRae,* proved too slow.

In the meanwhile Welles' board of strategy considered how the exits of the Mississippi might best be closed, and decided on establishing a station at the Head of Passes, where the river spreads its mouths through the delta, well below where the giant forts, Jackson and St. Philip, barred access to New Orleans. W. W. McKean, the flag officer in charge of the Gulf blockade, approved and sent up a squadron consisting of the screw sloop *Richmond,* the sailing sloop *Vincennes,* the sailing brig *Preble* and a little side-wheeler tug with three guns, *Water Witch,* all under command of Captain John Pope of *Richmond.*

On the night of October 12, 1861, Hollins attacked this force with his *Manassas* in the lead, followed by tugs towing fire-rafts and five various gunboats. It was an age when there were no searchlights, and since Captain Pope failed to post any picket-boats, *Manassas'* arrival came as a complete surprise. She rammed into *Richmond* and a coal barge alongside the latter, doing some damage to the sloop and more to herself, but producing something like panic in the Union squadron. *Richmond* had not steam enough to head the current; she drifted down river, with the two sailing vessels drifting after and the fire-rafts coming along behind. They did no damage; but both *Richmond* and *Vincennes* grounded on the bar at the mouth of the river and when the Confederate gunboats began to shoot, Captain Robert Handy, who commanded *Vincennes,* decided to abandon his ship and blow her up. He appeared aboard *Richmond* draped in an American flag to report what he had done. "Oh, God," said one of his sailors, "I have served that flag for forty years, and this is the first time I have run away from it"; but another crewman had already cut the powder train to the magazine, and *Vincennes* did not blow up after all, though she had to throw over most of her guns to get off the bar. The only damage from the Confederate fire was one shot found in a bureau drawer, and the guns of little *Water Witch* persuaded the attackers to retreat, but that was the end of the Head of Passes project.

It was also a good illustration of the state of the Navy at the time—good material below, like the seamen of *Vincennes* and those who fought *Cumberland* to the death; many good young lieutenants; but all reined in by old senior commanders who had never learned anything but the routine performance of non-combat duties. But at the head of the service there was still Gideon Welles, with his strong sense of duty, and Fox with his energy. The debacle at the Head of Passes set them to work on a new plan, that of getting past the big forts below New Orleans and occupying the city. No concept of how this might be done seemed valid until the arrival from the Gulf of Commander D. D. Porter, son of the War of 1812 Porter of *Essex* fame, who had been in charge of the paddle sloop *Powhatan;* he offered a plan for beating the forts into submission by means of long-range mortar fire, then running a fleet past them to take the city and hold it with troops brought from the coast through the bayous from the rear.

To command an expedition of such size one of the senior captains must be chosen, and the nomination fell to David Glasgow Farragut, the same Farragut who had served under Porter's father in the War of 1812 as a youthful midshipman. He had run afoul of the powerful Perry family early in his career and had been given little chance to distinguish himself in a half century of naval service, but he soon showed that he was a different piece of goods from most of his contemporaries. Instinct with energy, he was small but nimble, a skilled swordsman—also a man who gave as careful personal attention to every detail as Truxton had in the old days. He was named to a new West Gulf Blockading Squadron, with jurisdiction from Pensacola to the border of Texas, and his real objective was concealed by carefully loose talk about Mobile, Galveston, and other points.

Farragut's fleet consisted of one of the screw frigates, four screw sloops, the paddle-wheeler *Mississippi,* twelve gunboats and twenty schooners, each of the last fitted to carry a 13-inch mortar, these bombardment ships being under Porter's command. They assembled off Ship Island on March 7, 1862, crossed the bars with much straining and went up to the Head of Passes. The difficulties Farragut experienced were immense. His frigate could not cross at all; the screw sloops had to be towed through; he was short of medical supplies, anchors, coal, and even some kinds of ammunition. But he demolished all obstacles with indomitable energy and rowed through the fleet daily, visiting every ship and talking to the ordinary seamen. On April 16, he was ready to begin. The mortar boats moved up and began throwing shell into Forts Jackson and St. Philip.

The arrival of those shells was the first veritable news the Confederates had that a serious attack was intended from the seaboard flank of New Orleans. Secretary Mallory had grown very worried about the advance of the Union river gunboats from the north and ordered most of the floating defense forces sent upstream to hold Memphis and the forts above it against them. The big ironclad *Louisiana* was complete except that her engines would not work; she was towed down to lie beside the forts and aid in their defense. A second ironclad, *Mississippi,* was complete only in her wooden parts.

The Union attack was thus a strategic surprise. But Porter, who had promised that his mortars would break down the forts in forty-eight hours, soon found that though he did them considerable damage, they would still be shooting when his ammunition was gone. Farragut decided to run the fleet right through the guns on the night of April 24. The Flag Officer had every precaution taken; the sides of the ships daubed with mud to make them less visible; top-hamper sent below; obstacles piled around the boilers, sand on the decks—then sent all hands to sleep till midnight.

He knew what he was getting into; the Confederate forts were built of stone, the Union ships of wood and had no such superiority of firepower as in the attacks along the Atlantic, for there were more than one hundred sixteen heavy guns against them. To make things worse, a strong current opposed their progress. As the ships neared the forts, great bonfires sprang up along the banks, and down against the ships came huge fire-rafts pushed by tugs, while behind these in the murk loomed the Confederate river fleet: *Manassas* and nine gunboats. The screw sloops retorted to the forts with so hot a fire that many of the gunners were driven from their pieces under the curtain of flame and smoke, and the damage to the ships, though considerable, was less than expected. The flagship *Hartford* was almost set ablaze by one of the fire-rafts; *Brooklyn* was holed by the ram and one of the Union gunboats—commanded, incidentally, by a brother-in-law of the unfortunate Lawrence of the *Chesapeake*—sunk. As dawn came sullenly in, however, the Confederate river ships were all destroyed or driven into the bank, the forts were passed, and with another dawn the Union fleet was at the quays of New Orleans, the largest city of the Confederacy was in Federal hands, and the forts isolated into surrender.

It was a paralyzing shock, particularly in that diplomatic field where the Confederates had placed their highest hopes for success, and it came just at the moment when their prospects seemed brightest. From the beginning of the war their efforts had been concentrated on winning recognition from France and England—this was one of the reasons for the cotton embargo. This would automatically make it legal for the ships of these nations to trade through Southern ports, and in view of the exiguous state of the blockade and the profits to be made, would almost certainly provoke a clash between the two great European powers and the Washington government. Two Confederate commissioners, designated ambassadors, were sent out during October, 1861—James M. Mason to England, John Slidell to France.

Now it happened that at that time the screw sloop *San Jacinto* was in the West Indies searching for the raiding *Sumter*. Her captain learned that the pair were on their way to Europe aboard the British mail steamer *Trent*. This captain was Charles Wilkes, the explorer. His famous cruise had left him with a deep-seated dislike of the British as the result of an incident in which he lent his charts to an English officer who published them as his own. Wilkes was also an ambitious and unruly man, familiar with the story of the British searches of American ships that had preceded the War of 1812. It took him no time at all to decide to halt *Trent* with a shot across her bows and remove the Confederate commissioners by force, the date being November 8, 1861. *Trent* was in the service of the English government and had never come near the blockade; there were loud cries for war in England, and despite Congressional approval of Wilkes' action, only the common sense of Lincoln on the one hand and Prince Albert of Britain on the other settled the matter by the release of the prisoners to British custody.

The affair nevertheless left a strong undercurrent in England in favor of recognizing the Confederacy, and a still stronger one in France, where Napoleon III already had designs on Mexico. His plan was an offer of mediation, itself an effective recognition. The Navy's capture of New Orleans changed all that. The taking of Fort Henry, Fort Donelson, and Island No. 10 were of enormous strategic importance, but they occurred in an area as little known to most Europeans as the interior of Africa. New Orleans, on the other hand, was a world city, and if the Confederates could not protect it with the aid of a fleet and powerful forts, the chances for the survival of the new nation looked poor from Europe.

VI

Meanwhile events had been progressing on the Western rivers. When General Pope's troops were called overland for the move against Corinth, the Union river fleet on the Mississippi halted above Fort Pillow to wait the resumption of combined operations, and a program of long-range harassing bombardment by mortars was begun, with one of the river ironclads standing guard over the mortars. The fleet was now under C. H. Davis, Foote having gone home with a wound acquired at Fort Donelson, from which he never recovered. On the morning of May 10, *Cincinnati* was covering the mortars when a squadron of eight Confederate river rams came up so fast that the Union ships in the rear had no time to work up steam, struck the gunboat three times and sent her to the bottom. As *Mound City* joined the action, she was also rammed, and went into the bank disabled. The heavy guns of the other ironclads soon sent their adversaries drifting downstream, but it was a clear Confederate success.

General Halleck's operations against Corinth, though very slow, eventually pinched Fort Pillow out, and the Union fleet moved down the Mississippi toward Memphis. At the same time it was joined by four odd vessels, designed and commanded by an Army engineer, Charles Ellet, Jr. They were rams, but quite unlike the Confederate type; heavily braced internally to stand the shock of impact and lightened for speed by carrying no iron or guns at all. On June 6 they followed four of Davis' gunboats toward Memphis, where the Rebel fleet awaited the attack. All the people in the town came out with basket lunches to watch the battle.

It was hardly worth the time they spent making the sandwiches. The river filled with smoke as both sides opened fire and the Confederate rams steered toward the gunboats in a confidence born of their earlier success. At this moment there dashed through the ironclad line two of the Ellet rams, with Colonel Ellet waving his hat from the upper deck of *Queen of the West,* frantically cheered by the crews of the gunboats. The Confederate ram *Lovell* charged her, bows on, but at the last moment tried to turn and was nearly cut in two by Ellet's ship. Two other Confederates tried to strike the second Ellet ram, but she was too fast and they collided, disabling both so that they fell easy vistims to the gunnery of the Federal ironclads. The enemy was now in disorder; another Confederate ship was blown up, two more were crippled by gunfire, and only one got away downstream.

It was the only real fleet action of the war—one of the briefest and most decisive of record. Memphis surrendered that afternoon and the Confederate river navy was wiped out, except for the unfinished ironclad ram *Arkansas,* which had been towed down from Memphis and up the Yazoo River. There was now no substantial barrier between the upper and lower Union river fleets but Vicksburg, which had become a formidable fortress on bluffs 200 feet above the stream. Davis brought his squadron down there late in June.

Farragut had meanwhile been pushing his ocean ships toward the same objective through highly unappetizing conditions. His deep-draft vessels were almost impossible to handle in the narrow and tortuous channel; they were always going aground. He was beset by the same old shortage of coal; there were nowhere near enough mechanics to make the necessary repairs; the Confederates sniped from the banks with small arms and light batteries then ran away before retaliation could come; supply vessels had to be convoyed up four hundred miles of river by warships. Worst of all for the ocean sailors were the dysentery, malaria, enervating heat, and swarms of insects that came down on them like a blanket. Everyone was dissatisfied, tempers grew short, and the available land forces to co-operate with the fleet consisted of only three thousand men. The Gulf mortar boats came up to shell Vicksburg from long range.

The Washington authorities, who had no real knowledge of the conditions, expected Farragut to take the place as he had New

Orleans. On the night of June 26 he ran his squadrons past the Vicksburg batteries; but this was not New Orleans, with its water-level forts, and the fire of the ships was totally ineffective against guns mounted at such high levels, whose location could only be guessed by their flash. They were unhurt, but in return the Union ships took many casualties while *Brooklyn* and two of the 90-day gunboats could not make the passage at all.

When the fleets of Davis and Farragut met above Vicksburg, ocean and river sailors gazed at each other's strange craft, the like of which they had never seen, and there was much visiting back and forth. Though Farragut felt he had demonstrated that well-handled ships could run past any forts, the defect in the Washington strategic thesis appeared at once. At New Orleans and Island No. 10 the forts could be supplied only by the line of water; when ships got across that line the jig was up. But Vicksburg drew from all interior Mississippi, was not subject to naval blockade, and the handful of Union troops could do nothing against its steep slopes and well-manned defenses.

Farragut boarded one of the river ironclads and went down for a tryout against the batteries. A shot came through a porthole and killed a man at his side, whereupon the old man remarked that he was going out on deck where he felt safe. But it was clear that the ships could never beat down Vicksburg without land help, the Mississippi was falling to a point dangerous to the ocean-going ships, the Confederates were erecting more batteries all down the banks, and disease had reached epidemic proportions. There was a week or more of consultations with Davis, whose squadron was in not much better shape than Farragut's, the green-timber ships cracking open and racked by the pounding they had received, badly in need of repair. The two Navy commanders could accomplish little without troops.

Their decision was hastened by the *Arkansas* incident. By almost incredible exertions and ingenious compromises Lieutenant Isaac N. Brown of the Confederate navy had built a Rebel ram in a semi-wilderness on the banks of the Yazoo, which ran into the Mississippi a short distance above Vicksburg. On July 15 the *Arkansas* started down. Some news of her presence had been brought to the Union fleet by Negroes. It happened that that very morning the Ellet ram *Queen of the West,* the wooden gunboat *Tyler* and the ironclad *Carondelet* had been sent up the Yazoo to look for her. When they met there was no room in the river for *Queen* to work up speed for the use of her single weapon; she turned back down, followed by unarmored *Tyler* and then by *Carondelet,* whose commander thought he could do best by fighting his stern 42-pound rifles while warning the fleet below by the firing. *Carondelet* got the worst of this exchange; her guns would not penetrate the ram's armor, and just as she reached the Mississippi her steering gear was shot away and she was driven into the bank with many casualties. *Tyler* also was hard hit, while *Arkansas* rushed on down into the press of the Union fleet. Not a ship had steam up, and few had time to get gun crews completely ready for action. The river filled with smoke and thunder as the Confederate ram charged through the fleet, receiving the fire of and firing into each Federal ship as she passed, to come to rest under the batteries of Vicksburg.

The *Arkansas* was not undamaged. Everything outside the casemate had been shot away, her weak armor was penetrated, and there were many dead. She needed repairs and new men. The Confederate military authorities would not allow Brown to take any but volunteers, and few cared to volunteer after they saw the condition of the ram's deck. But to Farragut the *Arkansas* represented an immediate and formidable danger to the command of the lower river for there was nothing between her and Baton Rouge, or for that matter, New Orleans, but a few wooden gunboats. The admiral got all ready and ran through the Vicksburg batteries downstream that same night, keeping right on until he reached an area where his battered ships could be repaired. A week later Davis sent the ironclad *Essex*—commanded by another of the sons of Porter of the 1812 *Essex*—down to attack the ram where she lay, but in the falling light and rising shadows no damage was done, and *Essex* had to push on to become part of Farragut's command.

He made her station ship at Baton Rouge, the northern limit of Federal occupation. On August 5 the Confederates sent a land expedition against the place, and asked for *Arkansas* to furnish heavy artillery support, without which they could not crack the Union lines on land. The ram came down, but was delayed overnight by the failure of one of her engines, and after it had been repaired next morning, both engines gave out together and she ran into the bank, just as *Essex* came ploughing slowly upstream. *Arkansas* was in a position where she could not fire a gun; her commander, with tears streaming down his face, ordered abandon ship and set her afire, and that was the end of the Confederate ram, after a spectacular career of twenty-nine days.

It was also the end of the first Mississippi campaign. Davis moved his headquarters back to Helena, Arkansas, and nothing was done on the Union side until the end of the year.

VII

By this date there were major changes. In July, while Davis and Farragut were off Vicksburg, Secretary Welles got an omnibus Navy bill through Congress. It provided for the largest building program yet undertaken by the United States, also for the establishment of the ranks of Rear Admiral and Commodore, the old fears of a naval aristocracy having eroded under the pressure of war. There were to be retirements for age or cause, and the whole department was reorganized into five bureaus, co-ordinating through the office of Assistant Secretary Fox—a reform much needed, since under the old setup one office furnished a ship, another her guns, another her crew, and still another her supplies, without any of them ever making contact with the rest.

Part of the reorganization was a general reshuffling of commands. Louis Goldsborough had been in charge of the North Atlantic Blockading Squadron, which covered everything down to the South Carolina border. Under his administration a plan of Davis' strategy board for the penetration of the North Carolina sounds was pushed forward, since the almost continual bad weather around Hatteras made it difficult to blockade those sounds from the outside and the internal traffic along them was a matter of consequence.

A strange fleet of armed tugs and small craft was assembled for the purpose, with the help of an army corps under General Ambrose Burnside. The operation was substantially and successfully completed by the early part of 1862, but Secretary Welles got less pleasure out of it than the northern newspapers. He characterized Goldsborough with: "There are many such men on the list; good students who acquire promotion through study and must be given commands," but the man had "no hard courage." Goldsborough was replaced by S. Phillips Lee, one of the Lees of Virginia who stayed with the North and who had done well in the river gunboats. At the same time Theodorus Bailey, who had been Farragut's flag captain and led the line of battle at New Orleans, received the East Gulf Blockading Squadron in place of W. W. McKean, who was now so old and feeble as to be unable to attend to his duties. The ancient captains were going.

From the river command Welles recalled Davis as too intellectual for such a "rough and tumble" assignment and sent out the turbulent but driving David D. Porter, with the rank of Acting Rear Admiral. Porter reached the area in October and began a thorough reorganization, the fleet being now fully transferred to Navy administration. He found that while it was under the Army many men had been hired at above the prevailing Navy pay rate, and many more were worthless—"lazy deckhands," he called them. Six hundred of them were dismissed, many sick. To fill their places Washington was deluged with appeals for seamen, while in the meantime Porter hired as many Negroes as he could to be coal passers and handlers of deck gear and ammunition. "Women and children even," he reported to the department in one of his wails for help, but this may be taken as a characteristic piece of Porter overemphasis.

The material condition of the squadron he found somewhat better. Repairs to the old "Pook turtles" were progressing satisfactorily, five new ironclads of an improved model were nearly complete, and nine river monitors building, though these would not be ready for some time. Most important of all were the "tinclads." Davis, who had deeply felt the need of light-draft ships that could carry guns of some force up rivers too shallow for the ironclads, was behind this idea—fundamentally a scheme for plating light river steamers with boiler iron to make them safe against musketry and giving them any guns they could carry.

A handful were in progress when Porter reached the West. The moment he saw them, he knew they were just what he wanted for the task before him, and threw himself into the tinclad program with such energy that twenty-two were purchased by the end of the year and twenty-six more in 1863. Some of the smaller ones drew as little as twenty-two inches of water and none were very big; as Porter put it: "They could run on a heavy dew." The armaments varied

widely, but normally consisted of something like six 25-pound howitzers, with a piece of light rifled artillery added later in the war. Nothing
in the story of the fighting in the West is more important than the work
of the tinclads. The heaviest field pieces in the Confederate service
were 12-pounders, and the 6-pounder was more common, which made
the 24-pounders of the little ships a clear overmatch for anything but a
major military effort from the shore. Even then things were usually
somewhat more than equal. There was one case where a single tinclad
put to rout five thousand troops.

It was a hard service, and one unlike any other in the history of
naval war. As the numbers of the tinclads grew they were sent on
patrols and expeditions not only everywhere along the Mississippi,
but up every affluent—the Tennessee, the Cumberland, the White, the
Arkansas, the Yazoo. There was always the chance that they would
encounter the enemy, and they fought a hundred combats without
names. There was the continual likelihood they would be rushed to
some Army post, under attack by Confederate bands, which had sent
an urgent appeal for tinclad support. There might be a call to convoy
a valuable vessel through an area where it was likely the Rebels
would shoot her up. The Union ships had to anchor in the center of
the stream at night, and from the dark shore would come snipers'
bullets. Small Confederate artillery groups tried to ambush them
and sometimes did. Cotton speculators tried to bribe their captains.
Supplies were often difficult to come by.

But the Federal gunboats flowed like a corrosive fluid all along
the veins of the Confederacy. Even more than in the North, heavy
traffic went by the streams, the more so since the already limited railroad equipment had been cut down still farther in military operations.
With the coming of the tinclads it became impossible for supplies to
reach the eastern Confederacy from the producing lands in Texas
and western Louisiana except under the shadow of the new fortress
that presently grew up at Port Hudson to cover the mouth of the
Red River. Even though an individual or a boatload of men could
always slip across the big river, no important body of men or supplies
could make it.

With the Confederate river navy destroyed, Porter's major ships
became a floating wing of the Union army and their operations were
meshed together (which was a good deal easier in practice than in

theory since Porter at once established the most cordial relations with Grant and his leading subordinate, Sherman). The first combined operations campaign was underway in December, 1862. The plan was for Grant to pin the Rebel army defending Vicksburg well north of the town in an overland operation, while Sherman took thirty-two thousand men down the Mississippi, then up the Yazoo, and made secure Haynes' Bluff, thirty miles above Vicksburg. Once ashore on the high ground, the army could conduct a land campaign against the city, supported from the river. Porter sent on ahead up the Yazoo two of the new tinclads, with the ironclads *Cairo* and *Pittsburg*. The river was found to be full of that early form of mines then known as "torpedoes"—explosives on a pile, hung on ropes, or moored on the bottom. The tinclads, whose shallow draft made them immune to these obstacles, cleared a good many, but *Cairo* ran onto one and went down. Porter replaced her with *Benton,* the strongest of the older ships; on December 26 she and *Pittsburg* shelled out the rifle pits at the base of the bluffs and fought a duel with the batteries farther up the slope, in which neither ships nor batteries were much damaged. Three days later Sherman landed his troops and tried an assault on Haynes' Bluff.

It failed miserably. The plan had gone awry. Back in central Mississippi a Confederate cavalry formation had struck around Grant's army and burned out his supply base, destroying much of the railroad that supported it. Grant was forced to beat a hurried retreat to Memphis, and had no way of advising Sherman (since the message had to go by courier to Memphis and then down the river by boat) that instead of being pinned in central Mississippi, the whole Vicksburg army would be at Haynes' Bluff.

Sherman and the ships retreated to a temporary base at the mouth of the Yazoo. It is worth noting that there was no Confederate attempt at counterattack; the heavy guns of the gunboats and tinclads made a secure base of any place where the Union army could effect a lodgment.

But now a new feature entered the campaign in the person of General John A. McClernand, a politician-officer who had obtained from Washington a somewhat vague authority to raise new troops "and take Vicksburg." He arrived at Sherman's river base with fresh levies just after the Haynes' Bluff defeat, and assumed command of everything there under his mandate. After looking at the Vicksburg bluffs he decided the place was "too big a boo," so he went off up the Arkansas River to attack Fort Hindman, from which Rebel raids had been launched against the Mississippi area. Porter sent along three of the "Pook turtles" and eight tinclads. The expedition moved upstream and landed its troops on January 10, 1863, the idea being a military envelopment while the ships amused the place in front.

Fort Hindman had eleven heavy guns, well casemated in with armor, and they made good practice as the ships approached. But Porter noticed that the range-marks for their firing were placed at fifteen hundred to one thousand yards, at which point the Confederates expected his ships to lie. He closed right in to four hundred yards and at that range the heavy 8-inch guns of the ironclads shot the armor of the casemates through and through. Long after dark the crews of the ships heard the sound of hammer and chisel, as men in the fort made repairs, mingled with the screams of wounded horses, of which a large depot was inside the fort. Next morning the ironclads went in again, covered by the tinclads against snipers aiming at their ports. In a couple of hours of firing they dismounted every gun in the fort, and when the troops arrived they were to find a white flag up and the Navy in possession. Two of the gunboats rushed on up the stream, destroying supplies and depots as much as seventy miles beyond the fort.

With regard to naval operations, this reinforced the lesson of Fort Henry, that fortifications near the water level, no matter how heavily built, stood little chance against the armored gunboats.

However, into the general strategy of the campaign against Vicksburg it introduced an element which placed compulsions on Grant. He obtained an acknowledgment from Washington that he was in fact in command of all operations in the Mississippi area and superior to McClernand, but to make it stick, he had to go downstream in person. Now, as Sherman pointed out, the technically correct military procedure was to take all the troops back to Memphis and organize a new overland campaign against the rear of the fortress; but the victory at Fort Hindman, the presence of so many men in the Vicksburg area, would cause such a backward movement to be construed as defeat and retreat, and no one knew it better than Grant. He brought all his troops down to the neck of land opposite Vicksburg and began trying to think out a way to reach the high ground on the Mississippi side in a combined operation. One thing at least was certain—his communications were safe as long as they followed the river held by the Navy.

VIII

The Confederate effort at privateering attained only the most mediocre success, and that only in the earliest months of the war. Following the pattern of previous conflicts, the first privateers out were a collection of tugs, fishing schooners, and coasters, small craft armed with any guns available, which levied on traffic not far offshore. Privateers from the mouths of the Mississippi captured a few ships, but this enterprise withered from natural causes when Union shipping in the Gulf ceased because there were no ports to trade to. Small privateers from the Carolina inlets took a few prizes, but this effort also speedily wilted under the pressure of the blockade maintained by Union war steamers that could run down a sailing ship in almost any weather, and received further set-backs with the seizure of the exits of the sounds by Stringham, Goldsborough, and Du Pont. The only privateer that scored any real success was the fast ex-slaver brig *Jeff Davis,* which took several prizes off New England, and she was wrecked on the coast of Florida coming in. Well before the end of 1861 privateering had ceased as an industry.

The commerce destroyers commissioned by the Confederate government, operating on the lines of the great raiders of 1812, could afford steam engines and heavy guns that allowed them to compete with all but the larger classes of Union cruisers, and they speedily became a much more serious matter. The first out was *Sumter,* commanded by Captain Raphael Semmes, one of the outstanding men of the old Navy who had gone south when Alabama seceded, leaving a brother in the United States Navy still loyal to the old flag. Semmes—"Old Beeswax" his crew called him—wasted no time. The *Sumter* burned one prize in the West Indies, sent one in to New Orleans, which was recaptured on the way, and ordered six more into Cuban ports, where they were returned to their original owners by the Spanish authorities—the latest international doctrine and treaties not allowing such use of neutral harbors.

Without benefit of marine cables sea news traveled by the traditional process of sailing days, ships stopping to exchange tidings when they met, or captains gossiping in port. Of the six vessels looking for *Sumter,* the sloop *Iroquois* picked her up at Martinique but the French authorities told both that neither would be allowed to leave until twenty-four hours after the other. Captain James S. Palmer of the cruiser arranged with an American schooner in port to hoist one masthead light if the Confederate steered north, two if she went south; but the schooner's skipper could not be restrained from spreading the news, so that when Semmes left harbor he steered south just long enough to draw the lights and send *Iroquois* charging in the wrong direction before he turned north.

The same type of news source told Semmes about the loss of the prizes he had sent in to Cuba: now he burned the four prizes he captured in a cruise across the Atlantic. *Sumter* put into Cadiz and then Gibraltar in January, 1862, out of coal and with serious defects in her boilers. While she was there three Union sloops entered Algeciras just across the bay, an effective blockade. The ship had to be sold and Semmes and his crew were taken to England.

English yards had already produced one Confederate commerce raider. James D. Bulloch, the Confederate navy agent in England, had persuaded a firm of Liverpool builders to produce a light sloop on British navy lines. She was shifted through a series of dummy ownerships and in March, 1862, put to sea without weapons. Off an uninhabited island in the Bahamas, this ship met another carrying her guns and was christened *Florida,* but such equipment as sights, gunlocks, and elevating screws had been forgotten. Captain John N. Maffitt of the Confederate navy could obtain but twelve men for a crew and most of these were speedily on their backs with yellow fever. Proceedings in a British Admiralty court held the raider up for some time, but she was released and on September 4 appeared off Mobile. Commander George Preble of the sloop *Oneida* sighted her coming in, but *Florida* hoisted English colors. Preble took her for a British ship inspecting the blockade (as they had every right to do) let her get past before opening a fire which brought the proper flag to her masthead.

Florida's speed did the rest; she escaped into Mobile harbor and spent four months fitting out and gathering a crew. In January, 1863, she came down to try the blockade again. It now consisted of seven ships, but some were absent for coal or repairs, and *Oneida,* to which

Maffitt's ship passed nearest, did not get up anchor for half an hour because of a ship's general order about the way things should be done. *Florida* thus showed the blockaders a clean pair of heels, coaled in the British West Indies, and set off on a career of destruction that ranged from one end of the Atlantic to the other, during which she burned fourteen prizes and fitted out one as an auxiliary raider. The auxiliary took five more ships off New England before being brought to book; *Florida* herself went to Brest in friendly France, where she spent six months in a thorough refit before taking off for the South Atlantic under a new captain, Charles M. Morris, again coaling in British island ports on the way.

She put into Bahia, where she found at anchor the Union sloop *Wachusett,* Captain Napoleon Collins, a believer in direct action. A Brazilian warship promptly took up station between the two, but next morning at daybreak *Wachusett* got under way, circled the Brazilian and slammed into *Florida*'s quarter. The raider fired a few pistol shots; they were returned by a rattle of musketry from the Union sloop, whereupon the Confederate surrendered. *Wachusett* took her under tow and carried her off to Norfolk. It was an outrageous violation of Brazilian neutrality, promptly so recognized by the U.S. government, but as preparations were under way to return *Florida* to Brazil, an army transport ran her down and sank her in a quite unfortunate accident. Adequate apologies were offered.

By the time *Florida* put to sea on her original cruise in disguise, Semmes and his men were already in England, and Bulloch was busy with the much more important project of *Alabama,* constructed as a fast sloop to British navy specifications. The agents of Charles Francis Adams, American minister to Great Britain, had no difficulty in establishing that she was being built for anything but peaceful purposes and the Crown law officers recommended her seizure. The British authorities did exactly nothing, however, and on July 29, 1862, she slipped out to sea under pretense of a trial run. Two supply vessels joined her in the Azores with her battery, Semmes, and the crew. Now a full-fledged warship, *Alabama* cruised the North Atlantic for two months, during which time she took and destroyed twenty vessels, then headed for the West Indies.

Semmes had carefully studied his problem and made the most elaborate arrangements for refueling in remote areas. He estimated that two months on any cruising ground would be as much as he could allow before news of his presence would reach the United States and set the hounds on his slot. At Martinique he was found by the Federal sloop *San Jacinto,* a much more heavily armed vessel. The local governor enforced the twenty-four hour rule, however, and *San Jacinto* was too slow to overhaul the raider when she slipped out at night. There was another coaling off the Mexican coast, where Semmes picked up news of peculiar events at Galveston and of the Union reaction.

The Galveston operations had begun at the time of Farragut's retreat from the middle Mississippi, when he determined to caulk the hitherto leaky blockade of Texas by applying the Atlantic formula of seizing coastal points. Expeditions of Union troops occupied Galveston, Sabine Pass, and Corpus Christi by October, 1862. A regiment was garrisoned in Galveston and in the harbor were stationed two armed steamers, the ferryboat *Westfield,* a 90-day gunboat, and the revenue cutter *Harriet Lane.* General John B. Magruder assembled Confederate troops in the area and put artillery and riflemen aboard two steamers armored with cotton bales. At 3 A.M. January 1, 1863, when a strong ebb tide would make the Union vessels difficult or impossible to maneuver, his shore contingent charged the Federal guard regiment in overwhelming force, while the steamers attacked *Harriet Lane.* She had time to fire only a few shots before her deck was swept by volleys of musketry that killed the captain and first lieutenant; the junior officers could not hold the crew and she was carried by boarding.

She had been the best armed ship in the Union squadron and immediately bore down upon the rest. *Westfield* was hard aground, with no guns bearing; Commodore W. E. Renshaw decided to blow her up, but the powder-train burned too fast and the explosion killed him. The senior surviving officer was now Lieutenant R. L. Law; he decided Galveston was too hot to hold and steamed off with his three remaining ships, abandoning the blockade.

Farragut had Law court-martialed and suspended and ordered the powerful sloop *Brooklyn* with six gunboats to re-establish the blockade. This was the news Semmes picked up off Mexico, but he got it in the garbled form that the Union high command was dispatching a heavy force of troops to recover the lost city, and he immediately decided to strike for the transports. On the night of January 11, *Brooklyn* sighted the raider about twelve miles off. Since she had no steam up and her engines were under repair she signaled the armed steamer *Hatteras* to intercept the stranger. *Hatteras* was a small walking-beam side-wheeler with a battery less than half *Alabama*'s power; Semmes let her get close in and in a few minutes the Union ship was on fire, sinking, and with her walking-beam shot away. The flashes of firing were seen from *Brooklyn,* but long before she could work up steam the fast Confederate had vanished.

Alabama took two prizes in the West Indies; then Semmes headed for the hump of Brazil, where he took eight more before shifting to the Bahia area for a two-month cruise in which he made ten prizes, the Brazilian authorities giving him such liberty of action that Napoleon Collins later held himself fully justified in cutting out *Florida.* With his normal two-month stay in an area up, Semmes cut across to the Cape of Good Hope, where he cruised for a time without much in the way of prizes, then hearing that a Union cruiser was after him, bore away for the East Indies, where he stayed for six months and took seven ships. It was now March, 1864; the *Alabama*'s bottom was foul and she badly needed repairs. Semmes turned her back toward Europe and, on June 11, reached Cherbourg harbor. Permission for the necessary docking was delayed, and three days later the Union sloop *Kearsarge* came steaming into the harbor, took one look at the raider, and without stopping swung round to lie in the offing.

The layout of Cherbourg does not permit any such easy evasion as Semmes had practiced at Martinique. Moreover, if he waited to finish his refit, the number of blockaders would increase as they had against *Sumter* at Gibraltar. Further, the Confederate captain was fully aware of the gossip around the marine world about his being a raider merely, no true fighting seaman; and the sloops were of about the same class. On the morning of June 19, 1864, Semmes steamed out, while half the population of Cherbourg lined the bluffs to watch.

The ships approached each other, then began circling around a common pivot point, firing their starboard broadsides. To conserve ammunition Semmes had not held much target practice; but the captain of *Kearsarge* was John Ancrum Winslow, a descendant of the Pilgrims and a seaman of the old American school that reached back to Preble and Truxtun, an officer who believed in gunnery as something akin to religion. Though the weight of metal was nearly equal, a good part of *Kearsarge*'s was concentrated in two big 11-inch guns. The result was that *Alabama* hit *Kearsarge* hardly at all, while *Kearsarge* hit nearly every time, and every time she hit, she hurt. Great holes were torn in the Rebel raider's side; the crew of the after pivot gun had to be four times replaced, and an hour after the fight began, *Alabama* headed toward neutral water in sinking condition. She never made it. Semmes himself was picked up by a British yacht that had come out to watch the show.

The difficulty of dealing with such a raider is partly illustrated by the Union navy's efforts to find *Alabama*. Her appearance in the West Indies and the depredations of *Florida* there led the department to set up a "flying squadron" of cruisers among the islands under the dynamic Charles Wilkes. At one time he had sixteen ships under his command, both as an anti-raiding force and to control blockade runners. But he formed the habit of appropriating to his squadron any ship that came into his area, including two of Farragut's sloops belonging to the West Gulf Blockading force and *Vanderbilt,* one of the fastest ships in the navy and one that had been sent south under orders to follow *Alabama* wherever she went. A peremptory command from Washington finally forced Wilkes to release *Vanderbilt,* which missed her quarry at Cape Town by only five days, and Wilkes was ordered home. He reacted in a manner so public and so violent as to earn a court-martial.

There were other Confederate raiders but none of them enjoyed so long or so successful a cruise as *Alabama,* though one of them, *Shenandoah,* was sent against the North Pacific whalers and was burning ships in the Bering Sea eight weeks after Lee surrendered. She finally reached Liverpool, the Rip Van Winkle of the war, long after the Confederate government was dead.

The amount of damage these commerce destroyers did was individually impressive, but statistically utterly unimportant. Sea traffic continued to flow to Philadelphia, New York, Boston, as though they did not exist, and it was never necessary for the Union to put commercial shipping under convoy. But the raiders did succeed in damaging the American merchant marine beyond recovery. The effect was indirect; news of the operations of *Florida* and *Alabama* worked on minds attuned to tales of the privateers of 1812 to produce something like a panic in shipping circles. Not only did insurance rates rise to a point where the American carrying trade became unprofitable in competition with foreign shipping, but also the shipping men themselves sought the immunity of foreign flags. Over a million tons, nearly half the total, were transferred, mainly to British registry, while the construction of commercial shipping fell nearly to the vanishing point. The merchant seamen who had always formed the reserve of the navy were aboard gunboats on blockade or on double-enders penetrating the Confederate waterways. When the war was over, they would be unemployed.

IX

On the morning of January 31, 1863, there was a chill, low-hanging mist off the entrance to Charleston harbor, and the ring of blockading vessels lay close in because of the poor visibility. Through this mist there suddenly appeared the two small Rebel rams built at the city, *Chicora* and *Palmetto State,* each about half the size of *Virginia.* *Chicora* was onto the armed steamer *Mercedita* before she could fire a gun; tore a hole in her stern with a ram-blow and fired a heavy shell which exploded the steamer's boiler. She hauled down her flag. The fast side-wheeler *Keystone State* exchanged broadsides with *Chicora,* not damaging her a bit, then turned round and came back at full speed to ram. The Rebel ship stopped her with a hail of shells that tore her engines and steam equipment all to junk and killed a quarter of her crew; then the two Confederates went back to harbor, since other Union ships were gathering along the horizon and there was no way of taking the captured cripples in.

This raid produced a fierce controversy when the Confederates demanded that *Mercedita* be turned over to them as a surrendered ship, and took the foreign consuls down the harbor to get them to certify that the blockade had been broken. Probably more important was the reaction it provoked in Gideon Welles; he informed Admiral Du Pont of the South Atlantic Blockading Squadron that he would be assigned seven of the new monitors beside the big broadside frigate *New Ironsides,* and it was imperative that they move in and take Charleston. (The original *Monitor* went down in a storm off Hatteras in December, 1862.) Du Pont was skeptical; he pointed out that the monitors could fire only once in seven minutes and the successes hitherto achieved against forts had been through the fast smothering fire of many heavy guns. John Ericsson, being asked, said Du Pont was perfectly right; also he considered the Charleston fortified area too extensive to be taken without the co-operation of a heavy force of troops. But the war was going badly on land that winter and the most Welles would concede in his need for a victory was that Du Pont should experiment with monitors against some other and lesser fortification. The first test was made at Fort McAllister at the mouth of the Great Ogeechee on January 27 by Worden, now commanding the new monitor *Montauk*. She was hit fourteen times and not hurt, but neither was the fort, a fact of which Washington took no notice. More new monitors gradually trickled down the coast to join the squadron, and on February 28 *Montauk* went back to McAllister, under the protection of which now lay the fast English-built raider *Nashville*. At four hundred yards *Montauk* began firing and slowly shelled the raider into a flaming wreck in spite of the frantic efforts of the fort. Reports on this operation convinced Welles; he overruled Du Pont's protests and sent orders that the ironclads were to beat their way past the forts into Charleston harbor.

In addition to the seven monitors and *New Ironsides,* Du Pont had the experimental ironclad *Keokuk,* with curved sides, two non-revolving turrets and apertures through which the pivoted guns could fire. At three o'clock in the afternoon of April 7 the battle line was formed, with John Rodgers in the monitor *Weehawken* leading the way into the harbor. He was hardly at the entrance before he sighted a tangled mass of obstructions, with ropes and floats that meant torpedoes. At the same time over a hundred heavy guns began to shoot. The ships moved gradually along the line of forts at the entrance, firing slowly and doing some damage to Sumter within, but when Du Pont signaled to break off action at 5 P.M., the fire from shore was not visibly diminished. As the captains came aboard *New Ironsides* to report, there were sober faces around the Admiral's table; *Keokuk* was so badly hurt that she sank before twilight, all the monitors had been hit from forty to fifty times, had jammed turrets or guns out of action, broken armor, and smashed pilothouses.

There could be no question of renewing the attack, but only one man was killed and the thing looked very bad in Washington, where they were used to hear of ships running past forts. Secretary Welles told his famous diary that Du Pont "prefers living on his palace ship, the *Wabash,* at Port Royal. Officers under him are becoming infected by his tone, think inaction best." There was no question in Welles' mind but that Du Pont would have to go.

X

Vicksburg sat high on a bluff on the Mississippi side of the river. Grant could land his troops freely down the low Louisiana bank up river from the city. It should have been possible, though precarious, to steal a crossing at some lightly defended point on the eastern side, from which high ground could be reached. But a crossing in small boats would take so long that the expedition would be overwhelmed by assembling forces before it could grow large enough to defend itself—and how would an army on the east bank set up a line of supply?

The first project, suggested from Washington, was cutting a canal through the neck of land on the Louisiana side where the Mississippi swings an S-curve opposite Vicksburg. This would enable Union troops and supplies to be moved by water to a point down river from the city without coming under the fire of the Vicksburg batteries. Grant had little faith in it, but it kept the men from thinking about the misery of their wet camps during the winter. In the meantime, it was becoming an increasing necessity to stop the flow of supplies from the Confederate west down the Red River to Port Hudson on the Mississippi and the railheads on the eastern bank of that river. The only way to do this was by a naval blockade of the point where the Red entered the Mississippi. For Federal ships to reach this stretch of the Mississippi they would either have to be sent down-river past the Vicksburg batteries or upriver from Farragut's fleet past the Port Hudson batteries. The first attempt was from upriver. Young C. R. Ellet, nineteen years old, volunteered to take the ram *Queen of the West* down past Vicksburg on February 2, and made it, though hit twelve times by heavy shot. At the mouth of the Red he captured three ships and destroyed two, but eleven days later a treacherous pilot put his ship aground under a battery. *Queen's* engines were destroyed by a shell and Ellet and his men had to abandon ship and make the rest of their way to the mouth of the Red aboard a miserable captured steamer, where there was nothing to eat but water-logged wheat. The *Queen* was captured by the Rebels.

There they found the new Union ironclad *Indianola,* which Porter had sent after them past the Vicksburg batteries at night. She maintained the blockade of the Red, but on the night of February 24 the Confederates came down on her with the repaired *Queen of the West, Webb,* the last of the Hollins rams, and two armed boarding steamers. The action beautifully illustrated the conditions under which Porter had to operate. *Indianola* had two big guns forward and two astern, but no light, fast-loading pieces to make the enemy keep their distance, and her crew was only large enough to man one pair of the big guns. Her first two shots from the bow guns missed in the dark, and one of the Confederate rams struck her, racking her badly. The other ram got past upstream; *Indianola*'s gun crews raced through the ship, but before they could do more than get a shell into the ram, it hit from astern heavily, one blow tearing off a paddle wheel and another smashing the ironclad's rudder and placing her in sinking condition, so that she had to be run into the bank and surrendered.

The Confederates did not get much good out of her. Porter at once had the whole work force of his advance base at Milliken's Bend turn to on an old scow, building up to the simulacrum of a powerful turreted ironclad, with log casemates through which protruded log guns. The funnels were piled pork barrels with pots of pitch burning beneath. This fearsome monster drifted downstream on February 27, completely ignoring the Vicksburg batteries, and the Confederates, who had just got *Indianola* afloat and started to repair her, blew up their new acquisition.

But the fact that it was one of the most successful ruses of history did not solve the problem of blockading the Red. Porter could not spare a whole squadron from the operations above Vicksburg, while the fate of *Indianola* showed what would happen to one or two ships. But when Farragut at New Orleans heard of what was happening above, he made one of his characteristic snap decisions to go up and blockade the Red with his ocean ships. On the night of March 14 he made the attempt to pass the Port Hudson batteries, his own flagship *Hartford* leading, followed by the sloops *Richmond* and *Mononga-hela,* each of these three with a gunboat lashed to her off side to provide additional power; then the old side-wheeler *Mississippi.*

At Port Hudson the Mississippi River made a sharp bend around a long tongue of low land jutting from the Louisiana shore much as it did at Vicksburg, and the Confederate batteries on high ground along the east bank could lay down a concentrated fire on the narrow channel. Bonfires blazed out from the western shore as the Union ships advanced, silhouetting them for the Rebel batteries to the east. Both sides began to shoot; it was a still night, and soon so heavy a pall of smoke descended on the river that all were firing at flash and navigation was purely by instinct. In that pandemonium, where the ships were making only three knots against the current and shells were bursting everywhere, *Hartford* and her attendant gunboat barely made the passage; both *Richmond* and her assistant had their engines damaged and were forced to turn back; *Monongahela*'s bearings burned out and she drifted downstream, while the old *Mississippi* got hard aground under the fire of the batteries and had to be set afire and abandoned. The last man to leave the ship was a young lieutenant named George Dewey, who would be heard of later.

The Confederates counted this a success; only two of seven ships came through and one was destroyed. But all the same *Hartford* now lay in the mouth of the Red, oddly rigged out, with her lower yards on deck and chain cables hanging from them, surrounded by floats of cypress logs as a preventive against sudden ram attacks. The Red River was closed and General Richard "Dick" Taylor of the Confederate Trans-Mississippi command complained that twelve ships were held in the stream, one of which alone was carrying a quarter-million pounds of bacon.

Farther north the season of spring rains had come, and was used by Porter and Grant in efforts to outflank the batteries along the bluffs of the Yazoo north of Vicksburg by running ironclads through the tangle of bayous in the wide diamond-shaped jungle at the foot of the high ground. The first try was launched from one hundred fifty miles up the Mississippi where a levee was cut to allow the river to flood an old channel and permit the ships to cross to the upper Yazoo via its tributary, the Tallahatchie. Two Union ironclads, with six tinclads and two rams following, pushed in, covering an expedition of several thousand troops. It was a weird form of warfare, where the obstacles were furnished by nature; overhanging trees swept away smokestacks, boats, and everything movable on the upper decks; the ships were aground a dozen times a day, and progress was a crawl. But on March 11 they reached the junction of the Tallahatchie and the Yazoo, only to find a new fort on high ground rising from the surrounding ooze. The ironclads tried to shell it out, but they had no luck. One of them was *Chillicothe,* sister to the unfortunate *Indianola,* a ship so badly built that many of her people were hurt by bolts driven out of the armor and right through its wooden backing. There was no dry ground on which to land the troops for an encircling attack, and Lieutenant Watson Smith, who commanded the expedition, had a nervous breakdown, so the project was abandoned.

The other drive was headed by Porter himself, with five of the old "Pook turtles," through the bayous and passes at the southern end of the Yazoo delta. Spring floods covered the bottom land and it was hoped the gunboats would be able to use small streams to avoid the Confederate fortifications on high ground and work their way around behind Vicksburg. It was as peculiar a voyage as any ships ever undertook. The stream chosen was so winding that from the flagship those following could be seen pointing in four different directions at once. Overhanging branches tore everything away topside and strange collections of animals driven into the trees by the flood dropped on the decks and quarreled there. Huge piles of burning cotton lined the banks, drifting smoke and heat across the narrow channel. There was no fort to stop this expedition, but it encountered an area where the waters spread wide across impenetrably tangled willows, in which a tug and then one of the ironclads stuck fast, and it took the combined efforts of the fleet to pull them out. Confederate snipers were thickening on the banks around. Porter had to unship his rudders and let the ships drift backward down the current, anchoring at night in midstream with the sides of his ships heavily greased as a protection against boarding. Nobody was hurt and General Sherman's men arrived along the banks in time to clear out the sharpshooters during the last stage of the journey, but it was clear that no foothold on the high ground could be won north of Vicksburg.

Now Grant took over, with a new plan of campaign. On the night of April 19, seven of the ironclads ran south through the fire of the Vicksburg batteries with three transports, and a week later, six transports more. Two of the total were sunk during the process, but the remainder were ample to carry an army across the river. The troops meanwhile marched down the west bank, which had now dried out after the floods. On April 29 the gunboats tried to shell out the newly erected Confederate guns at Grand Gulf, sixty river miles below Vicksburg, but the batteries were on high ground and the naval effort against plunging fire failed, as it had earlier at Fort Donelson. Grant moved still further downstream and won his crossing at Bruinsburg, where the east-shore bluffs are three miles back from the riverbank. The Confederate high command was no little confused by a simultaneous feint by a Union gunboat squadron at the old Haynes' Bluff position on the Yazoo to the north of Vicksburg, carried out so vigorously that the ironclad *Choctaw* was hit sixty-one times in action with the forts.

This distracted the attention of Confederate General Pemberton in Vicksburg to the north: Before he could assemble his wits or his forces, Grant was well on his way to Vicksburg from the south, abandoning communications, marching like a streak up the east bank of the Mississippi and hitting like successive flashes of lightning. On May 15 the crews of the gunboats saw men capering on the long-unattainable bluffs; they wore the Union blue. Vicksburg was closely besieged and everything Grant needed could come flowing down the Mississippi until the place surrendered on July 4, 1863.

That is, the campaign that took Vicksburg was a genuine combined operation. The fleet without the army had failed when Farragut came upstream in 1862; the army without the fleet failed when Grant tried the overland route. But once the operations were dovetailed the force became irresistible and the war on western waters thenceforth was mainly in the hands of the tinclads.

XI

The replacement for Du Pont in the South Atlantic command was Admiral John A. Dahlgren, slight, pale, ambitious, something of a genius in mathematics and ordnance, a remarkable character who had been told he was going blind at the age of thirty and had cured himself. For nearly twenty years he had been kept ashore as head of the Bureau of Ordnance, and in the early, confused days of the Lincoln administration, when the loyalty of many officers was in doubt, he had won the confidence of the President. Now he was panting for a command afloat—and received it with orders to capture Charleston. This time, however, the operation was to be by stages instead of the *coup de main* Du Pont had tried. Dahlgren was assisted by three thousand troops under General Q. A. Gillmore; they were to land on Morris Island at the south end of the harbor entrance and reduce Fort Wagner at its tip, with the help of the ironclads, then erect new batteries which would beat down Fort Sumter and cover the removal of the obstacles so the monitors could steam in.

Before this new campaign opened, word reached the Federal authorities that the Confederates were building a new ironclad named *Atlanta* on Wassaw Sound in Georgia. The monitors *Weehawken,* Captain John Rodgers, and *Nahant* were sent down to see about it. *Atlanta* poked her nose out on June 17, 1863, bringing with her the high hopes of the Confederacy, which had set afoot a number of such ships as blockade-breakers, and a parade of excursion boats to see the new titan demolish the "abolition kangeroos." It was just breaking day when *Weehawken* came in range. *Atlanta* fired a broadside that missed; *Weehawken* fired an 11-inch shell that glanced from the Confederate's armor, then a 15-inch that went right in, wounding sixteen men and knocking forty more to the deck. A second 11-inch shell cracked *Atlanta*'s armor; another 15-inch smashed her pilot-house and killed the helmsman, and the Confederate ironclad grounded out of control and hauled down her flag. *Nahant* never got a chance to fire a shot.

This was the sort of thing the monitors could clearly do. Dahlgren was less sanguine about his ability to handle heavy fortifications with the number of ships he had, and moved up toward Fort Wagner on July 6 with something less than confidence. The troops were landed with four monitors moving in to help them, a thrill of cheering going through the fleet as Dahlgren's flag broke out from *Catskill,* leading the line in person. The fighting against the forts was long and very fierce that day, the troops being repulsed ashore and *Catskill* taking sixty hits. Next day the ships came back, Dahlgren now leading the line in *Nahant,* and this bruising battle continued for more than six weeks, the monitors and *New Ironsides* going in to fight Fort Wagner almost daily, taking long-range shelling from the other works around the harbor while the soldiers drove siege parallels under a rain of artillery fire. In the iron cases of the little ships, the heat was intense, the racket of constant explosions terrific, and the shock of heavy shot striking their turrets hard to bear. Man after man was sent home, simply worn out by the ordeal. Dahlgren himself grew so weak he could hardly rise from his chair and walk, but as of the same day he set this fact down, he recorded: "Led the monitors in to attack."

Inch by inch the parallels ashore crept forward and the resistance of Wagner decreased. The Confederates formed the habit of sending new guns into the fort by night, so Dahlgren posted a monitor around the point each twilight to cut off this traffic. Light-draft blockade runners had been seeping close inshore around Fort Moultrie at the northern entrance, but late in August one was forced to lie overnight under the guns and *Catskill* set her afire. At the end of that month the Confederate commander in Wagner reported that the place would become untenable in two days; his working parties could not repair damages as fast as they were now being inflicted, and on the night of September 6 he pulled out in the dark.

Union guns replaced the Confederate in the captured fort and were turned inward, toward Fort Sumter, which was presently reduced to a heap of rubble by the bombardment from sea and shore. On the night of September 7, after a terrific gunfight at the entrance of the harbor, in which the monitor *Passaic* was hit ninety times, an attempt was made to take Sumter by a boat attack. It failed.

Dahlgren now reported to the department that he believed he could beat up the harbor to Charleston, but not without losing ships to gunfire, obstructions, and torpedoes, and he would need six additional monitors to make good the losses he expected. Welles acknowledged failure by replying that the actual capture of the city was now "merely a point of honor."

The monitors went back to Port Royal for repairs; *New Ironsides* and the wooden ships remained on blockade, through which there still occasionally skipped one of the specially built blockade-runners, low and very fast, painted dark gray, carrying cargoes that netted every man aboard a competence. But the Union fleet was not yet through with its difficulties off Charleston. On the night of October 5 *New Ironsides'* watch saw something mysterious emerging from the harbor, hailed at three hundred yards, and was answered by the discharge of a shotgun. The next moment there was a terrific explosion aft and a tall column of water went up alongside the ironclad. She had

been hit by the first mobile torpedo ever used in war, borne on a spar
at the prow of a semi-submerged vessel called *David*. The wave of the
explosion nearly drowned the torpedoboat and most of her crew
were taken prisoners, but two of them managed to get back aboard
and work her into harbor. *New Ironsides* was damaged enough to
be sent in for extensive yard repairs.

The second (and last) Confederate mobile torpedo attack also
came off Charleston, on the night of February 17, 1864, when the
lookout on the screw sloop *Housatonic* sighted something moving in
the water one hundred yards away. The ship slipped her cable and the
quarterdeck called for steam, but before she could get under way she
was rocked by an explosion that tore out so much of her side that she
sank in less than five minutes. Her attacker was *H. L. Hunley,* a
cigar-shaped craft designed as a submarine and powered by a row
of men turning cranks. It was supposed to attack underwater, towing
a torpedo beneath the target ship. But the submarine was so poorly
designed that the hatches had to be kept open most of the time before
submerging to avoid suffocating the crew, and when the hatches
were open a single wave could sink her. At Mobile, where she was
built, three crews were drowned in this way before she was finally
taken overland to Charleston, where another crew was lost before
she took off to sink *Housatonic*. This was her final voyage. She attacked on the surface, but even so a fifth crew of incredibly nervy
volunteers went down with her when she perished in the explosion
that destroyed the sloop.

XII

The Red River expedition of 1864 was hatched in politics and stank
of it throughout; this was why it became more costly to the navy than
the genuinely military campaigns against New Orleans and Vicksburg. French bayonets had placed Austrian Maximilian on a tawdry
throne in Mexico; Secretary of State Seward was worried lest the old
claim to Texas be asserted or the independence of that state recognized, and wanted some points seized and strongly held to demonstrate that it was U.S. territory. The first try was at Sabine Pass in
September, 1863, with a considerable squadron and four thousand
troops. Only four armed steamers could get across the bar, however,

and they proved no match for the batteries, two of them having their boilers blown up so they were forced to surrender.

The full-dress expedition planned for the spring of 1864 was to be a combined operation up the Red River from the Mississippi to take Shreveport, capital of Confederate Louisiana, as an advanced base. The main body of troops would come from the occupation army at New Orleans under General N. P. Banks, with a second column striking cross-country from Union bases in Arkansas. A corps was borrowed from Sherman's army for a strictly limited time to get the new base established. It was assumed that communications could be maintained by the river after the first objective was achieved.

Porter assembled the most powerful fleet yet seen in the west—ten ironclads, eight tinclads, and three of the new river monitors, with paddle wheels in humps at the stern. From the beginning in early March it was evident that Banks was far more interested in politics— and other things—than war. He dawdled, holding local elections and making appointments, and above all gathering in highly profitable supplies of cotton. There was a Confederate strong point with case-mated batteries, Fort De Russy, halfway up to Alexandria, but the experience at Fort Hindman had given the Confederates a poor idea of the ability of such works to resist armored gunboats, and the enemy pulled out without waiting for land attack.

With no little difficulty the Federal ships pushed upriver through a belt of stony rapids at Alexandria, where Banks ensconced himself in the best hotel and held elections. The ships ran out of coal; Porter sent landing parties out to gather fence-rails, and on both banks piles of cotton were fired, darkening the sky with low hanging smoke. The heavy ironclads could not go much farther. Porter pushed on with two tinclads and two of the river monitors into channels that were filled with snags and shoals and were crooked enough to drive pilots mad. He was one hundred ten miles north of Alexandria when word came on April 7 that Banks had been heavily defeated at Sabine Cross Roads, fifty miles to the south, and was retreating as rapidly as possible.

The position of the fleet instantly became acutely difficult. The whole operation had been predicated on the annual spring rise in the Red River, but this year, for the first time since 1855, the freshets in the upper waters failed, and now the stream was dropping fast. The

Federal ships could only crawl down river and were under constant attack from the shore. The ironclad *Eastport* ran on a torpedo, was with difficulty kept afloat. Two hump-boats that came up to help her were smashed by Confederate artillery from the banks, while the refugee Negroes they had taken aboard were killed in the water by the Rebels. In the same action the little tinclad *Cricket,* with Porter himself aboard, was hit thirty-eight times and lost more than half her crew, the tinclad *Juliet* was nearly as badly hurt, and *Eastport* had to be abandoned and blown up. Only the appearance of one of the Union monitors saved the situation. At Alexandria, Porter found Banks making himself very comfortable. In an action at Pleasant Hill the Confederates had been beaten off by the troop borrowed from Sherman, but General Banks for the first time in the campaign showed determination. He was determined to retreat to the mouth of the Red, and told his companions that the whole river fleet was not worth one day's rations for the army.

At this point it was not unlikely that the Union river fleet would be lost, for at the rapids there were less than three feet of water in a twenty-foot-wide channel, whereas the shallowest of the ironclads drew seven feet. The savior of the situation was Colonel Joseph Bailey of the 4th Wisconsin, a lumberman who remembered that when they wanted water to float logs down the river in his country cribs were built out from the bank to make an artificial lake, suddenly released. With difficulty Bailey extracted three thousand soldiers from Banks to do the hard labor. They scoured the countryside, gathering logs, stones, the timbers of cotton mills, anything that would hold, while all the blacksmiths in the fleet made iron clamps. The armor was taken off the ironclads to lighten them, but just as things were almost ready, the barges at the neck of the cribs washed out and only three ships went through. Bailey unhesitatingly built another set of cribs, higher upstream, and at last the ships rocked through to safety. But in the meanwhile two of the ironclads, convoying seized cotton for one of Banks' generals, were caught by batteries and shelled into destruction.

As Vicksburg was a high point in combined operations, so the Red River campaign was the low one. The basic strategy, dictated from Washington, made the unjustifiable assumption that communications for a couple of hundred miles up the Red could be kept open by water, which would only have been true if there were enough deep water to carry tinclads to convoy supply vessels, and ironclads to cover the tinclads. That is, geography was ignored. What was more important the operations never truly combined; there was no meeting of the minds between Banks and Porter as there had been when the admiral dealt with Grant and Sherman. This lack of co-operation brought out the fact that there was no real top-level command.

XIII

April, 1864, was a bad month for the Union navy. On top of the Red River defeat there was a disaster in the North Carolina sounds, where an indomitable Confederate captain named J. W. Cooke built the small ironclad *Albemarle* in an open cornfield up the Roanoke River. She mounted only two 100-pounder guns, but had solid armor and a strong ram bow. Cooke brought her down the river on April 19 to find the Union converted ferryboat *Southfield* and the double-ender *Miami,* linked together by chains in the hope of catching *Albemarle* between them with the idea of boarding her and throwing explosives down her funnel. Cooke prevented this by maneuver; drove his ram into *Southfield*'s side, and leaving her sinking, engaged *Miami* with the guns. Commander Charles W. Flusser of the latter was killed by a shot that rebounded from the ironclad's flank, and his ship was in a state of near-wreck before she retreated. Plymouth, the Union post on the Roanoke, was left without naval support and fell to Confederate troops.

The difficulty of dealing with *Albemarle* was the fact that the Federal navy had no armored ships that could get across the bars into the sounds. This had been foreseen and it produced the singular episode of the shallow-draft monitors. Early in the year the Navy Department asked John Ericsson to design a monitor with one turret and one gun, not to draw over four feet water, for just such service. Ericsson calculated and reported the requirements impossible; the design was turned over to Alban C. Stimers, who had much to do with the outfitting and handling of the original *Monitor*. He was a good man, but while the twenty light-draft monitors contracted for were still building, the department introduced additional items of equipment, and one of his clerks made an error in arithmetic. The result was that when the first of the ships was launched, the dismaying discovery was made that she would not float. None of them was ever of any use.

There were thus nothing but wooden ships to send into the sounds and four double-enders were ordered in under Captain Melancton Smith, with four armed steamers, several carrying nets to foul the iron-clad's propellers, and *Miami* back for revenge with a spar torpedo on her bow. There was not a ship in the squadron with a gun of more than 11-inch caliber, and the double-enders were too weak in the prows for ramming, but they fought *Albemarle* from 4 P.M. until dark, trying to net her propellers, ride her down, or get a shot into one of the ports. *Miami*'s steering gear had been working badly since the earlier encounter and she could not drive home with her torpedo. The double-ender *Sassacus* took a shot in the boiler that killed her whole engine-room crew, and several of the other Union ships suffered badly. But one of *Albemarle*'s guns was blasted off at the muzzle and her funnel was so riddled that her speed dropped to little over a knot, which made it impossible to use the ram weapon, so she steamed back to her berth at Plymouth.

At this point Captain Cooke's health broke down, but there is no real explanation of why the Rebel ram was kept lying at her dock from May to October. In the meanwhile, two New York engineers had been attentively studying the Confederate torpedo attacks off Charleston, and reached the conclusion that the planning was all wrong. They designed a torpedo craft of their own—a thirty-foot launch with engines geared to run silently, the torpedo on a long spar cocked over the bow out of water, but so arranged that it could be lowered and fired by the skipper, standing forward with reins in his hands. Three of these craft were built and sent out at once to the scene of action in North Carolina, where the need was the greatest. One foundered at sea, one was cast on the Confederate-held part of the Virginia coast and taken. The third arrived on October 20, under command of William B. Cushing, a young lieutenant who had been restored to the Navy after expulsion from the Naval Academy for, among other things, drawing caricatures of a professor—and who had promptly made a name for himself in the service for unusual daring. Cushing and his seven men were worn out and weak from the ordeal of the voyage, having lived on spoiled biscuit and water for a week. Simultaneously with his arrival came a State Department request to have him put on trial for some petty violation of blockade regulations.

David D. Porter had lately been brought East to command the North Atlantic Blockading Squadron in preparation for an assault on Fort Fisher, the fortress that guarded the mouth of the Cape Fear River, gate of Wilmington, the last of the major blockade-running ports. Porter was fond of officers who violated rules in the national interest; when Cushing expressed a desire to go in after *Albemarle* at once, the admiral packed the court-martial, got the lieutenant acquitted, and sent him in with Godspeed on the night of October 27.

As Cushing approached up the Roanoke, he was hailed from the ram; he ordered full speed ahead, at which point a fire of musketry broke out from ship and shore and a bonfire was lighted on the bank, revealing a heavy boom of logs around the ironclad, placed there to block just such an attack. Cushing circled to gain momentum, and while bullets tore through his clothes and one of *Albemarle*'s 100-pounders slowly depressed, he manipulated the complex lines to control and fire the torpedo. Torpedo and 100-pounder went off in a double shock and Cushing found himself swimming. Twice he dodged Confederate boats full of armed men and finally pulled himself ashore in a swamp, where a Negro took heart at the sight of his torn blue uniform, gave him something to eat, and told him the ram was sunk. By night and cloud he worked his way to the shore, where he stole a boat and rowed out to the blockading fleet. Cushing was the only survivor except for three prisoners the Confederates fished from the water. Porter instantly promoted him and made him flag captain of the fleet.

XIV

After the capture of New Orleans, Farragut had wished to attack Mobile at once, but Washington insisted on using the seagoing ships against Vicksburg. When that place fell Grant offered a plan for a second bisection of the Confederacy, on a line down from Nashville and along the Alabama River to Mobile, the attack to be made simultaneously from both ends. But the troops were siphoned off for the fighting around Chattanooga and Banks' Red River expedition and the project never got beyond the talking stage. Thus by the spring of 1864 nothing had been done about Mobile, and Forts Morgan and Gaines, on the sandspits facing each other at the entrance, had become very strong. The situation was complicated by the fact that at Selma, up the river, the Confederates were busy building a fleet of ironclads, and on May 20 floated the first one across the bar at the river mouth into the bay and began to fit her out, under command of Admiral Franklin Buchanan, who had led *Virginia* during the first day of her sortie.

The new ironclad was named *Tennessee,* a ram of the usual Brooke-Porter type, but more heavily armored than any other, with 5-inch armor; two 7-inch and four 6-inch rifles. With the three light gunboats that accompanied her she offered a serious problem to Farragut, for he had nothing but wooden ships under his blockade command. He begged and pleaded for monitors, but they were all needed before Charleston or in the James, where the Confederates had built two new ironclads at Richmond. It was not until July that there arrived in his squadron four ships fresh from the yards—two new Ericsson monitors, *Tecumseh* and *Manhattan,* with a pair of 15-inch guns apiece, and two from the Mississippi, *Chickasaw* and *Winnebago,* Eads jobs, with turtle-back decks and two turrets, each containing a pair of 11-inch. It was 150° F. in the cabin of *Chickasaw;* young Captain Perkins went around in his shirt and an old straw hat and had to sleep on deck; the crew were pale and always panting. But Farragut at once prepared to run the forts, having obtained two thousand troops to invest the entrance forts.

Fort Morgan was the more important and dangerous work—on the right of the entrance, the only deep-water channel lying under its embrasures. A triple line of one hundred eighty torpedoes—mines, they would be called today—closed all this channel except a hundred-yard gap left for the use of *Tennessee,* which placed herself across it with the gunboats as the Federal ships came in. Farragut had three heavy wooden sloops and four lighter ones, to each of which was lashed a gunboat on the off side, as at Port Hudson, in case of disabled engines. They formed a starboard line, led by *Brooklyn* under James Alden, another son of the Pilgrims and one of the last of the senior captains, who demanded this honor. The monitors were in line to port, headed by *Tecumseh.* The wooden ships took some pounding from *Tennessee* and the forts before they could open fire; when they did a blanket of smoke puffed out across the water level, so that Farragut climbed into the mizzen rigging, where a sailor lashed him fast.

At this moment *Tecumseh* swung across the line of black buoys that marked the torpedoes, in haste to get at *Tennessee*. One of them exploded; *Tecumseh's* screws came up in the air and she was under water in a matter of seconds, carrying down her captain as he courteously stood aside to allow his pilot to precede him up the escape ladder. Behind, the buoys had been sighted from *Brooklyn* and her attendant gunboat. She stopped, swinging into a position where she lay across the head of the line, raked both by the fort and the Confederate ironclad, and the other ships began to pile up behind her. "What's wrong there?" shouted Farragut from the rigging.

"Torpedoes! Torpedoes!"

"Damn the torpedoes! Full speed ahead!"

Farragut's *Hartford* swung to port to lead the line across the ominous black buoys, and those aboard heard the primers snap, but never a torpedo went off. The line straightened by magic and the ships were through into the bay. One of the Confederate gunboats was destroyed by a broadside from *Hartford;* another sought safety up the bay but was run down by the fast double-ender *Metacomet*. As the ships totted up casualties, there was a puff of smoke from under the guns of Fort Morgan and here came *Tennessee* to attack the whole Union fleet.

"I did not think old Buchanan was such a fool," remarked Farragut, and in fact there were many more intelligent things the Confederate commander could have done, including beating out through the now unguarded channel to attack the Federal transports outside. The wooden sloops tried to attack the monster by ramming; one, two, three they charged her and damaged nothing but their own prows, their shot glancing from her side. *Tennessee* came flank to flank with *Hartford,* the guns bruising the Union flagship sorely and setting her afire. *Manhattan* fired one shot that broke the ironclad's armor, then dropped out with engine trouble. But the monitor *Chickasaw* with young Perkins prancing on one of her turrets in his shirt-sleeves, hung right under *Tennessee's* stern, firing her 11-inch "like a pair of pocket pistols." She shot away the steering chains, got a shot through a port that wounded Buchanan, jammed the ironclad's port shutters with another, and with her funnel down, casemate filled with smoke and unable to fire effectively, *Tennessee* surrendered.

"If it hadn't been for that damned black hulk under our stern we would have beaten you," said the Confederate captain as he came aboard to deliver up his sword.

X V

Mobile was the story; the end of the Confederate States Navy. The other ironclads up the river could never get across the bar, for they had to be without guns to negotiate it and the Union gunboats in the Bay prevented that, while the troops speedily made an end of the entrance forts from the sandspits on which they lay. The Charleston ironclads were faced by an overwhelming force of monitors, and when the three built at Richmond made their only sortie down the James, they encountered the new double-turreted monitor *Onondaga,* which cracked their armor with her first shots, so they were destroyed at their docks.

Since the beginning of the war Wilmington in North Carolina had been the great port of the blockade-runners, and they made fortunes in the business. By 1863, a whole class of English-built special vessels was engaged in the traffic. They loaded mainly at Nassau in the Bahamas from cargoes brought by deep-water freighters, war materials mostly; would approach the coast hull down from the outer ring of blockaders and hover till dark, then slip in under the loom of the land, almost invisible. One runner taken in the fall of 1863 had three hundred cases of Austrian rifles and a hold full of saltpeter. The outbound cargo was always cotton, compressed to the smallest possible space; the ordinary profit was £30,000 a round trip, and at this price the blockade-runner paid for herself in two runs.

When the fall of Mobile threw into relief the importance of Wilmington and the arms-running traffic through it, General Grant became very anxious that the trade be brought to a halt by the capture of Fort Fisher, a work three-quarters of a mile long on the sandspit at the entrance to the harbor, with a five-hundred-yard crosswork on the land face. Porter asked for one hundred sixty seaborne guns to dominate the sea side. The Department gave him more, three of the big screw frigates, *New Ironsides,* four monitors, ten gunboats, six double-enders and twelve armed steamers, with a corps of eight thousand troops under General Godfrey Weitzel—the largest American expedition launched to date. It was intended not to achieve by surprise or speed like most of the others, but to crush by overwhelming force— a concept new to American naval thinking, but one that was to have no little influence.

The expedition assembled at Hampton Roads, where Porter took his ships out daily for exercises in fire and maneuver, which was a new concept at the time, but the sailing seemed almost endlessly delayed by a series of conferences in the military command. Behind this lay the fact that Weitzel's corps belonged to the department of General Ben Butler, the marplot politician officer who was so influential that even Grant found it hard to oppose him successfully. Butler was insisting on his right to command the troops of the expedition in person, expecting to win glory as cheaply as he had at Hatteras in the early days of the war. He made it stick, and in addition imposed on Porter a plan of his own for beaching a ship loaded with one hundred fifty tons of powder on the sea face of the fort and blowing the work all to pieces.

The explosion ship was towed in on the night of December 23 and the train was set alight; but when the Navy moved in next morning there was no visible sign of damage, nor was there any actual harm, some men inside having slept through the shock. All day the ships fired, the monitors close in, trying to knock out guns by direct hits, the wooden ships outside pouring in a volume of shellfire that burned the barracks and drove gunners from their pieces. The transports arrived too late for disembarkation that day; but next morning, Christmas Day, the men were set ashore some distance up the sandspit, while the ships kept up a fire that held the fort quiet. The troops worked to within one hundred yards of the place, but that night General Butler sent off a letter to the fleet, saying that he considered Fort Fisher too strong for anything but siege operations, and was therefore re-embarking his men.

The dynamic Porter's fury over this performance can be imagined, and it communicated itself so far that for the first time in the war Ben Butler found that his influence had run out. He was summarily removed and the expedition put back under A. H. Terry, a real fighting officer. Fort Fisher had been considerably strengthened since the first attack, but when the monitors moved in to do counter-battery work on January 13, the shore guns found it impossible to reply adequately to the wooden ships. That night Terry landed his men and worked in. On the night of the 14th Porter set ashore some sixteen hundred bluejackets from the fleet for a frontal attack. The ships kept up their fire. On the 15th the double assault was delivered. The naval branch of it failed; the sailors had no training in land warfare, were armed only with cutlass and pistol, and could make little reply to the Confederates who lined the parapets, shooting them down with musketry, nor could they cross the wide ditch in front. But Terry effected a lodgment in the main works, and there now developed a series of battles along the traverse embankments in the fort, with wooden gunboats very close in, firing support, and the monitors just behind them to take care of any artillery that opened. A confused struggle in a dark shot with flame lasted until midnight and after. At that hour a young ensign named Robley Evans, lying in the ditch with four bullets in his body, listening to the wounded around him crying for water, lifted his head to see a man with a torch signaling that the fort was taken, and heard as an echo the tempest of cheering that broke forth on sea and shore.

When Welles reported the event to Lincoln, the President said, with an air of surprised realization: "Why, there is nothing left for your ships to do"; and it was perfectly true. The naval side of the Civil War was over.

Under the dynamic leadership of Welles and Fox, the Navy had successfully carried out a fantastic expansion program: From 1861 to 1865, the number of ships grew from 90 to 670; of officers, from 1,300 to 6,700; of men, 7,500 to 51,200; and of budget, from 12 million to 123 million dollars. The result was the most experienced, and one of the most powerful, navies in the world. It remained to be seen whether the vital role the Navy had played in the Federal victory had won the public support needed to keep it in the first rank.

★ ★ ★ ★ ★

6

The Long Sleep; the Slow Awakening

AT THE CLOSE OF THE WAR of the Rebellion the United States had the largest and most powerful Navy in the world. But it was a Navy of special ships for special jobs. The river ironclads and tinclads were obviously only useful in their special element and were early sold out of service. The monitors were almost as obviously suited chiefly for work in inshore waters, and though they were widely imitated abroad, and one of them made a voyage around the Horn as a demonstration of seaworthiness they were far from seagoing general-purpose ships. *New Ironsides* was the only American example of the "broadside ironclad," a type built in considerable numbers in Europe and forerunner of the modern battleship. American or foreign, they suffered from the general disability of being horribly slow. The big broadside wooden frigates that were the pride of the Navy at the beginning of the war could not deal with ironclads of any type.

Besides these the United States Navy had a class of vessel little imitated elsewhere, the wooden screw cruisers, outgrowths of the screw sloops-of-war. They were intended to run down Confederate commerce-destroyers on the seas and to cut off blockade-runners before they could make the shelter of the shore, and in the latter role they succeeded better than any other type of blockading craft. In response to what may be called a naval law of evolution, they tended constantly to grow in size; and in response to the always ominous threat of war with Britain over the international side issues of the Civil War, they grew in power. The last numbers of this series were the fifteen cruisers of the Wampanoag and Java classes, none completed until after the war. They were some of the most remarkable ships ever built by the Navy, armed with ten 9-inch and three 60-pounder rifles; the hull designs by the famous clipper-ship builder Donald McKay; the engines furnished by Benjamin Franklin Isherwood, who deserves mention as the greatest steam engineer in the history of the service, as Ericsson was its greatest inventor.

Wampanoag of this class did a good seventeen knots on a 24-hour trial in 1869, at least three knots better than any British liner or British cruiser. The reports of her phenomenal speed had no small influence in determining the British to arbitrate American claims against them for damage caused by *Alabama,* which they had hitherto rejected. A nation that could put fifteen such ships on the ocean had to be treated with kid gloves.

But these big cruisers were built of green timber as were the hulls of the large double-turreted monitors, and they warped and rotted. Congress and the country were content to let them rot. The current theory of naval defense was the protection of the coast and harbors, which were menaced by nobody, with raiding cruisers on the high seas as a counter-threat. The nation had become intensely interested in transcontinental railroads, in filling up the empty acres of the West, and in making money. There were few to worry about a sea commerce that had fallen to less than one-third of its former size. Laws on the books prevented re-transfer to the American flag of the ships that had sought refuge under foreign colors during the war, or the purchase of foreign-built ships for the American merchant marine.

The result was that there was hardly any merchant marine to protect and no feeling for the need of a Navy. In addition, Admiral Porter, who had become the effective head of the Department, thought up an ingenious scheme for getting at least some new ships (since Congress would vote none whatever) under the guise of repairing old ones. But Secretary of the Navy George Robeson, one of the leading boodlers who hung around the Grant regime, managed the business in such a manner that his own firm showed enormous profits. Congress, presently becoming aware of this, passed a law that no ship should be repaired for an amount more than a small fraction of its original cost.

The combined result of these factors was that between the Civil War and 1883—eighteen years—American shipyards went completely to sleep. Two small gunboats were the only new ships laid down for the U.S. Navy, and it completely missed the period of experiment with iron and steel hulls, improved steam propulsion, compartmentation, and breech-loading guns. The flag was still shown in foreign ports—aboard wooden cruisers, one of which was visited by a French officer, who patted a smoothbore pivot gun and remarked: "Ah, yes, on the old system. Why, I can remember when we had those in our Navy!"

As with the ships, so with the men. In spite of the retirement provisions introduced during the Civil War, the officer list stagnated as it had between 1815 and 1861 because there were so few ships left in commission. Many of the more energetic men quit the service. Among those who stayed, lieutenants who had seen half a dozen battles by the age of nineteen were still of the same rank at thirty-eight with little prospect of promotion. They had not the slightest experience with modern steel warships and but little with machinery; the directive was for ships to use sail as much as possible to save coal. The reserve of trained seamen from the merchant marine dried up with the merchant marine itself; they were somewhere in the West, homesteading along the line of the railroads. Their places were filled by out-of-work foreigners from the great wave of immigration. It became convenient for officers to speak three or four languages to communicate with their crews. By 1881, the U.S. Navy ranked twelfth in the world, below those of Chile, China, and Denmark, and its men were some eighty per cent foreigners.

II

In the meantime the world itself had become smaller and it was obvious to anyone who cared to look that our Navy was no longer capable of fulfilling even the limited strategic plan of defending harbors and striking back by means of raiders. The first man who looked was William H. Hunt, Garfield's Secretary of the Navy. He convoked a board of officers to report on the service, and it recommended the construction of thirty-eight cruisers, a figure which so terrified Congress that it exerted political pressure to have Hunt kicked upstairs into an embassy, then authorized two cruisers, but without appropriating money to pay for them.

Hunt's successor was William E. Chandler, manager of the Republican campaign committee, with a mandate to clean things up before opponents of the administration could make political capital out of the situation. Chandler got through an appropriation for three small cruisers and a dispatch vessel, and then began to make unpleasant discoveries. The first was that there was no one in the United States who could design a modern warship; he had to buy his plans from England. The second was that a lieutenant named Evans (the same who lay wounded in the ditch at Fort Fisher) had inserted in the specifications a requirement that the ships should be built of American-made mild steel, and there was not a rolling mill in the country that could produce it.

Chandler spanked Evans by putting him on a board to inspect antique lighthouses, but although the ironmongers were willing to learn the new trade of rolling steel plate, and though this was ultimately the foundation of the U.S. steel industry, they could not pick up overnight. The administration's term ran out before the ships were finished.

The new Navy Secretary was William C. Whitney and the administration he served was the Democratic one of Grover Cleveland. It was decidedly to its interest to find something wrong with the proceedings of its predecessor. Whitney found plenty: The contracts for all four Chandler ships had gone to a Philadelphian named Roche, who was a large contributor to Republican campaign funds; the dispatch boat had engines so far above her waterline that a single shot would wreck them and she was well below her contract speed; the cruisers were hogs for fuel, very slow and of an off-beat design which indicated that the British had been experimenting with novelties on American money. Whitney flatly rejected the dispatch boat and the contractor went broke; then the Secretary set out to start a real navy.

The first authorization was for two armored cruisers, or light battleships, three light cruisers, and one torpedo boat, the last a new type of vessel, designed to use the equally new self-propelled torpedoes. Once again recourse was had to England for design and Whitney was swindled. There is no other word for it. The armored cruisers were of an experimental type, supposed to give all-around fire to their big guns, but the result of the arrangement was that their salvos tore their decks to pieces unless the big guns were trained right abeam. The engine design for the light cruiser *Charleston* proved to be a combination of three sets of plans for similar ships produced in British yards, and the machinery simply would not work until basic changes had been made. When the 1887 program for two more cruisers came up, Whitney had lost patience. He advertised for competitive bids on design and construction, both to come from the United States, with penalties for non-fulfillment and bonuses for exceeding specifications.

This proved the key piece in the combination. The subsequently famous American "know-how" had not yet been invented, but it had now become accepted doctrine that the U.S. was to have some kind of navy, and the designers turned to to make it qualitatively superior, in much the same spirit as frigate-builder Joshua Humphreys in the 1790s. They were helped by the fact that although Congress continued reluctant to spend money for ships there was a revolution in Chile in 1891. The revolutionaries bought a ship at San Francisco, loaded her with munitions, and put to sea. Now this was precisely the issue on which the U.S. had laid claims for the damage caused by *Alabama* during the Civil War and made good its claim. An American cruiser followed the filibuster, stopped her, and sent her back. But the Chilean revolutionists won, and a wave of the most intense anti-American feeling was sweeping the country when the cruiser *Baltimore* put into Valparaiso in October and sent a liberty party ashore. The men were set on by a mob; the police helped the mob with pistols and clubs. Two were killed and eighteen wounded and a war threat rose like a full moon.

The matter was settled by diplomatic action and the polite firmness of Commander Robley Evans (still the same Evans), who reached Valparaiso with the gunboat *Yorktown* just as *Baltimore* was leaving, but it underlined a fact that the Washington authorities could not miss. Chile possessed a battleship; only one, but it was strong enough to have taken on the whole U.S. Navy at the date. Up to this time nearly all the talk in naval and congressional circles, as well as all of the building, had been in terms of fast cruisers and how much damage they could inflict on an enemy's commerce—the legacy of 1812, translated into something like a fixed idea. To be sure, there were dissenters to this theory, mostly centering around the new

Naval War College which Admiral Stephen B. Luce had set up in an abandoned poorhouse at Newport in the face of fierce opposition. *"Teach* the art of war!" said one of the old-line officers, when he heard of the project. "Well, I'll be damned. You have Cooper's 'Naval History'; what more do you want?"

But Luce persisted and named to his staff a certain Commander Alfred T. Mahan, who had already written one book and was meditating on the influence of sea power upon history, a topic that eventually became the title of one of the most influential works of the coming age, not for Americans alone, but for the world. It set forth the theory that national greatness and national commerce depended not upon menacing a potential enemy's sea traffic, but on *control* of the sea lanes. That any great ferment had resulted from this at the time of the Chilean incident may be regarded as uncertain; but the ideas were there and the existence of the Chilean battleship lent them point. Congress was persuaded to authorize three "coast defense battleships"—the designation as a gesture in the direction of the old prejudices. In 1893, they were launched and soon followed by a fourth.

Like the Humphreys frigates, like other ships of American design, they excited derision abroad. It was also remarked that the new American cruisers that accompanied these battleships were too heavily gunned for their displacement, insufficiently armored, and incapable of standing long cruising. The battleships themselves rode too low in the water, had poor stability, and lacked protection for the ammunition hoists of their secondary guns.

Nevertheless the Navy was out of the doldrums at last.

It was at this time for example that it got its first submarine, John P. Holland's *Plunger*. She was only one hundred sixty-eight tons, but she carried a torpedo tube and could make ten knots submerged. The *Plunger* never saw battle, but she was a significant addition to that long line of historic American undersea craft that began with Bushnell's *Turtle*—and has culminated in the atomic *Nautilus* of today.

III

This was the material condition of the Navy when the nation stumbled into war with Spain in 1898. The proximate cause of the war was the explosion which destroyed the armored cruiser *Maine* in Havana harbor, where she had gone because of the long-continued unrest in Spanish Cuba, with resultant loss of life and property to Americans, a condition which Spain seemed unable to correct. It is unnecessary to go into the controversy over whether the explosion was caused by Spaniards, interior conditions on the ship, or Cuban revolutionists seeking to embroil Spain with the United States. The dominant fact is that there was war, and it was obvious that the war would be primarily naval.

In the four battleships and two new armored cruisers, with the older armored cruiser *Texas,* the U.S. enjoyed at least a paper superiority in first-line ships over the Spanish fleet, whose backbone was made up of seven exceptionally heavy armored cruisers. The latter were rated faster. The proportion of lighter ships in the two navies was about the same, while the U.S. had six modernized monitors, of which the Spaniards had none. But it is instructive to compare the historical results with contemporary opinion in European naval circles. Even in England, which was favorable to the U.S., it was held likely to be a long, difficult war, only to be decided by Anglo-Saxon staying power. On the Continent there were free references to the lack of discipline aboard American ships and their bad gunnery; the sailors were described as "3,000 Swedish mercenaries" who would probably desert in action, and there was general agreement that there would be something like panic among the American coastal cities, forcing the government to keep its ships at home.

On the last point the outside observers were near the mark. The declaration of war was rapidly followed by news of the sailing from Spain of four of the big armored cruisers, with an escort of torpedo-boat destroyers, and a tremendous outcry went up all along the coast for naval protection. It was so vigorous that it could not be altogether ignored, and the Navy was forced to adopt the strategically unsound plan of splitting off from Admiral W. T. Sampson's main fleet at Key West a "flying squadron" of two armored cruisers, two light cruisers, and a battleship, based on Hampton Roads under Commodore W. S. Schley, who as a lieutenant had commanded the *Monongahela* at Port Hudson.

But most of the other opinions of our Navy held abroad reflected simple ignorance of American conditions, and especially ignorance

IV

The day after *Baltimore* reached Hong Kong with her ammunition came news of war, and Dewey's squadron was given twenty-four hours to quit the port, steaming out with all wooden articles already thrown overboard, past British vessels which manned yards to cheer them. What they thought of the lonely venture of the American squadron was expressed in one of their wardrooms: "A fine set of fellows, but we shall never see them again." In fact, the odds seemed insuperable. The Spaniards had twelve small cruisers and gunboats in Manila Bay, some of them of wood, but they would be under cover of the heavy batteries surrounding Manila city, or those of the Cavite arsenal opposite. There were forts at the harbor entrance and the channel was supposed to be mined.

But George Dewey had been with Farragut at Port Hudson; he did not believe in the efficiency of Spanish mines and he did not believe shore batteries could stop ships at all, unless they were mounted high for plunging fire, which these were not. On the dark night of April 30 he took his fleet past the entrance to Manila Bay, leading the line in *Olympia*. If there were mines they did not go off; the entrance batteries fired only a few shots. May 1 was a misty morning, with the first shafts of light just picking out the steeples of the city. The American fleet pushed into the bay toward where the Spaniards lay off Cavite and held on until sounding showed shoal water. *Olympia* swung westward; at 0548 Dewey said quietly: "You may fire when you are ready, Gridley," and the whole line of guns opened.

Spanish shells kept dropping round the ships and one of them hit *Baltimore* as the American line ran to the limit of range, turned back, then back again, like Du Pont at Port Royal, four times passing the Spanish fleet through veils of smoke in which it was difficult to make out anything but the masts of the enemy. An officer told Dewey that ammunition was running short; he took the fleet into the offing to count casualties, check supplies, and have breakfast. Ship after ship signaled that there were no casualties at all and the ammunition supply satisfactory; Dewey turned back to find two of the Spanish ships burning uncontrollably, all the others badly hurt and trying to get behind Cavite Point. In half an hour more they were finished. *Balti-*

more was sent in to deal with the batteries and shell the arsenal; she took a hit that wounded six men and two officers, the only American casualties of the battle.

It was, in fact, hopelessly one-sided. But this takes no credit from Dewey. When he went out to the Eastern station, he had prepared by studying every book and magazine in print that had anything on the Philippines or the Spanish Navy (like Matthew Perry before Japan), and knew exactly what he had to face. That is, he approached his task in the same spirit of dealing empirically with the matter in hand that led Bainbridge and Stewart to plead with Madison to let the frigates go to sea in 1812. It has always been one of the most valuable traditions in the U.S. Navy.

V

There are few events in American naval annals more remarkable than *Oregon*'s run around the Horn to join the fleet in the Atlantic. At least one-third of the crew was of men so green that one of them complained to Captain Charles E. Clark: "The fat man in the cellar wants me to sleep in a bag." From the beginning it was dreadfully hot in all the interior spaces and the engineers said that if they had to take salt water into their boilers, speed must necessarily drop off. Captain Clark piped all hands, told them the score, and asked whether they would accept reduced water rations to help the ship get there earlier. The men willingly agreed, and on their own volition voted that the men in the engine room should have all *Oregon*'s small stock of ice. This small event may be taken as indicating a turning point; it was no longer a Navy of officers, where the crew were "mercenaries" or hired hands, but one in which the men were treated as intelligent human beings and co-operation was invited, instead of everything being settled by order.

The *Oregon* ran down the zones to winter and icy storms in the Straits of Magellan, which forced Clark to anchor overnight. But the clearing morning showed a needed collier, dispatched by Roosevelt. At Rio on the way north there was definite news of the declaration of war, and that Dewey had attacked Manila. But the story—a preliminary dispatch from French and Spanish sources—also said there were two hundred dead in the American squadron. This looked ominous and it was accompanied by tidings of the sailing of the four big Spanish armored cruisers under Admiral Cervera, who might well be hunting for the *Oregon*. Clark assembled his men again and told them that if he met the Spaniards, he meant to make a running fight, not because he was afraid of them but because the *Oregon* would be outgunned in a broadside action. On the other hand, he pointed out the Spanish ships mounted only one big 9.4-inch gun forward each, while *Oregon* could bear over her stern two 13-inch and four 8-inch rifles.

No Spaniards were met; on May 18 the battleship pushed into English Barbados, where Clark learned that Cervera's fleet had visited Martinique four days before and left, with the ships in need of many things. *Oregon* steamed on across the Caribbean and was presently moving down a cheering line of ships, while *Indiana*'s band played her in.

In the meantime the Department had sent two modern double-turreted monitors to join Sampson who took them out of Key West for Puerto Rico, where Cervera might reasonably be expected. The monitors were a terrible nuisance; they dragged at the end of tow-lines, while one of Sampson's battleships developed engine trouble. He went back to Key West after finding San Juan empty, just in time to meet *Oregon* and the news that after visiting Martinique Cervera had surprisingly put into Curaçao for coal, where an American agent reported that his crews looked half starved.

The news reached Washington before it did Sampson, and the strategy board, with Mahan at its head, promptly dispatched Schley and his Flying Squadron to the south. There were three ports in Cuba that would take a fleet—Havana, Cienfuegos, Santiago. It was now unlikely that the Spaniards would go to San Juan, not only because it was now watched, but also because it was pretty far east to be reached from Curaçao by a squadron which apparently wished to remain elusive. Sampson added a second battleship to Schley's battleship and two armored cruisers and sent them to look in at Cienfuegos and then Santiago, while with the remainder of his fleet, including the monitors, he stood guard over Havana. Schley took his look at Cienfuegos and found no Spaniards there; his ships were now low on coal, and though he had a collier with him, it was too rough to attempt fueling at sea—so he went back to Key West without visiting Santiago.

This was the famous "retrograde movement," which later brought a furious controversy that spilled over into the press, and this was the reason Schley gave for it. The Commodore was undoubtedly wrong, since there were plenty of bays nearer than Key West where he could have put in for coaling before going on with his mission. When Sampson found out what had happened, he sent the junior commander back to Santiago under peremptory orders, himself following closely with the armored cruiser *New York,* his fastest ship, with the remaining units coming along behind. On May 29 Schley reached Santiago and sighted ships inside. On the 31st he ran in with his battleships for a trial bombardment of the forts and established the fact that the place held Cervera's whole squadron. The next day Sampson arrived with *New York* and *Oregon,* and the door was locked.

But not satisfactorily. There was a chance that the Spaniards would made a sudden night torpedo attack, in spite of the fact that the American fleet formed a circle around the entrance, keeping its searchlights on the narrow neck of the channel; another chance that a hurricane might disperse the blockaders; and there was always so much difficulty about coaling that the fleet could not be maintained at full strength. On the night of June 3 Lieutenant Richard P. Hobson volunteered to take the old collier *Merrimac* in and sink her to block the narrow outlet. The ship was spotted, Spanish battery fire carried away her steering gear, and she ended up in the wrong position, though Hobson was saved, to become a congressman and a famous advocate of Prohibition.

The coaling difficulty was solved by the marines from *Oregon,* who forced a landing at Guantánamo Bay on June 10, drove off the small Spanish guard, and established a station which has ever since remained an important American naval base. On June 22 an army of seventeen thousand men under General William R. Shafter landed twenty miles down the coast from Santiago and began to work toward it to drive the Spanish ships out.

It was one of the most mismanaged expeditions in the history of combined operations. Shafter was a fat veteran of the Civil War, who had lost his energy. The War Department had neglected to supply him with artillery or adequate medical facilities; the Cuban jungle was adhesive, and the utility of naval gunfire support had been so completely forgotten that the General neither asked for nor approved it. But on July 2 he sent word to Sampson that he could not proceed farther until the navy forced the harbor and destroyed the Spanish ships.

This seemed somewhat odd to the Admiral, since the army had come in the first place to drive those ships out, but on July 3 he hung out a signal to disregard the movements of the flag, and took *New York* down the coast to confer with Shafter.

In the meanwhile the Spanish Governor of Cuba had informed Admiral Cervera that his position had become untenable and the ships must make their escape to avoid being included in the inevitable surrender. On the same morning when Sampson went down the coast, Cervera led the way toward the harbor entrance aboard his flagship *Infanta Maria Teresa,* followed by the three other armored cruisers and two destroyers.

The American squadron was in its usual semicircle, bows pointing inward toward the harbor, with Schley in the armored cruiser *Brooklyn* at the extreme west of the group. As the Spaniards rounded the buoy and turned to run west along the coast, with all the guns speaking out, *Brooklyn* obviously had to turn parallel with them; and she turned outward, through gunsmoke already thick, almost running down *Texas,* which had to take violent evading action. But the enemy shells were missing and three battleships were concentrating on their flagship. A pair of 8-inch shells destroyed her after-turret, a 12-incher from *Iowa* smashed her steering gear, and she ran ashore on fire and with magazines exploding.

The last of the Spaniards out was *Oquendo;* she was carried down the whole American line by her speed and took the fire of every ship, also reeling early into the beach. *Brooklyn, Texas,* and *Oregon* cut down the third Spanish cruiser, *Vizcaya,* her wooden decks blazing, while Captain Philip of *Texas* called to his crew: "Don't cheer, boys, the poor devils are dying."

Out ahead *Cristobal Colon,* best found of the Spaniards and their fastest ship, was gaining. But now *Oregon,* the supposedly slow battleship, came tearing past all the rest, even past the fast *Brooklyn,* while her stokers bent yelling to their task as they heard the big guns go off above. The shells pitched right over *Colon* and the battleship behind was gaining; the last of the Spaniards ran into the coast like the others and gave up, while away behind the two enemy destroyers were sent down without getting off a torpedo.

Except for a few minor coastal bombardments and inshore cable-cutting expeditions, this was the war from a naval point of view. Afterward the statisticians demonstrated that the Spanish opposition was so weak and inefficient that only monstrous American blunders could have produced any other result. But the point was that the blunders were not made; the American ships turned out to be well designed, well manned, and well fought, and the United States came out of the war with overseas dominions that made a seagoing Navy an obvious necessity.

★　　★　　★　　★　　★

7

The Navy of a World Power

Under the influence of Mahan's theories, the American concept of a Navy had begun to change even before the Spanish War, but the change was largely internal, in the way leaders and men thought of their service and its responsibilities. The accession of Theodore Roosevelt to the presidency in 1901 and the acquisition of such outlying areas as the Philippines, Hawaii, Guam, and Puerto Rico, not only made this internal change permanent; there was also introduced an entirely new theory of the place of the Navy in the life of the nation. The old concept of a navy for coast defense, plus raiding cruisers to discourage an attacker, disappeared almost as completely as privateering. It was no longer necessary to refer to "coast line battleships" in asking appropriations from Congress. The new dominant concept was a line of battle powerful enough to defend American interests anywhere in the world and to protect the coasts by fighting at a distance from them.

This was good classic Mahan doctrine and it was implemented by a steady program of building battleships and big armored cruisers, which within ten years brought the United States from a minor naval power to a temporary position as the second in the world, at least in capital ships. After 1905 all the new battleships were like the new British *Dreadnaught,* all big-gun ships with all their striking power concentrated in the heavy guns of the main batteries, paired in turrets. Each year more battleships joined the fleet, always bigger and stronger—and more expensive. And now too the Navy got more and more of a wholly new class of fighting ship. Originally called torpedo boat destroyers, and designed as a counter weapon, these small fast ships took on more and more duties until as destroyers they became among the most useful vessels in the Navy.

Mahan, with his eyes on the days of sail, had also insisted upon the vital importance of a merchant marine, not only as a school for sailors, but also to carry the seaborne commerce which he regarded as the secret of a nation's true greatness. Not even the drive of Theodore Roosevelt could provide the country with the kind of merchant marine the strategist had in mind.

The trouble was economics. By the early years of the twentieth century the American standard of living had already become so high that it was quite impossible for our shipyards to compete in the world market with those of Europe and Japan, where lower wages were paid, and for American ships to compete in the world carrying trade with nations which could employ lascars and coolies under conditions little short of barbarous. To these drawbacks were eventually added those of American corporation taxes, which made it difficult for shipping lines to set aside reserves from the occasional high profit years to cover the deficits of the years of non-profit. No business is subject to such violent fluctuation as the carrying trade.

The bad effects were partially overcome by such restrictive legislation as that which allowed only American-built ships in the flourishing coastal trade, and by various systems of subsidy enacted from time to time in a rather fitful manner. But the outstanding fact about the post-Spanish War Navy remained that it was not a natural outgrowth from and protector of a booming merchant marine, as that of Britain was, and as Mahan thought ours should be. It was rather a purely military arm of the state, having few roots except in the state itself. There was no such institution as that which enabled the Royal Navy to take over commercial ships, complete with crews, as auxiliary cruisers on the outbreak of war.

Yet, however this might fly in the face of theory, it was less important in terms of national defense than Mahan believed. In the days of 1812 the shift from a merchant sailor to a navy seaman was easy; the skills learned in one profession were perfectly adaptable to the other. But with the coming of the mechanical warship everything changed. Only a coal-passer or an engineer from a commercial vessel would find himself fully at home aboard a cruiser. Gunners, signalmen, armorers, even quarter-masters and lookouts had to be specially trained in tasks that had no direct civilian cognates. Because of their relatively high standards of living and education, the young Americans who enlisted in the Navy could be and were trained into very good sailors indeed, and during the early years of the century, the Navy was doing so many interesting things that the rate of re-enlistment was high.

The situation in the building yards was somewhat analogous. It was possible for business men to be indifferent as to what flag carried their goods abroad or where the ships were built; but there is only one place where a first-class navy can be built, and that is at home. In view of the general lack of demand for large-sized, American-made commercial shipping, there grew up a whole group of constructors who were pretty much warship specialists, and they were backed by a steel industry that had grown to roaring proportions since the days twenty years before when nobody in the country knew how to roll a mild steel plate. The designers kept step with the builders; they had no customer but the government, but their work was subject to the practical criticism of how much they were getting out of a given tonnage as compared with foreign designers, and to the interest of a well-informed President. Europe, which had begun by laughing at American ship design, turned to respect and then to imitation, and world naval opinion was that the U.S. had possessed itself of a very fine Navy indeed.

Yet it was a Navy whose composition reflected the somewhat artificial conditions of its nature. In the years between the accession of Theodore Roosevelt and the Wilson Navy Bill of 1916, which marked a new era, the U.S. built thirty battleships and ten armored cruisers, but it laid down only six true cruisers. In most navies cruisers outnumbered battleships by three to two and in the British almost two to one. The U.S. Navy thus had a powerful battleship line and practically nothing else down to destroyers—exceptionally large destroyers, but not by any means ships that could fulfill the duties of scouting and screening in the face of enemy cruiser opposition. Congress was willing to appropriate for battleships in a spirit of national pride and the American cult of bigness, but repeated requests for cruisers met not the slightest response, and the British need of them for commerce protection obviously did not hold for American conditions. Less understandable was the fact that the submarine service also lagged, with small, poorly armed vessels—and these used with little imagination.

II

Any virile institution develops internal stresses as its members try to enforce points of view in which they see the only route to progress, and the U.S. Navy in the period following the Spanish War was no exception. The first strain came over Schley's "retrograde movement" from Cienfuegos and the turn away from the enemy his *Brooklyn* had made at Santiago. Admiral Sampson was cold and unapproachable; Schley made himself popular with the newspaper men and in the beginning was given all the credit for winning the battle. This aroused opinion within the service and some outside it. E. S. Maclay, the naval historian, well connected in the Navy, presently wrote a history of the Spanish War in which Schley was denounced in such terms that he demanded a court of inquiry. It gave him a vote of censure.

This might easily have developed into an embittered controversy had not Roosevelt been President. He not only smoothed things over, but soon brought out a far more interesting controversy for people to talk about. There came to him a letter from a young commander on the China Station named William Sowden Sims, who wrote right over the heads of the admirals to the President of the United States, in complete disregard of official procedure. The letter was sweepingly and violently critical of the design of American battleships. Their portholes were too large, the armor belts so low they would be under water in action, and so on. But the sharpest criticism, and the one that drew Roosevelt's particular attention, was of American naval gunnery. Sims pointed out that during the Spanish War our ships had made only five per cent hits out of the shots fired, and this was not only a wretched record on any computation, but one that would doom us to defeat in a contest with a major opponent.

Was it true? Roosevelt ordered firing tests under the conditions used by the British Navy, with reports to him personally. Their gunnery had recently been rejuvenated by the director firing method of Sir Percy M. Scott, and they were getting eighty per cent hits under target conditions, while the U.S. Fleet could do no better than thirteen per cent in the trials the President ordered. Roosevelt immediately cabled for Sims, and by executive order placed him in charge of all Navy target practice for eighteen months, with word to "cut off his head" if he had not achieved something by that time.

Sims did; and it was well that he did, for the Japanese crisis arose just when he completed his work. This had its origin in the conference Roosevelt called at Portsmouth, N. H., and the peace made between Russia and Japan there under his auspices, almost under his domination. The Japanese felt they were badly cheated by the terms. They had expected to receive at least Vladivostok and a slice of Manchuria; and there were riots in Tokyo, with American shops stoned. At this precise moment the San Francisco school board chose to come out with a ruling that Japanese children must be segregated in the schools.

In Japan there was such an outburst of rage that Lloyds offered even money that there would be war within the year, and the Japanese battle fleet, strengthened by captures from the Russians, went on maneuvers in the Bonin Islands under war conditions. But Roosevelt called the San Francisco school commissioners "infernal fools," and ordered sixteen battleships to the Pacific under Robley Evans, now an admiral.

The voyage was wholly peaceful and wholly successful. Evans's big ships reached San Francisco, then pushed on right across the Pacific to Japan itself, and from there to Australia, Ceylon, and around the world. Nothing like it had ever been done before by any navy, and the fleet moved with precision, efficiency, and good conduct on the part of the sailors through twenty foreign ports. The American Navy had reached the status of a world power.

In the meantime technology was giving forward-looking Navy men something new to think about. Ever since Theodore Roosevelt had become Assistant Secretary, the Navy had been keeping a sharp eye on attempts to fly heavier-than-air craft and in 1898 had joined with the Army in a study of Professor Samuel P. Langley's experiments. After the successful flights of the Wright brothers and the development of other aircraft, enthusiastic officers urged the Navy to invest in an airplane of its own. It was not until 1911 that the conservative seniors allowed the Navy to buy three planes, however, and in the meantime a civilian flier, Eugene Ely, had given a dramatic demonstration of the possibilities of teaming planes with ships when in 1910 he flew a Curtiss plane off the deck of the cruiser *Birmingham*. Although a special launching deck had been built for the take-off run, this hinted at the possibility that ships might some day carry their own aircraft with them—and the development of plane catapults soon afterward made it even more likely.

A few months after his *Birmingham* take-off Ely went one better. Lines were stretched athwartships on the deck of the cruiser *Pennsylvania,* and weighted with sandbags. This time Ely took off from shore and put his plane down on the deck, the lines snagging the undercarriage and bringing the aircraft to a halt before it went in the drink. Here were the essential elements that make possible the huge aircraft carriers of today—although it was a good many years before the Navy recognized it. Simultaneously, the usefulness of aircraft at sea was being multiplied many times over by the increasing reliability of wireless telegraphy. When a plane could radio its reports back to the fleet it was obviously a highly valuable scout.

III

When war came to Europe in 1914 the service had slipped somewhat from its earlier statistical position, not so much from internal causes but because Great Britain and Germany were engaged in a furious armament race, and neither of the two administrations that followed Theodore Roosevelt chose to compete. In addition there had developed on the fringes of liberalism a well-heeled and highly vocal pacifist opposition to naval expansion. The pace of American battleship building fell off while that abroad speeded up, and ours remained an unbalanced fleet, without cruisers for eyes, and short of destroyers.

The Navy that looked out on a warring world in 1914 was becoming a far different organization from any the United States had known. When Wilson became President, he appointed to the Navy Department Josephus Daniels, an amiable and liberal-minded North Carolina editor. His Assistant Secretary was a new, Democratic Roosevelt—Franklin D. Like everyone else in an administration that made "the New Freedom" its watchword, the new Secretary believed that the time had come for changes. He found plenty to change. Promotion exclusively by seniority had brought to the head of the list a group of aging admirals, whose mere presence threatened another period of officer stagnation, and who were so conservative that only President Theodore Roosevelt's personal intervention had prevented them from having Sims court-martialed for insubordination over the gunnery business. Officers of all ranks formed a tight caste, almost as exclusive as it had been in Truxtun's day or in the 1820s. No matter what a man's technical accomplishments were, he was set apart from this caste by an unbridgeable gulf. Desertions had become so frequent as to be a specific disease. Contractors, especially for supplies, were making an extremely good thing out of the service.

Daniels struck at these and other matters which he considered abuses, by a series of measures that aroused an acrid storm of criticism both in the Navy and the press. One order prescribed a certain number of promotions from the enlisted list to officer rank; another made it possible for enlisted men to obtain appointments to Annapolis as the result of competitive examinations. Daniels asked that sons of naval officers not be appointed to the Academy, and with infinite labor and many changes of form, finally got through a method of selecting specific officers for promotion on merit, rather than having them wait for seniority. His effort to have a series of government-owned plants set up to supply such items as guns and ammunition was balked by Congress, but he did succeed in expanding the navy yards to the accompaniment of highly favorable political reactions, and several of them became capable of building major warships. Finally, he introduced the prohibition ruling; there was to be no more liquor served aboard American warships or in the shore establishments.

The last item evoked the bitterest criticism of all, especially in the service. The new officers from the enlisted ranks were given rather a thin time by their seniors, who called them "jackass officers," and assigned them to such jobs as the command of tugs and target scows. The selection method also drew fire. But in retrospect, all the Daniels reforms have turned out well, with the single exception of that keeping the sons of naval officers out of the service; it proved unnecessary, since the caste system was breached along other lines of approach. The conditions of the war that presently supervened brought a demand for small craft whose officers clearly could not be supplied by the number of Annapolis graduates, and the men promoted from the enlisted ranks were one of the best sources of supply. Desertions stopped almost at once when it became apparent that a career in the Navy did not mean a man must stay in a subordinate position forever. Even the much-ridiculed prohibition order became not only accepted but fully approved by the vast majority of the service. As ships grew more and more complex mechanically, lightning-fast, unclouded reaction in handling them was obviously necessary.

Over all this loomed the ominous shadow of the European war, ever nearer. In the early days, when Wilson was enforcing strict neutrality, he was deeply concerned over the totally new definitions the British were giving to blockade. They placed food on the contraband list. It had never been illegal for neutrals to purchase the merchant ships of belligerent powers in the neutrals' home ports, and British interests had so bought many American ships during the Civil War; but when the U.S. attempted to buy interned German ships and use them, the British calmly confiscated. They controlled traffic between the U.S. and Holland—two neutrals. They put out a blacklist of firms dealing with Germany, some of them American-owned and American-operated, and declared that all property belonging to such firms should be sent to H.M. courts for adjudication. American merchant vessels were stopped on the high seas and arbitrarily ordered to British ports for examination, where, even if found innocent, their voyages were long delayed and British shipping correspondingly favored.

In short, the restrictions were not too dissimilar to those before the War of 1812, and Wilson paced the floor in worry. Nor did there seem anything particularly practical that could be done about it. The progress of the war had shown that the older battleships, built before H.M.S. *Dreadnaught* inaugurated the day of ships with all big guns and heavy armor, were death traps in the face of the new monsters. Of this new type the United States (thanks to the building slow-up) had only ten and the British thirty-nine; that is, the earlier favorable position had been lost by technical progress.

But the accumulating resentments against the British were quickly wiped out by the fact that in February, 1915, the Germans announced a "war zone" around the British Isles, which neutral vessels might enter only at their peril, and in May they backed this up by torpedoing an unarmed American ship in this area. Six days later, on May 7, 1915, a German submarine sent down the unarmed liner *Lusitania* with a loss of 1,198 lives, including 124 Americans. This was not blockade by any recognized method, but blockade by murder and terror, for the Germans lacked the force to make it really dangerous to approach the British coasts. A wave of indignation swept the United States. A series of increasingly strong notes of protest were dispatched to Germany, and finally Wilson interrupted one of his pacings to cry: "Let us build the biggest navy in the world and then we can do as we please!"

It took months to get the program through Congress, but when it came out it provided for ten giant new battleships, six battle-cruisers, ten light cruisers, fifty destroyers, and one hundred submarines, with personnel increases in proportion. They were all to be built in three years.

IV

This was in August, 1916. That same week there reached the White House a communication from our embassy in Germany; the militarists there intended to resume the submarine campaign (which had been relaxed somewhat after the furor raised by the *Lusitania* sinking) against all shipping approaching Britain on a wholly unrestricted basis. The pledges, earlier given in answer to protests, that neutral shipping would be respected and merchant ships warned before sinking were regarded in exalted Berlin circles as a cover to gain time for the construction of more submarines, through which the Germans hoped to starve Britain before any assistance could become effective. On January 31, 1917, the Germans officially announced the new program. One American ship a week would be allowed to visit England, painted in zebra stripes and flying a checkered flag; the rest must stay out of a zone completely surrounding the British Isles or be sunk.

It was now only necessary to wait the first overt act before war came. Rear Admiral William S. Sims, who had been one of Daniels' strongest critics, was selected to go to England and co-ordinate matters with the British, and arrived to find that war had been declared a week before he landed. It was not until he sat down with Sir John Jellicoe at the British Admiralty, however, that he understood the basis of the calculation on which the Germans had taken the gamble of bringing the U.S. into the conflict. They were sinking British

shipping at three or four times the admitted rate, over 500,000 tons
in February, over 600,000 tons in March, and the April sinkings
would probably total 900,000 tons. The pace was ruinous; Britain
would really be starved into submission by the end of the summer.
The difficulty lay in the shortage of anti-submarine vessels, particularly destroyers, the only ships fast enough to use effectively the recently developed depth charges. There were only two hundred British
destroyers, and half of these were needed with the Grand Fleet: Britain's shield in case the German battleships came out.

Sims' first question was why the British did not institute a system of convoy, instead of parceling out the available ships in area
patrols, as they were doing. The reply was that convoys would involve intricate maneuvers at night without lights, which merchant
skippers could not perform, that a convoy would be a big target, etc.,
etc., that the opinion in favor of convoys was untrained opinion.

For the time being the American admiral accepted this, and on
April 14 sent an urgent cable to the Navy Department for all the
destroyers and other light, anti-submarine craft that could be mustered to come to Britain at once. At the Department they thought
either that he was crazy or had been talked around by some Britisher.
The war plan, which Sims himself had helped to draw, provided only
for patrols off the American coast and down into the Caribbean in
case of the appearance of submarines in the west; ultimately for escorts to cover American land forces bound for France. It took a
series of further cables (pointing out, among other things, that England had only three weeks' food on hand) and the visit of a special
British mission to produce a sense of urgency.

On May 4, the first American destroyers arrived at Queenstown
(now called Cobh) in southern Ireland, a token force of a single division of six, under Commander Joseph K. Taussig, who astonished
the British port admiral when the latter asked when they would be
ready for sea. "We are ready now, sir." They were, too; the British
found that these American destroyers were not as fast as their own,
nor could they turn as rapidly, but they were better sea-boats, could
stand up to the Atlantic gales, and make more prolonged cruises.
By July 5, thirty-four of them were on duty, no inconsiderable reinforcement when it is remembered that the British had only one
hundred of their own on patrol in April.

In the meantime several other events had supervened. British opinion against convoys was by no means unanimous, and when Sims came back at Jellicoe after the first rebuff, his argument was backed by the admiral at Gibraltar, who was allowed to try sending a group of ships to England under convoy. Not a one was lost through collision or submarine action, and the sample tasted so good that the system was extended. In the second place the British admiral at Queentown fell ill just as a group of ships was due to sail from the U.S. Sims put them into convoy by radio and took the destroyers off the Queenstown patrol to see them in. There was some loss among the inshore shipping thus left uncovered, but the convoy reached port without damage. The new system was a success; merchant ship losses began to fall off to well below the figure the Germans had graphed as necessary to winning the war.

Yet with over 500,000 tons of shipping sunk in each of the months of July and August, the graphs were not yet at any point that indicated Allied victory, merely a decision held in abeyance. During the period of waiting there came into play a factor utterly neglected in German calculations—the industrial power of the United States, translated into marine terms. A vast program of building cargo ships from standardized parts was undertaken. They were not every good ships and the production rate was by no means up to the optimistic preliminary estimates, but still ships were turned out in such quantities as never seen before, and their very existence canceled out so great a quantity of the submarine sinkings that the curve on Allied ships in service rose steadily. The building of the huge Wilson Navy was laid aside; the yards turned to on a program of two hundred fifty-eight destroyers (or as many more as needed) of a new type, very large and fast, standardized like the cargo ships. None of the six German submarines that crossed the Atlantic to the American coast produced the slightest diversionary effect on this effort; their total bag was only a few small fishermen and coasting vessels, with one old armored cruiser that fell prey to a submarine-laid mine.

There were also the new weapons. At the beginning of the war the British and French had assumed (wrongly) that submarines would be mainly shoal-water craft, and ordered from American builders a number of small motorboats for work along the coasts. The American war plan called for patrols along our shores by similar vessels. But American coastal waters are relatively deep and stormy, so Loring Swasey of Boston was called into re-design the Allied motorboats for greater seaworthiness. He produced a design for a 110-foot craft, built in wood, with three screws and a Y-gun that could fire depth charges, and it was ready just as America entered the war. Some production began at once; a group of the little ships was at New London, with no particular patrol work to do, when a board of inventors, working under Captain Leigh of U.S. Submarine Headquarters, developed an underwater hydrophone to pick up the noise of submarine engines.

It was a relatively clumsy device, with two receivers at a little distance from each other, which the operator turned until the sound coming in each ear was exactly equal, thus giving the direction, if not the distance of the submarine heard. But the direction was enough if three hydrophone ships were working together; the position of the submarine could be obtained by triangulation.

The British were highly skeptical when Leigh took his device to London in October, 1917, with a group of listeners he had trained, but they loaned him three trawlers and a tame submarine for a trial. It proved so complete a success that as many hydrophone sets as America could produce were ordered, and since the key of the operation was the skill of the listeners, they had Leigh set up a school.

Now the question arose as to which ships should have the new device. Clearly destroyers would not do; they were needed for convoy work and it would be dangerous to have two or three of them standing around with idling engines while the listeners listened. But the little 110-foot submarine chasers were just the thing. Orders were placed for more and more until the total number reached four hundred forty, and though some of them went to the French and British, the majority remained under the American flag. These submarine chasers —the "splinter fleet"—were frail craft, whose skippers were yachtsmen or ensigns just out of the Academy, and their crews a wild assemblage of college boys and riffraff from everywhere; one had a deckhand with an M.A. in Arabic and a Greek cook who had been a lemonade butcher in a circus. Neither was life aboard them very easy; the first group of thirty-six had to cross the Atlantic unescorted through one of the wildest winters the old ocean had ever seen, with zero temperatures, ice a foot thick on their wooden decks and cooking done on an oil stove with the ship rolling 30°. "Put me back on my raft again," begged a sailor who had been picked up by one. "It's more comfortable there." But the sub chasers came through and the thirty-six went on patrol in the English Channel in March, 1918, at which point submarine sinkings immediately began to drop.

One of the most effective anti-submarine operations of the British had been mining the Strait of Dover, with patrols operating on the surface over the field, using flares at night. As early as April, 1917, Sims proposed to Jellicoe that since the Germans had almost given up using the Channel exit for their submarines, a mine barrage should be laid right across the North Sea from the Norwegian coast to Scotland. Jellicoe said that the project had been considered but abandoned; it would take 400,000 mines, more than could be produced in five years. This temporarily silenced Sims, but it did not quiet the Navy Bureau of Ordnance, which had developed a new type of antenna mine covering a far greater area than the standard model, and was already setting up a plant at St. Julien's Creek, Virginia, that could turn out 20,000 of these new mines a month.

The British were finally brought to agreement when Secretary Daniels offered to set up the mine barrage as a purely American project, and Sims pointed out that it was not necessary to make the barrier absolute. If one submarine in ten were sunk in such a screen the effect on enemy morale would be staggering, and if the figure reached one in five the result would be fatal. The rest was a matter of organization: A belt conveyor plant for making the mines; twenty-four big, low-slung lake steamers brought down to transport the product to western Scotland; a system to carry the mines across to Inverness and Invergordon on the east coast; the alteration of eight large coastal liners to minelayers, and the training of their crews to work with the two old cruisers already converted for minelaying duty.

The squadron put to sea on its first mission on June 7, 1918, and on that day placed nearly 4,000 mines, while the British also planted. Down through September every day of reasonable weather saw the minelayers at work. It was a hazardous task in ships bulging with explosives, which had to be constantly guarded by destroyers against submarines and by heavy ships against surface raiders, but it was carried on until over 70,000 mines spanned the North Sea, 56,000 of them American, covering a belt thirty miles deep. As early as July 9 the field collected its first dividend, a submarine badly damaged while homeward bound, which was almost better than sinking her, since she carried word that there were now mines in open ocean, where none had been before. Presently an outward bound submarine was so badly hurt she had to return; then the sinkings began and mounted steadily, until in September three U-boats went down in one day and another crawled home with her bows blown off. The point at which one submarine in five was striking a mine had now been reached and Admiral Sims was proved perfectly right. There was a mutiny in the submarine service; no orders could any longer make men go aboard the dangerous craft, and in October the submarine war slid to an end.

The war on the U-boats was enthusiastically joined by the Navy's now burgeoning air arm. Back in 1914, the abandoned Navy Yard at Pensacola, Florida, had been turned over to the naval aviators, and as the European war loomed closer to our shores a million dollars had been appropriated for naval aircraft the following year. When we entered the war, naval aviation went at once into high gear with a host of other naval air stations hastily commissioned and a rapid training program started for pilots and ground personnel. Air bases for anti-submarine patrols were established in France, Britain, and Ireland, and American pilots enthusiastically went to work encouraging the German U-boat skippers to keep their heads down, or bombing shore targets in Belgium and submarine pens along the Channel.

Building an air force took time, and the Navy's planes saw only a few months of action before the Armistice. Nevertheless, the approximately 20,000 officers and men who got overseas carried out 22,000 flights and dropped some 99,000 pounds of bombs. From now on it was obvious that the men with the golden wings on their jackets were going to be an important part of the U.S. Navy.

V

It would be futile to make any case that the U.S. was the dominant factor in winning the war against the German submarines. The British did it; of the submarines sunk, only one was positively identifiable as sent down by American ships, though there were assists and probables on several others. Aside from the great mine barrage, the American contribution was logistic and defensive—in building ships, furnishing supplies, in providing convoy escorts and patrols which not so much destroyed submarines as kept them impotent. Incident: on October 2, 1918, a squadron of Italian ships bombarded Austrian Durazzo (Durrës); it was attacked by submarines, which were promptly driven off with damage by American sub chasers.

Yet this contribution was not only essential; it was made at a time when neither British nor French could have made it for themselves. Thus on the part of the American Navy it was an unspectacular war, a war of statistics, in which the effort was counted in terms of ships *not* sunk, of goods and troops and arms delivered; and it was too large for the individual action to be marked or remembered. Also it was a war that showed that for current conditions at least, it was possible to expand a sound body of personnel into a vast and efficient organization almost overnight. The training stations that turned out men for dozens of destroyers and hundreds of submarine chasers with only small cadres of experience behind them were perhaps its most arresting feature.

★　　★　　★　　★　　★

8

The Rising Tide

I N 1921 Warren G. Harding became President of the United States. The trend in America was toward isolationism; economy was the watchword in Washington, and there was a general belief in the air that a long era of peace was at hand if only a few small spots could be rubbed out. When Harding summoned a general disarmament conference at Washington he was met by an enthusiastic response from England. Her fleet was wearing out and she was in no position to build against the Wilson Navy, already on the ways or in the water; or even against Japan, where the military caste was already close to effective control and was flexing its muscles in the direction of China. The response of France was qualified and that of Italy watchful, but they came; that of Japan reluctant, but delegates were sent.

At the very beginning the French refused to hear of any limitation of land armaments, and as France had the biggest land army, it perforce became a purely naval conference.

Secretary of State Charles Evans Hughes opened the meeting with a dramatic proposal for a general program for scrapping capital ships to bring the U.S., Britain, and Japan to a 5:5:3 ratio. The U.S. would sacrifice nearly all the new battleships then in various stages of construction, and all the old pre-dreadnaughts. The British would abandon plans for three new ships and the carcasses of a considerable number of older ones, to bring their tonnage to a parity with the American. The Japanese would similarly scrap planned and building battleships plus their pre-dreadnaughts. Mr. Hughes also indicated that he expected concessions from Britain and Japan in the cruiser categories, where they had a superiority over the American Fleet, and was willing to grant concessions in destroyers and submarines, where we outnumbered them. Smaller quotas were fixed for France and Italy.

Except for some grumbling from the Japanese, who regarded the acceptance of any inferiority as a loss of face, the battleship program went through without a hitch. To be sure, Japanese indignation over being in a minor place had to be appeased by a treaty prohibiting the construction of fortifications in the western Pacific. On the other hand, Britain and Japan abandoned their treaty of alliance, which the United States had long considered a threat.

But when ships other than battleships began to be mentioned there was trouble. The English delegation talked passionately about the necessity of protecting world-wide trade routes and would hear of no limitation on cruisers except as to size, which was to be 10,000 tons, and 8-inch guns. (Britain had five new 9,750-ton cruisers mounting 7.5-inch guns.) The French refused to accept any limitation on size, numbers or performance of submarines, insisting they were purely defensive weapons, and they were backed by the Japanese. The conference further agreed that the battleship proportions should be allowed to apply to aircraft carriers, and the U.S. and Japan were allowed to convert to this class two unfinished battle-cruisers each. The conference then guaranteed the integrity of China and went home, while all the papers declared a wonderful blow for world peace had been struck and a new era was dawning.

Experts are still arguing over who won the conference. Conservative naval opinion in all three of the big powers bitterly attacked the outcome. British admirals deplored the surrender of the Royal Navy's world supremacy. They conveniently overlooked the fact that the American building program already under way would have destroyed that supremacy by 1924—and Britain was in no condition economically to carry out a similar program of her own. Japanese conservatives attacked their country's acceptance of a subordinate Navy.

In America, the treaty was criticized for abandoning superior battleships actually under construction, which would have made the U.S. Navy the strongest in the world, in return for the scrapping of ships either obsolescent or not yet started. It is questionable, however, whether an economy-minded country would have accepted the heavy expense of completing the new super-dreadnaughts in any case.

More to the point were criticisms of the failure to limit non-capital ships, which left the Royal Navy, rich in cruisers and destroyers, with over-all superiority in strength, despite the equality in battleships. Even more disadvantageous were the limitations on further fortifications of bases in the Western Pacific. Britain and Japan already possessed strong bases in the area, and freezing of the status quo undoubtedly left us in an inferior position.

Our position in relation to Japan was further threatened by internal events in that country. At the outset liberalizing forces were in temporary control of the Japanese government and a militarist *coup d'etat* planned for 1923 had to be called off because of a devastating earthquake. But in 1924, the American Congress passed the quota immigration bill; it classed the Japanese with utterly undesirable Orientals who were not to be admitted to the United States under any circumstances, and the militarists had the ammunition they needed for arousing national resentment. From this hour on they were in practical control of the situation and any observance of treaties was purely coincidental and a matter of tactics.

There were indications of what was coming even that early. During the four years after the treaties were signed the U.S. laid down no warships at all, Britain one small cruiser, and France five submarines; but Japan began construction on twenty-two ships, and eight of them were 8-inch gun, or "heavy" cruisers. Moreover, when the experts began examining the characteristics of these ships, they became quickly convinced that the four later ones were well over the treaty limit, which later proved to be the case. Japan was going to build the kind of Navy she wanted and talk about limitation as long as anyone cared to listen.

In the meantime Britain, France, and Italy, had laid down their first new cruisers under the treaty, and as might be expected, built right up to the limit of permissible size—10,000 tons and 8-inch guns. Like the Japanese, the aggressive Mussolini government in Italy built over the limit in fact, and this was a source of no little concern to France, as was also the fact that Italy was building a number of very fast and dangerous light cruisers, with a big fleet of submarines and heavy destroyers. The United States, now under the definitely pacifist leadership that culminated in the Kellogg treaties "outlawing war," had decided to set a good example by not building.

Ultimately, the naval officers succeeded in getting an appropriation for two of the new cruisers—at a date when the three European signatories had at least three afloat and the Japanese eight. An extensive study had meanwhile been devoted to the new type of ship, and American officers decided they were just what the U.S. Navy needed—hard-hitting enough to take care of themselves in any cruiser company and, with the long steaming radius afforded by their size, able to operate to the limits of the Pacific. The British, on the other hand, found the new type excessively expensive and the long steaming radius was no use to the nation which had bases every eight hundred miles around the world.

This was the background of the conference called by President Coolidge at Geneva in 1927 to discuss the categories of ships not covered at Washington. It may be described as the first of the non-limitation gatherings. France and Italy refused to send delegates at all, only observers. Japan offered a bland proposal for the total abolition of battleships and a "common upper limit" on cruiser construction, which, as she had the strongest cruiser line afloat, would promote cruisers to the rank of capital ships with her in the lead. But the most shocking surprise came from Britain. She demanded a cruiser limit of 478,000 tons per nation, a figure almost equal to the total tonnage of any navy afloat, and amounting to no limit at all on cruiser construction. In addition, Britain now wished cruisers cut to 7,500 tons and 6-inch guns. Japan promptly agreed, with the "common upper limit" proviso. A treaty that provided for unlimited cruiser building while restraining the United States from the one type it wanted seemed so unreasonable that Coolidge broke up the conference.

The next meeting was in London in 1930, as provided in the original Washington treaties. By this date Herbert Hoover was President, and he had proclaimed his disbelief in "disarmament by example." The American delegates had behind them a Congressional authorization for twenty-five heavy cruisers. There seemed to be progress, but once more it was an illusion, and chiefly at the expense of the United States. Heavy cruisers were limited in number; the light cruiser tonnage limit was shoved up to 10,000; the Japanese obtained an increase in proportionate destroyer tonnage and parity

with the U.S. and Britain in submarines. France and Italy refused
to take part in tonnage limitation. Matters were adjourned to 1936,
when the Washington treaties were to expire.

Even this limitation treaty, which limited nothing but how far the
signatories might expand their navies, was carried out by Japan in
the spirit usual to her militarists. Their new destroyers were in fact
several hundred tons over the treaty limit; they announced the laying
down of six "8,500-ton light cruisers," which turned out to be heavy
cruisers of 15,000 tons; and in 1934 they announced they would
not even sign any more and withdrew from the whole Washington
treaty structure.

Even before this the Japanese long-range aim had become obvious.
In September, 1931, General Hayashi, commanding the occupation
army in Korea, moved his troops into Manchuria without bothering
to inform his government. They could do nothing but try to explain,
and the U.S., nothing but protest that the integrity of China was an
essential part of the whole treaty structure, a protest which Britain
endorsed, but which she refused to back up by any positive action.
The Japanese militarists assassinated their leading liberal opponents,
and the war for the conquest of China was on. The imperialists felt
they had achieved a reasonable naval security on their side of the
Pacific, and so they had; the U.S. Fleet could not operate that far
from its bases with anything like full strength.

But in 1933, Franklin D. Roosevelt became President of the United
States. He was fully conscious that both the militarists of Japan and
the very similar movement embarked on by Hitler in Germany had
world domination as their ultimate objective. For that matter they
made no secret of these intentions, but the American isolationists
and pacificists thought it was too silly to believe or too far away to
matter. Roosevelt did believe it and he believed that the forces opposed to those aggressive dynamisms abroad were so inadequate
that the attack must ultimately come washing around the shores of
the United States, having gathered accretions of strength that would
make it very hard to deal with. He was also a former Assistant Secretary of the Navy in the Wilson administration, which had believed in
building the biggest Navy in the world and then doing just as we
pleased. He came in in the year of the deep depression, when the
banks closed and Congress voted enormous sums for public works

to get the economy back on its feet. Roosevelt thought no public works were more important than an adequate Navy and squeezed out every dollar he could to get a building program started—the new heavy cruisers, a group of 10,000-ton light cruisers, new destroyers, two carriers, preparations for two battleships to be laid down as soon as the treaties permitted in 1936. In the following year he persuaded Congress to pass the Vinson-Trammel bill, which authorized building the Navy up to treaty limits by 1941.

It must not be supposed that this was easy. The year 1934 was the one in which a Senate investigating committee discovered that some munitions firms, shipbuilders, and bankers had made tremendus profits during World War I and managed to avoid much of their taxes. It also found that there was collusion and profiteering in the postwar building programs, extensive lobbying by shipbuilders, and attempts to stimulate international naval competition. One result of this sensational revelation was the attempt to pass bills "to take the profit out of war." These measures largely died in committee and the net long-term effect was to strengthen isolationism. Typical of this attitude was the singular Neutrality Act that forbade the shipment of arms in time of war and would not allow Americans to travel on the ships of belligerent nations. Roosevelt signed the bill, but he also pushed the Vinson-Trammel Act through, and when Europe blew up, and it became evident that the Germans were much more formidable than anyone had realized, added to it the "Two-Ocean Navy Bill," which gave him practically unlimited authority for further construction.

As matters turned out this was a very good idea.

II

The inner story of the Navy during those years was one of how narrowly it avoided the decay that set in after the Civil War. When the Armistice with Germany was signed in 1918, the reservists who enlisted for the duration wanted out; within a year personnel fell from 500,000 to 200,000 and it kept right on going down. Many of the new destroyers were not finished until after the Armistice, and when they had been formally placed in commission, barely ran trials before being laid up in long rows at San Diego or Philadelphia.

Under Coolidge things became even worse. He was an honest man, but a narrow one, and his world did not include the Navy. Appropriations were less every year; more warships passed out of commission, and it was even difficult to find money for necessary repairs. Many ships were manned only by partial crews and re-enlistments practically vanished. In addition the "hump" in officer ranks caused by the absorption of reserves into the regular service and increased classes at Annapolis during World War I made itself painfully felt; there had to be a ruthless policy of elimination, and no young lieutenant knew how long he would be allowed to stay in.

The coming of the Hoover administration brought no relaxation in pressures, in spite of the fact that the officer list had been fined down and the government was at least willing to provide money for new building. The depression hit hard; money was wanting for ammunition, for conducting maneuvers, for furnishing adequate facilities at bases, even for typewriters. The salaries in all ranks and grades were reduced, and the only thing that kept a cadre of experienced officers and technical specialists from bleeding completely away was the fact that a civilian life in which there were millions of unemployed offered few attractions. There was an over-all decline in efficiency, and duties were performed mechanically, rather than out of understanding and a desire for improvement.

To this there were two saving exceptions—the Marines and Naval Aviation. When the Marine Corps was founded during the Revolution and refounded with the birth of the United States Navy, the men of that organization were supposed to fulfill three functions. They were very importantly ships' police, apart from the sailors, to maintain order and prevent mutiny; in battle they supplied small-arms men who fired on the enemy from decks or tops; and they were to lead landing parties by men armed with shoulder weapons. These functions remained reasonably valid down through the Civil War, but with the coming of the steel warship, rapid-firing guns, and longer ranges, there was no need for riflemen in a naval action, and a general improvement in discipline made the police assignment unnecessary.

This left the landing party task, and the Marines performed it in all sorts of odd places: against seal poachers on the islands of the Bering Sea, bandits in Panama, and a fort in turbulent Korea which fired on American shipping without reason. But such emergencies arose only rarely, and aboard the vessels that carried them the Marines had little to do with the ship's work or ordinary duties. This general condition of idleness, combined with the need for instant combat readiness early attracted the attention of the heads of the service, and their solution—not attributable to any one man, but an obvious general drift—was to make the Marines a *corps d'elite*, very difficult to enter, and which received more severe training and sterner discipline than any other group in the American military service. When new volunteers marched through the company streets at a marine base, they were received by a lineup, which chanted in unison: "You'll be sorry." It was early prescribed that cooks and messengers, radio men and aviators, should receive full infantry training; that is, that every Marine should be able to take his place on the firing line.

During World War I, the Marines expanded, like all other military organizations, and ultimately reached a strength of three brigades, one of which was incorporated as a unit in the 2nd Army Division. At Belleau Wood and later at Soissons this unit made a terrific battle record and was classified by the Germans as one of special shock troops. The achievement failed to endear itself to the Army, which took the not altogether unreasonable view that the existence of special volunteer shock troops not under its own control tended to lower the general standard of the Army in land operations. When the Second Marine Brigade reached France, it was broken up and assigned to miscellaneous guard duties at harbors and bases.

This left the Marines in something of a quandary at the close of World War I. Precisely what would their function be if they survived as a service? One answer seemed to lie in the Caribbean. As early as the first Wilson administration, conditions in the Dominican Republic, Haiti, and Nicaragua had become so utterly chaotic that all three were running sores of anarchy. Not only were all debts repudiated, but also Europeans as well as Americans were attacked in a continuing series of revolutions, and the European countries more than intimated that if the U.S. wished to keep the Monroe Doctrine alive, it had better do some intervening before they did. Marines were sent in, and they remained in Haiti for twenty years, on the whole doing a good job and training local forces that could maintain order. But this was obviously and avowedly a temporary mission. There was no real point in maintaining a special force of ship-borne troops for such police work.

Through the early part of the 1920s there was a good deal of thinking and discussion of where the Marines fitted into the modern world, with the conclusion that the main function of the Corps as a part of a major Navy would be beachhead operations; the establishment of a foothold ashore under the fire of the fleet and its retention until more numerous Army troops could be landed. As early as 1925 a directive sets forth that the Fleet Marine Force, which is to exercise this duty, is the premier body of the Corps.

The operations off Cuba in the Spanish War and the British failure at Gallipoli were studied closely. Experimental landings were made at Culebra in the Caribbean and on the coast of Hawaii, with a sharp eye on such matters as the proper type of naval gunfire support, how it should be co-ordinated by shore observers, what units should land first, and how they were to be supported. A weakness early discovered was in the boats used for landing. In the Spanish War, ships' boats were used, and many of them capsized in the surf, leaving the men struggling ashore, drenched, and in no condition to fight. A boat builder named Higgins, of New Orleans, was induced to construct experimental landing craft that could ride right up onto the beach. They were tested under combat conditions, with live shells flying overhead.

Another difficulty was getting an early supply of hand-borne automatic weapons into the beachhead; the Marines designed their own, since the existing types were too heavy. By the date when the Roosevelt revival gave new impetus to the Navy, the Marines had developed a solid body of doctrine on amphibious war and were pushing for further experiments.

Naval air took a somewhat similar course—one independent of what was going on in the other arms of the service. The war was hardly over before one of the Navy's big flying boats—the type was almost exclusively an American product—flew the Atlantic in a series of hops via the Azores, the first plane of any kind to do so.

And now the pioneer work of Ely a decade before began to bear fruit. An old collier was given a flat deck and became the Navy's first aircraft carrier, the *Langley*. She became a center for training aviators at sea. And the scrapping of partly built ships under the naval treaties was not an unmixed drawback to this service. It permitted the conversion to aircraft carriers of two battle cruisers, the largest in the world; if *Lexington* and *Saratoga* did not join the fleet until 1929, it was because the intervening time was spent in developing their gear and training pilots. The Philadelphia Naval Aircraft Factory was the development center; it worked out a satisfactory arrester for carrier landings, and improved catapults that enabled battleships and cruisers to use scout and spotting planes.

At Pensacola, where the main naval air station was established, hundreds of young ensigns came in for flight training, attracted by the romance of the service and the fifty per cent extra pay it offered. Through the blank years before the Roosevelt administration, Naval Air was the most vital arm of the service, the youngest and most energetic, and by the time the upturn came, it had learned a great deal.

For instance, dive-bombing. This seems to have originated with the Marines, who were interested in furnishing close air support for their beachhead operations, and did not believe that high-level bombing could give the necessary accuracy. The basis of the complaint was the bombing tests held off the Virginia capes in 1919, when that somewhat tarnished saint of the Army Air Corps, Billy Mitchell, claimed that an airplane could sink any battleship. He did sink one, too—an old surrendered German ship in poor condition, which he insisted on having anchored at a given distance and location. To naval flyers this seemed to have little relation to the conditions bound to obtain in sea warfare, where the ships would be neither old, crippled, motionless, or at any specific location, but would on the other hand be well supplied with anti-aircraft guns. From the beginning the naval aviators trained for real combat conditions, and when the new carriers began to come out their air groups worked on such problems as long-range scouting, navigation, recognition, and co-ordinated attacks by dive-bombers from above and torpedo planes low along the water.

One branch of Naval Aviation flourished mightily, only to die from a combination of crashes and speeded-up technology in other types of aircraft. This was the huge lighter-than-air dirigibles, the American equivalent of the zeppelins that the Germans had sent over

London in World War I. A series of beautiful and enormous airships
were built, some in the United States and some in Germany under
the Versailles Treaty, but all came to tragic ends. The American-
built *Shenandoah,* launched in 1923, split apart in a squall over Ohio,
in 1925. The *Akron* plunged into the sea after less than two years
of service, carrying with it Rear Admiral W. A. Moffet, one of the
great pioneers of Naval Aviation. In 1935, the *Macon* was lost at sea
due to structural failure. The end result was that lighter-than-air
work was left to the smaller non-rigid types, which eventually proved
their worth on anti-submarine patrol in World War II.

III

When the war in Europe broke out Japan was already in possession
of key areas in North China and the whole coast down to the border
of French Indo-China, but was having considerable difficulty in sub-
duing the interior, and American opinion over the aggression was
thoroughly aroused. France collapsed the following spring and the
Japanese extended their hold still farther by assuming a "protector-
ate" over Indo-China, which included a monopoly of the valuable
rice crop and the possession of the air and naval bases. There was
no doubt what the Japanese were driving for: domination of the East
Indies and its resources in metals and oil. Especially oil; Japanese
representatives had already informed the Dutch that the oil resources of the islands would henceforth be developed "jointly."

For oil had turned out to be a basic necessity for the Japanese imperialists. A flaw had appeared in their theories. They assumed earlier that naval superiority in the western Pacific would be adequate
to protect them against any interference beyond notes of indignation
while they were executing their ambitious project against China, and
they had discovered that even their naval advantage rested on a basis
of resources in steel and oil. Japan had no oil of her own. And she
lacked sufficient amounts of the scrap that must be mixed with iron
ore to produce steel. These things came to her mostly from the U.S.,
and there was early in the game a reluctance here to furnish Japan
with such means of aggression. In July, 1940, after the capture of
French Indo-China, this reluctance was translated into action. President Roosevelt placed an embargo on the shipment from America to
Japan of aviation gasoline and certain classes of iron scrap. In Sep-

tember, he followed it up by an embargo on all classes of scrap iron and steel.

An oil embargo was now just over the horizon, and in July, 1941, it came, together with the freezing of Japanese assets in the U.S. so that she could no longer implement an earlier procedure of paying for Dutch East India oil in cash. War was now inevitable; the Japanese militarists would accept nothing but complete American co-operation in their effort to conquer China, and this was one thing Washington was unwilling to give.

As the hour of destiny approached, the Navy had pretty well recovered from its morale troubles of the Hoover administration. The appropriations behind it were no longer inadequate, although there was still a shortage of personnel. The individual vessels were in a fairly high state of efficiency, and those in the Atlantic had gained valuable experience and some sense of the urgency of war through running convoys to Iceland against the threat of the German submarines, one of which had already torpedoed the destroyer *Reuben James*. The new ships of the Roosevelt Navy were coming off the ways, and though only some of the cruisers and destroyers had finished their shakedowns and were fully fleeted in, two battleships were in the shakedown period and construction was in progress on four new carriers, and eight more battleships. A vigorous program of training young men just out of college as naval aviators was in full swing, and the training was rigorous, both mentally and physically.

Whatever defects there were lay near the top. Franklin D. Roosevelt was very much his own Secretary of the Navy, and he was a man who did not like to be contradicted. The result was that many of those he chose for the highest commands before the war had a certain willingness to accept the presidential point of view, to a degree where they became almost irresolute without its support. Admiral J. O. Richardson, commanding the Pacific Fleet, objected to a Roosevelt order to base it on Honolulu, on the ground that a well-serviced and fully-manned fleet on the Pacific coast would be far more of a deterrent to the Japanese than an incompletely-manned fleet at Hawaii, and added to his objection by pressing his view on Senators and the State Department. Roosevelt relieved him in February 1941. The replacement chosen was Admiral Husband E. Kimmel.

★ ★ ★ ★ ★

9

The Days of Defeat

WHEN THE BOMBS began to rain down on Pearl Harbor on December 7 1941, the U.S. Fleet in the Pacific, even with the potential help of England and Holland counted in, was inferior to the Japanese in every class of combat ship. With the utmost reluctance and in response to one of the Roosevelt directives, Admiral H. R. Stark, the Chief of Naval Operations, had split the Fleet, sending three of the best battleships, three carriers, and attached cruisers and destroyers to the Atlantic in the face of the German threat. To upset the odds further, the Japanese had secretly built four new carriers and had more coming, for it was the belief of Admiral Yamamoto, their naval high command, that Naval Air would be the controlling weapon in modern sea war. Thus the Japanese had ten carriers in the Pacific to three for the United States.

There were eight separate official investigations as to responsibility among American commanders in the attack on Pearl Harbor, aside from what private efforts turned up. The synthesis of these is that a great deal of the blame rested on Washington, where adequate information of the coming attack had been received, but was not coordinated; nor was any urgent warning sent. Washington was aware of massive Japanese troop and ship movements toward the south and thought that any attack must come in the Indies; and at Pearl Harbor, Kimmel's staff felt the same. Nor did Kimmel have enough planes to fly adequate patrols.

Yet the facts remain that he did not fly patrols at all; that he found himself so busy with an urgent training program that he took almost no precautions; that the eight available battleships of the

Pacific Fleet were tied up in Pearl Harbor, with the crews on normal peace-time liberties on the morning of December 7. Of the Army anti-aircraft batteries that were supposed to protect the Fleet, few were manned and none had any ammunition. Practically all the Army defensive planes were in neat rows on the airstrips.

The Japanese came in five waves of dive-bombers and torpedo planes from six carriers, and within an hour all eight battleships of the Pacific Fleet were severely damaged, two of them permanently, one with her magazines blown up and the second capsized. All the others but one had their keels on the bottom and it would be a year before more than three of them were repaired. There were 2,403 dead and 1,178 wounded, more than the Navy had lost in the Spanish War and World War I put together. For all practical purposes the battle line was eliminated, and the Japanese were free to capture the Philippines and to conduct their expansion southward into the oil areas of the Indies.

The attackers' success had been quite up to their best expectations, but it contained three elements of miscalculation. They had counted heavily on the efforts of their submarines, of which twenty were deployed off Pearl Harbor, and on five midget submarines, launched from larger craft, that were to penetrate the anchorage. All five of the midgets were sunk without accomplishing anything; the big submarines sank a couple of ships off California and lost one of their own number. They utterly failed to interrupt traffic to Pearl Harbor, which assumed enormous proportions at once.

The second miscalculation was on the psychological effect of the raid and the damage to the American battleships. The Japanese fully believed that they had established one of those moral superiorities so important in war and to which they attached particular value. They had reason to expect this from the experience of their similar surprise attacks on the Chinese in 1894 and the Russians in 1904, after each of which the defeated party entered every subsequent action with an expectation of further loss. That is, they counted on American dismay, on the idea that American admirals and captains would enter action with a sense of approaching doom, fatal to effective performance. Nothing of the kind happened; the reaction in the American Navy was one of fury, quite uncomplicated by the least sense of inferiority.

The third miscalculation was perhaps the most important of all. Admiral Yamamoto, although the great advocate of naval aviation in the Japanese service, believed that air operations must be a preliminary, and the ultimate decision in naval war would be achieved by the guns of the battleships. This theory was also widely held in the American Navy at the time, in spite of some notable dissenters, including Admiral Jonas Ingram. But the Pearl Harbor disaster had deprived the U.S. of its line of battleships. As a result, whatever American operations were conducted in the Pacific during the next year had to be of necessity accomplished by task forces built around carriers. Yamamoto, on the other hand, was never given a chance to lose his faith in the ultimate decisive effect of the battle line. The full impact of the new task force strategy would not be felt until later; but the seed was planted at Pearl Harbor.

II

In one respect the Washington intelligence estimates were perfectly right: The Japanese had shifted the major weight of their forces southward. Now they displayed an unexpected capability for simultaneously launching strong offensives against the Philippines, Dutch Borneo, and British Malaya. American forces in the East consisted of the Asiatic Fleet: one heavy cruiser, two light cruisers, thirteen destroyers, a squadron of twenty-eight patrol planes, and twenty-nine submarines. The British had two battleships at Singapore, with a destroyer squadron of four; and in the Indies a heavy cruiser and two lights, with three destroyers; the Dutch could contribute three light cruisers and seven destroyers beside about twelve submarines. Against these small and scattered groups there was deployed the full strength of the Japanese Navy. In addition, the enemy threw in hundreds of land-based planes, flying from Formosa, Indo-China and, after the second day of the attack, from newly-seized bases in northern Malaya.

Arrangements had been made for the co-operation of the three nations' naval forces. Admiral Thomas Hart of the U.S. Asiatic Fleet, one of the few officers who took a wholly realistic view of Japanese intentions and strength, was already drawing his forces down toward the Dutch islands when the enemy struck. In the first two days of the war the Japanese planes dealt two crippling blows.

On the morning of December 9 there was an air alarm at Clark and Nichols fields near Manila, where the bulk of the American land-based planes were stationed. An all-clear was sounded and the planes came in. There has never been an explanation of why they were lined up in careful rows, but it is clear that there was a complete breakdown of communications from radar and coastal warning stations. When a heavy force of Japanese dive- and high-level bombers arrived just after noon only two planes were in the air. At one blow over one-third of the American fighters and more than one-half the bombers were destroyed. The next day the Japs came back; at Nichols Field they overwhelmed the defending fighters, while the remainder attacked Cavite Navy Yard without air opposition and completely wrecked it, together with one of the submarines that was in dock.

That same day Admiral Tom Philips was taking his two British battleships up the Malay coast in the hope of catching the enemy transports reported landing troops all along the eastern side of the peninsula. Singapore warned that it could give him no land-based air cover, as all planes were needed for the support of ground defense, already crumbling in the face of heavy enemy forces, but the Admiral persisted. At about the same hour when Cavite and Nichols Field were hit he was attacked by more than fifty bombers and torpedo planes. Within a little more than an hour both ships were on the bottom, the heart had gone out of the defense of the Indies, and it was established that heavy ships could not stand up against land-based air —something that happened to be true at the time, but impermanent, though it greatly darkened strategic counsels later.

The main current fact was that the Japanese had complete air control of the Philippines and complete naval control of its waters. They could pour in as many troops as they wished in the novel landing craft they had learned to build and handle during the Chinese campaign, and the defense was condemned to a series of retreats, occupying as many enemy forces and inflicting as many casualties as possible. On May 6, 1942, Corregidor Rock, the last American stronghold in the Philippines, surrendered after submarines had taken off nurses and important personnel, including General Douglas MacArthur.

III

In January, 1942, the ABDAflot (American-British-Dutch-Australian) command was set up, with headquarters in Java and the objective of defending the Malay Barrier, the islands that sweep from Malaya to the north of Australia. From the first this command was beset by disagreements and the lack of any real co-operation. To the British nothing seemed so important as holding Singapore, the key of the Indian Ocean. To the Australians and Americans the major issue was stopping Japanese penetration of the southwest Pacific, and they agreed with the British that Java could not be held. To the Dutch only Java counted. In addition there was no real over-all command: The co-operation among ground, naval, and air forces was achieved by one commander asking another for help "if convenient." The Dutch insisted that the high commander afloat should be one of their own men. He was Admiral C. E. L. Helfrich, a cautious man who could enforce no strategic ideas of his own in the face of British insistence that Singapore was the key of the situation and the first duty of the little combined fleet was to convoy troops and supplies thither.

Admiral Hart, who had turned over seaborne operational command of the American forces to Vice-Admiral W. A. Glassford, was all for using what forces were at hand to strike as heavily as possible at the Japanese as they came down Makassar Strait to the east of Borneo and the South China Sea to the west. Helfrich violently disagreed; he insisted that only a kind of passive defense was possible until more planes had come. But there were no more planes to send, not even in the United States, and when on January 20 word came in that the Japanese were landing at the great oil port of Balikpapan in eastern Borneo, the Dutch Admiral let Glassford take the two American light cruisers and four destroyers up to see what they could do about it.

The light cruiser *Boise* tore her bottom badly on an uncharted reef, and had to go all the way back to the United States, out of the campaign. The light cruiser *Marblehead* had engine trouble; the destroyers pushed on by themselves on the night of January 23 and got right in among a convoy of twelve transports in the dark. Four destroyers charged back and forth through the lines of anchored ships, firing torpedoes and guns in a pandemonium of smoke, explosions, burning ships, and shellfire, and got away without losing a man for the first clean, if minor, American success of the war.

It was minor because out of forty-eight torpedoes, only five sank ships, though some others were damaged. Behind these disappointing results was a problem that was to harry American torpedo craft, especially the submarines, for the next two years. The torpedoes were no good. The twenty-nine American submarines and twelve Dutch should have made things extremely hot for the Japanese in the comparatively constricted areas where they were driving their invasions home. All told, there were more of these submarines operating than the Germans had at sea during any month of World War I, and they carried out their patrols with courage and navigational skill. The Japanese defensive arrangements were fairly good, but only fairly; they succeeded in sinking only two submarines aside from the one bombed at Cavite. But in the campaign for the Indies, American submarines accounted for only twelve ships with a total tonnage of 50,000.

The torpedoes were no good. *Seadragon* had a beautiful broadside shot at a big freighter, and fired five, of which four missed and the one that hit was a dud. Five submarines got into Lingayen Gulf when eighty Japanese transports were sitting-duck targets; they sank only one, all the other torpedoes missed. It was past belief that boats so well handled, so successful in getting into firing position and evading the enemy, were incompetent in the single detail of firing their torpedoes. The submariners themselves protested with some vehemence that at least 37½ per cent of the torpedoes must be defective.

The fact was that not long before the war the Navy had developed a new magnetic exploder, which was intended to set the torpedo off as it passed under the keel of a ship as a result of entering the ship's own magnetic field. It was so secret that only commanders of ships knew about it and no one knew how to service it; and it did not work. The device had been designed and installed at the torpedo station in Newport and magnetism in the South Seas is quite different from that in the Northern Hemisphere. Even before orders had gone out to de-activate the magnetic exploders, another defect had been discovered; the torpedoes ran consistently several feet below the depth they were set to run. Like the magnetic exploder, the depth setting had been developed in the comparatively shallow waters of Narragansett Bay and nearby areas and then under a regime that could not afford ships for targets. Meanwhile the Japanese had been blowing up dozens of ships under conditions approximating those of war and developing the finest torpedoes in the world.

It was not until 1943 that the American Navy began to get fully functioning torpedoes. In the meantime, the enemy was pressing down the straits toward Java. They were reported landing on the island of Celebes, across Makassar Strait from Borneo, and all the Allied forces not engaged in the Singapore adventure were assembled at Surabaya for a strike toward Makassar town under the Dutch admiral, Karel Doorman. These forces consisted of two Dutch light cruisers, the heavy cruiser *Houston,* the light cruiser *Marblehead,* and four destroyers of each nation. They steamed out a minute after midnight of February 4. Nine in the morning found them off Bali with a warning message that thirty-seven Japanese bombers had left an enemy-held airfield in eastern Celebes for Surabaya; a few minutes later the planes were overhead and attacking.

They were heavy bombers, which came in four distinct groups. *Marblehead* was hit forward, taking bad leaks, then by a heavy bomb aft that completely knocked out her steering gear, and a third hit set her afire amidships. *Houston*'s after turret was hit and every man in it killed. The ships turned back; it was only by something like a miracle that *Marblehead* reached Tjilatjap on the southern coast of Java, where her bow was repaired enough to let her make the voyage clear across the Indian Ocean, steering on her engines.

Now overwhelming Japanese forces came down to take Timor and Bali, cutting Allied communication with Australia, while on February 14 Palembang in Sumatra fell, followed by Singapore the next day. What was left of the Allied fleet was isolated and surrounded in the Java Sea. It now consisted of the damaged *Houston,* one British heavy cruiser, two Dutch light cruisers and an Australian, with eleven assorted destroyers from the three nations. Down against them and Java in the last days of February came the Japanese with four battleships, four carriers, and an advance force of two heavy and two light cruisers and fourteen destroyers, with all the land-based and carrier air cover they could use, leading a convoy of forty-one transports. Doorman sallied with his little fleet on February 27, trying to reach the transports. He had been on a futile search for the enemy for two days and all hands were at the last point of fatigue. When contact came the Japanese had planes to spot the fall of shot and he had none; their heavy cruisers counted twenty big guns to his twelve; language and signal differences made communications difficult.

Yet the Allied command did not do too badly during the first two hours of a confused, twisting battle through clouds of gun and funnel smoke, with evening closing in. Then the British heavy cruiser was badly hit and turned away out of line; several other ships followed her and the Japanese launched one of their ceaseless torpedo attacks into the confusion. Two Dutch destroyers and one of the British went down, another ran on a mine, and as darkness closed in tight, both Dutch cruisers were torpedoed. *Houston* and the Australian *Perth* reached Surabaya, then tried to get out of the trap through Sunda Strait. There they found a great Japanese invasion convoy of 56 ships just putting men ashore, and before the rapidly assembling Japanese forces could sink the two cruisers, they destroyed at least four of the enemy.

The only ships that escaped the fatal Battle of Java Sea were four American destroyers that slipped out of Bali Strait, while the old carrier *Langley* was caught south of Java by Japanese carrier planes and destroyed. The Empire had now attained the objectives for which it went to war—not only the oil supplies of the Indies, but all the other resources needed, with a chain of island bases to protect the area. The only force that could have been capable of interfering was out of action for a long time.

IV

Farther north in the Pacific the Japanese had taken the Gilbert Islands without trouble to round out their defensive chain, and on December 11, 1941, they launched an attack on Wake Island. It was held by a Marine defense battalion and the attackers caught a tartar, losing two destroyers and having other ships badly hit. They came back with heavier forces supported by carriers on December 22, and after two days of desperate fighting, made the invasion stick. A task force built around the carrier *Saratoga* under Admiral F. J. Fletcher had been dispatched from Pearl in time to have effected a relief, but he lost many hours refueling his destroyers and when Wake radioed that it was already under attack the expedition was called off from headquarters.

This was at least partly due to the fact that Kimmel had been relieved shortly after the Pearl Harbor attack and was on his way home, while his replacement had not arrived, and the interim commander was unwilling to bring about a serious battle before the new chief came. The failure left a distinctly bad taste, and officer morale at Pearl went down almost to the point the Japanese had expected. It picked up at once with the arrival of the new Commander in Chief Pacific.

He was Chester W. Nimitz, who came from the Bureau of Personnel with a reputation for handling men. He was quiet in manner, gentle in speech; possessed of an immense capacity for work and an equal one for co-ordination. At Pearl Harbor he instantly established himself by announcing that instead of making a clean sweep of the staff, as might be expected, everyone would be kept in his place until he had shown he could not fill it. Behind Nimitz in Washington there was now Commander in Chief of the Fleet Admiral Ernest J. King, whom Roosevelt had been somewhat reluctantly persuaded to appoint; a hard man, as little willing to accept opposition as the President himself, but with a strong sense of strategy and of the possible.

In his office King drew a line on a map from Midway to Hawaii, Samoa, Fiji and Brisbane in Australia, telling Nimitz it must be held at all costs. Samoa and Fiji were the obvious weak points, for the Japanese had just taken Rabaul in New Britain, which placed the whole chain of the Solomon Islands within bombing range, and they seemed bent on extending the southeast corner of their huge triangular sea empire until it severed connections between the U.S. and Australia.

Marines were embarked for Samoa in January and covered by Admiral Fletcher's task group of cruisers and destroyers around the carrier *Yorktown* (just arrived from the Atlantic) and Admiral William B. Halsey's similar group around *Enterprise*. King was very anxious for some kind of counter-attack in the central Pacific islands to discourage the Japanese from expanding farther, and on the way back from the Samoa coverage, both carrier groups ran in on the Marshalls and attacked Japanese bases at Wotje, Kwajalein, and

Jaluit. As strikes these operations were not notably successful, for very little damage was done, but as the first counter-offensive of the war they gained great publicity and raised morale all along the line. They were presently followed by carrier raids on Wake and Marcus islands, which had more material success and added to the confidence of the flyers.

Meanwhile Admiral Wilson Brown with the carrier *Lexington* task force ran right down into the Coral Sea for a try at a raid on Rabaul from south of New Guinea. He was spotted by Japanese scouts and, on February 22, two formations of nine heavy bombers each came out to attack the carrier. They ran into something, to wit: *Lexington*'s famous Fighter 2 squadron, considered one of the best in the fleet. While the carrier's crew cheered as wildly as at a football game, plane after Japanese plane streaked down the sky, and only one of them got away to carry the news to Rabaul that if you were unescorted by fighters an air attack on an American carrier could be costly. The American strike against Rabaul was given up, but shortly later the Japanese landed troops at Lae and Salamaua in eastern New Guinea, and Wilson Brown repeated his raid. This time the *Yorktown* group was attached to his force, the planes flying northward over 15,000-foot mountains. They caught Japanese shipping in the harbor and smashed it up badly, then turned back to Pearl, after a raid which was to have a strategic effect that counted for more than material damage.

At the same hour there was already being mounted a raid which was to have still deeper strategic results. *Saratoga* had picked up a submarine torpedo and was in for repairs, but the new carrier *Hornet* had just reached the Pacific and it was decided to employ her in a surprise attack on Tokyo. No Navy plane could fly the distance without bringing the carrier too perilously close to the Japanese coast line, but the Army co-operated heartily by supplying a squadron of sixteen B-25s under the famous Jimmy Doolittle. They filled the carrier's whole deck; she avoided sea traffic by steering far to the north, where she picked up *Enterprise,* and both bows turned toward Japan. On April 18 picket boats were encountered, 668 miles from land and well short of the proposed launching point; Halsey and Doolittle decided to launch anyway, and in a sea so heavy that it was breaking over the carrier ramps, got the planes away. They reached Tokyo just at noon, and though the material effect of the raid was small compared to those that came later, it provided a moral shock that became one of the main influences in changing the whole course of the war. Most of the planes crash-landed in China; seventy-one of the eighty flyers survived.

V

The importance of Wilson Brown's raid over the New Guinea mountains lay in its influence on Japanese strategic planning. The great over-all Japanese scheme for setting up a system of island barriers that would protect the southern resources area was well ahead of schedule at most points, but Brown's raid revealed a weakness at the southeastern angle of the barrier system, and there were signs of an Allied air build-up toward eastern New Guinea. The Japanese high command determined that the key point of Port Moresby on the south coast must be taken and the whole chain of the Solomons not merely brought under Japanese air domination from Rabaul, but made a forward base area for further operations southeast against the New Hebrides and New Caledonia to close the sea and air lanes between the U.S. and Australia.

The operational plan was one of typical Japanese complexity. It called for an invasion force covered by a light carrier and other ships to move straight down through the Bismarck Sea and around the eastern tip of New Guinea to Port Moresby. Another Japanese force was to enter the southern Solomons and set up a base at Tulagi. And still a third force, at the heart of which were two major carriers, was to circle the Solomons, destroy any Allied ships that entered the area south of Tulagi, then run in and knock out the air bases of northeast Australia.

In the latter part of April, American Naval Intelligence decided that something was in the wind in the Coral Sea area, and action was indicated. The *Enterprise* and *Hornet* task groups were still on their way back from the Tokyo raid. Nimitz sent the only force he had available, the *Lexington* and *Yorktown* groups under Admiral Fletcher, with the other two carriers to follow in support as soon as they had replenished at Pearl Harbor.

Fletcher's two carriers were in Coral Sea on May 3, at some distance from each other and refueling, when word came through Australian long-range search planes that the Japanese were already landing at Tulagi. Without waiting for *Lexington,* Fletcher took *Yorktown* up south of the Solomons and flew strikes across mountainous Guadalcanal island against the harbor. The material damage was less than the flyers believed, but it was still not inconsiderable, and aboard the carriers they were happily talking about having turned back the Japs and being due for a spot of leave in Sydney as the ships turned west.

May 6 was the day Corregidor surrendered. That night the major Japanese carrier force was in the eastern edge of Coral Sea, and early next morning flew searches southward to make sure no American carriers were behind them as they steamed northwest to join in the support of the force headed for Port Moresby, which was now rounding the eastern tip of New Guinea under the wing of the light carrier *Shoho.* The searchers reported that they had found an American carrier escorted by a cruiser, and the Japanese flew off full strike groups southward. They reached their targets all right, but it was only the oiler that had been refueling Fletcher's ships and though they sank her and her destroyer escort, it kept them from finding the American carriers that day.

Fletcher, now far to the west and north, had meanwhile located *Shoho.* He launched no less than ninety-three attack planes; they caught the Japanese carrier just turning into the wind, and in five minutes hit her with ten heavy bombs and fifteen torpedoes. *Lexington*'s radio crackled with the jubilant shout of Lieutenant-Commander Dixon of the air group: "Scratch one flat-top! Dixon to carrier. Scratch one flat-top!"

This time the Japanese force really was turned back; the Port Moresby invasion convoy was ordered to retreat to Rabaul. Japanese Admiral Hara, however, with the two heavy carriers kept pressing into Coral Sea while Fletcher was steaming southeast. That night each force was aware of the other's presence, something like a hundred miles away, and several Japanese planes were shot down when they mistook the American carriers for their own and tried to land.

At dawn both sides flew off strikes. A weather front had come down and the Japanese were under cloud cover with frequent squalls, while our ships were in the clear. The enemy attack got at least three torpedo hits on *Lexington* and a big bomb into *Yorktown;* the American counter-stroke was hampered by torpedoes that ran badly or did not explode, but achieved three bomb hits on the carrier *Shokaku* that nearly wrecked the ship. Later in the day, when the attacks were over, gasoline fumes released aboard *Lexington* by the torpedo hits suddenly exploded; the ship was soon burning uncontrollably and had to be abandoned, while her people stood on the decks of rescue destroyers with tears unashamedly streaming down their faces.

Tactically the Battle of Coral Sea was a Japanese victory. Numerically and in tonnage they suffered the lesser loss. But it was the incidence of the loss that counted. The air groups of both big Japanese carriers had been practically wiped out and they had no such reserve coming up as that provided by the American pilot-training program. As a result, they pulled both their big carriers out of the Coral Sea and back to Japan, where they were immobilized for months. The Port Moresby project had failed and the Japanese never did succeed in getting around that eastern cape of New Guinea.

★　　★　　★　　★　　★

10

From Midway to Guadalcanal

FOR SOME TIME there had been a violent dispute in the Japanese high command between the Naval General Staff, which favored maintenance of the perimeter of the sea empire, with extension only to the southeastward, and the fleet command of Admiral Yamamoto, who insisted the Empire would never be secure until the United States Fleet was destroyed. The specific step he proposed was the occupation of Midway Island. It was within long-range bombing distance of Hawaii, and once it was taken the Americans would surely be forced to commit whatever ships they had to an effort at recapture. This controversy was settled in typical Japanese fashion by sitting on both chairs. The Naval General Staff continued its preparations for a southeastward advance toward New Caledonia, while Yamamoto drew his own plans. A determining factor was the Doolittle air raid on Tokyo; it was felt as an intolerable loss of face by everyone in the Japanese government, and though they did not know the raiders had come from a carrier they were quite sure that the seizure of the Midway outpost would prevent anything like that from happening again.

Events in the Coral Sea only reinforced this resolution. The view in Tokyo was that it had been a clear-cut Japanese victory; they were certain that both American carriers had been sunk, and there was bitter criticism of the admiral who ordered the withdrawal. The plan for the Midway attack and occupation was therefore laid on for early June, and it involved practically the whole combat force of the Japanese Navy—eleven battleships, their four biggest carriers, and heavy cruisers in the striking force, an invasion group to follow in transports, and a strong diversionary attack group to strike in the Aleutians and occupy their outer islands. Yamamoto's plan was to destroy the local Midway defenses by overwhelming air attack from the carriers and take over the island. When the American fleet came out to recover it, he would deliver a preliminary carrier attack, then go in with the big-gun battleships and finish matters.

It was a plan based on the assumption that the Americans would do what he thought they would do, and on ignorance of how much Pearl Harbor knew. Since before Coral Sea, American cryptographers had been reading Japanese cipher messages. At the date when Yamamoto's armada sortied from Japan, Admiral Nimitz had long been informed as to the exact composition of their forces and what they intended to accomplish. Enough of the Pearl Harbor battleships had been salvaged to work up a line of seven powerful, if slow, battleships. They put out of San Francisco in the latter days of May as linebackers in case the Japanese broke through, but Nimitz did not really expect to use them. He was going to base his defense of Midway on air forces. Army and Marine land-based planes were rushed to the island and long-range bombers made ready at Hawaii. The damaged *Yorktown* steamed fast north from Coral Sea, and a repair job that experts estimated as requiring ninety days was completed in forty-eight hours of hectic round-the-clock labor by yard workmen who were told this was a desperate emergency. *Enterprise* and *Hornet* were made ready for battle. Since Halsey had fallen ill, they were placed under command of the cruiser admiral Raymond A. Spruance.

It was one of the best choices ever made by Nimitz or anyone else. Spruance had no experience in carrier war, but he submitted everything to a process of cold, remorseless logic, and was known in the fleet as "the thinking machine." Yamamoto had thrown out a screen of scouting submarines to detect American movements from Hawaii. Before the scouts arrived Spruance had divined their coming and taken his carriers to sea in the area northeast of Midway, the spot least likely for the Japanese to find them. There he was presently joined by *Yorktown* with Fletcher, who was senior officer afloat and therefore in technical tactical command. Fletcher lacked an air staff, however, and left a good deal to the junior admiral.

This was the background. The great assault opened on June 3, when planes from two Japanese light carriers came through the mist and clouds that perpetually shroud the Aleutians to launch an attack on the American bases at Dutch Harbor. They found it much larger and better equipped than they had imagined. On the way back to their carriers the Japanese aircraft were suddenly set upon by Army pursuit planes, which had no business there at all, since by Japanese information there was no American airfield anywhere in the neighborhood. Harassed and perplexed, the Japanese admiral withdrew westward and settled for occupying the uninhabited islands of Kiska and Attu. His diversion had not diverted a single ship or plane from the American defense.

June 4 was a Thursday, with light winds and small clouds over the American carrier force, while the Japanese were well covered under a weather front. Nagumo, the Japanese carrier admiral, launched his strike against Midway early: one hundred eight planes, with the deck crews shouting the banzai as each one cleared. Half an hour later another one hundred eight followed. Radar warning sent every plane on Midway into the air—patrol planes back to Pearl Harbor out of trouble, a formation of Navy torpedo planes, one of Marine glide-bombers, and twenty Army planes going out to counter-attack; fighters up. The Japanese bombers burned out a fuel tank and a hangar, and their more numerous fighters got rid of most of the American defensive planes, but they did so little damage to the island that the Japanese flight leader radioed back that another strike would be necessary. The counter-attacking American planes were equally futile; the majority of them were shot down without producing a single hit on the Japanese ships, and Admiral Nagumo turned north under the cloud cover to refuel and rearm his planes.

At this moment there entered the combination a force of whose very existence the Japanese were ignorant—Spruance and the American carriers. *Yorktown* had flown the early morning search and located the Japanese carriers; Fletcher dropped back to take in his planes and sent Spruance on ahead with *Hornet* and *Enterprise* to act as he pleased. That admiral had expected to run in to within a hundred miles of the Japanese position before launching strikes, but the news of the attack on Midway gave him the idea that he just might catch the Japanese planes on their carrier decks, rearming. In spite of the fact that he was at so great a distance that he could probably count on losing many planes through running out of fuel, he flew off full strikes—every plane on the decks of both carriers. Half an hour later and nearer, *Yorktown* also launched, but only half a strike.

Spruance's was one of the key command decisions of the war, but for some time it seemed that it might utterly miscarry. Nagumo's turn had taken the Japanese carriers well away from the positions where they were originally reported. The American planes had to hunt for them, and in the drifting banks and levels of cloud, fighters, dive-bombers, and torpedo planes became separated from each other. The result was that the torpedo planes, low over the water, reached the Japanese first and without fighter cover, receiving the undivided attention of the enemy combat air patrol. They were shot to pieces. Only four of them ever got back to the carriers; in *Hornet*'s Torpedo 8 squadron there was a single survivor, Ensign George Gay, who floated in a rubber boat, settling himself just in time to see the most tremendous spectacle of the war.

For the four Japanese carriers had been forced into such radical maneuvers by the torpedo men that they could not get their planes away, and they were still on the decks, fueled and armed, when there came through the clouds the dive-bombers from *Enterprise* and *Yorktown*. The Japanese fighters were at the low levels where they had been killing off the torpedo planes; the dive-bombers had no opposition except anti-aircraft fire as they streamed down on the twisting carriers. Aboard *Enterprise* they could hear on the radio the fervid swearing of Squadron Leader McClusky as the first three bombs missed. Then the hits began—thousand-pound bombs from close in. Aboard three of the Japanese carriers vast sheets of flame leaped up to engulf everything; the gasoline tanks of the loaded planes burst, the torpedoes and bombs they were carrying let go with the heat, the decks of the carriers folded back as though they were cardboard, streams of fire ran through their fueling systems and Ensign Gay on his rubber raft gazed with no little satisfaction at the long line of blazing giant ships, wracked by explosions. In five minutes the battle was decided.

But it was not yet over. One Japanese carrier, *Hiryu*, had slipped away north from the rest and was not hurt. About noon she began flying off strikes at *Yorktown*, which had lagged behind the other carriers and been seen by Japanese search planes. The strength of the

American fighters was well down; at the cost of more than half their planes the Japanese got in on *Yorktown* and hit her with three bombs, one of which seriously damaged her engines. As a result when a torpedo attack came two hours later the Japanese got two crippling hits, and the carrier was under tow and helpless when a Japanese submarine sank her two days later.

In the meantime *Hiryu* had been located by American search planes and a powerful strike was flown against her from the two intact carriers. Her effort against *Yorktown* had nearly stripped her of planes, and she took the same treatment as the other Japanese carriers, bomb hits that stripped off nearly her whole flight deck and left her all afire inside. She sank at dawn; and in the meanwhile Admiral Yamamoto got the word that instead of a single American carrier being present, as he had at first assumed, there were three.

He made one more try. During the night, as the exhausted pilots aboard the American carriers drank coffee, discussed the events of the day and friends who were missing, then flopped into their bunks without even undressing, the Japanese fleet steamed eastward, trying to bring about a night surface action with the guns. But Spruance had also turned away east and toward morning the Japanese admiral realized that he would have no gunnery action, but instead would receive at dawn more attacks from those deadly dive-bombers, while American submarines were reported all around. He turned back to Japan, therefore, standing on the bridge of his flagship and brooding with staring eyes as he sipped rice gruel.

More Japanese died that day than on both sides in any naval battle of World War I. And as at Coral Sea it was not so much the total loss that counted, but where the loss fell. Four of the six Japanese carriers that led the attack on Pearl Harbor were gone, with practically all their air groups, planes, and pilots, the best in the Japanese Navy, which should have trained others. Even Yamamoto was aware that he had lost the initiative.

II

This was clear to both Admiral King and Admiral Nimitz, and they decided to take the offensive. It was, however, a difficult decision to implement. At the heads-of-government level it had long been determined that Allied policy would be that of beating Germany first, as she was the more dangerous enemy. All the trained troops, with whatever ships and planes were necessary to support them, were already earmarked for the European operation, to be opened in French North Africa, for which the offensive plans were already made. Any stroke against the Japanese would have to be carried out by the unaided resources of the Navy. (This paralleled an earlier situation when the Japanese themselves had rejected their Navy's idea of a direct offensive against Australia because the Army declined to supply the necessary troops.)

The first American Pacific offensive of the war was therefore scheduled for the Guadalcanal-Tulagi complex in the Solomon Islands, at the extreme southeastern corner of the Japanese domain. The land striking force was to be furnished by the 1st Marine Division, then in New Zealand. On August 7, a fleet of cruisers and destroyers convoyed the Marines to the sound between the two islands of Guadalcanal and Tulagi. The key positions on Guadalcanal were quickly seized, but on the smaller island the Japanese had dug in in limestone caves, and Tulagi was only secured by hard fighting—an earnest of what was to come later. There were enemy air raids down from the big Japanese base at Rabaul both the first day and the next, and on that second day, Admiral Fletcher, in command of the three carriers covering the operation from south of Guadalcanal, left at once, notifying the shore commanders that it was too dangerous for him to remain in the area.

Not one-third of the supplies for the Marines had been unloaded, and that night there was a serious conference among Admiral Crutchley, the Australian who commanded the Naval forces, Admiral R. K. Turner of the Amphibious Command and General Vandegrift of the Marines. While they were talking, at 0130 in the morning, five Japanese heavy cruisers and two lights suddenly appeared off Savo Island at the entrance of the sound, firing guns and torpedoes. They had been sighted on their approach down the island chain but a failure of communications kept the news from getting through, and on all ships there were only night watches when the Japanese appeared. In less than eighteen minutes three American cruisers and an Australian were fatally hit; *Chicago* had her bow blown off by a torpedo, and two destroyers were badly damaged.

That was the Battle of Savo Island, the worst defeat ever suffered by the American Navy. The surface covering force for Guadalcanal was practically wiped out and the transports had to leave so rapidly that they never got more than a percentage of the supplies ashore. Fletcher was altogether too nervous about his carriers, taking them away at the precise moment when their planes could have given warning, but the main point was the lack of alertness, the fact that the U.S. Navy had hardly considered night fighting or being attacked at night. It was a bitter lesson and it was thoroughly learned— but for the present this was small comfort to the Marines cut off on the island, living on captured Japanese rice and with the enemy in the jungle all about them.

III

There then ensued the most furious and prolonged struggle our Navy had engaged in since the country became a major nation. The details are confused and confusing, but the general lines are clear. The night belonged to the Japanese. Ashore they staged night attacks, and at sea they bombarded the Marine positions and ran in reinforcements for their troops aboard destroyers or small fast transports that hid among the upper islands until dark gave them cover. After August 20, when our Marines placed the Guadalcanal airstrip in operation and received a complement of planes flown in from some distance, the day belonged to the Americans. They won back all ground lost during the dark hours, and their planes mercilessly harried everything Japanese afloat within range.

The Marines were better armed, better co-ordinated, and on the whole better trained than their opponents. Above all, they had better logistic support, though it might not always seem so to the men who ate skilly from mess-kit tins in the jungle. By a fatal coincidence every enemy ship carrying medical supplies to the beleaguered island was sunk, and the Japanese lost so many men from wounds and disease, that although it is a commonplace of war to overestimate the enemy's casualties, the Marines ultimately discovered to their astonishment that they had killed twice as many Japanese as they had thought.

This was the general picture of the fighting on the island, a war of close-in combat by night and day, with the thin American line of the perimeter around the airfield always under pressure. That airfield was the key of the strategic situation; if the Japanese could win it, they could keep American ships at a distance, pushing the frontier back to the New Hebrides and New Caledonia. Besides their general system of slipping reinforcements in aboard destroyers at night, they gradually developed a strategy of running in major reinforcement groups under cover of full fleet operations designed to break American naval strength, while they filled the waters south of Guadalcanal with submarines to grind down the ships supporting the American operation. They had superior forces in the area and the first big effort came on August 24. It was a typical Japanese attack in several separate forces, one headed by the light carrier *Ryujo* to draw American air strength, while two major carriers swept out at a distance to strike the American ships, and a transport group ran down through the islands.

This was the Battle of the Eastern Solomons. The Japanese plan succeeded all too well for its makers. *Ryujo* did indeed attract attention, but she was set upon by air groups from *Saratoga* and *Enterprise,* which came tearing up from the south and sent her to the bottom in flames; several other Japanese ships were badly battered. The enemy flyers found that the proportion of fighters aboard American carriers had been greatly increased. They scored three bomb hits on *Enterprise,* but did not even put that indestructible entity out of action, and they lost nearly all the planes that took part in the attack. The enemy troops got ashore on Guadalcanal all right, but they consisted of only fifteen hundred men of a special storm troop known as the Ichiki Detachment, Japanese Intelligence having reported that the Americans on the island were fewer in number than originally believed and that they had suffered a "loss of spiritual power." The Marines killed all but twelve of them.

The Japanese now began to build up their forces more gradually for a major attack on the airfield from the inland side, while their submarines were to cut off American reinforcement. In one sense they were successful; during late August and September they succeeded in damaging the carrier *Saratoga* so that she was out of action for many months, hit the battleship *North Carolina,* and on September 15 sank the carrier *Wasp.* But they failed in the objective of stopping supplies for the Marines on the island, and the land assault bloodily failed in the Battle of Edson's Ridge.

Early in October the Japanese program was changed to one of running in strong reinforcement groups by night under cover of a cruiser squadron, which would then bombard the airfield. Admiral R. K. Turner developed the counter-plan of sending in a whole regiment of Army troops to reinforce the tiring Marines under escort of Admiral Norman Scott with four cruisers and a destroyer group; the ships to remain off Guadalcanal until dark, then hunt Japs. Scott's was the first American force to be trained for night fighting, with the men on duty from dark till dawn. On October 11 he saw his convoy in, then steamed out past Cape Esperance at the northern tip of the island.

That night the Japanese decided to come down with three heavy cruisers and eight big destroyers. As they rounded Savo Island they came right on into Norman Scott's formation, placing him in the position of crossing the T. New radar on one of the American ships gave warning; out blazed the guns and in fifteen minutes one of the Japanese heavies was rolling over and another running away with over forty hits that kept her in dock for many months. They were caught disorganized but not helpless; a salvo burned out the whole forward end of the light cruiser *Boise*. An American destroyer went down, but for that the Japanese paid with three destroyers of their own. Cape Esperance: It was the first surface victory of the war, the first night victory, after the Japanese had hit us so hard at Savo Island. In the surface Navy it, rather than Midway, was regarded as the real turning point of the war, and the harried Marines on the island plucked up in heart and in spirit.

The effect was not to discourage the Japanese, but to make them change techniques. The method of running men in aboard destroyers by night had worked very well; now they extended it, bringing in a picked division, one of the best in the Japanese service, during the month of October for an attack on the airfield through jungle trails at the rear. The cruiser bombardment program having encountered difficulties, the enemy sent in battleships to do the preliminary work, and on the night of October 13 two of them came down the slot between the islands and shelled the field for over an hour, disabling more than half the planes and so cutting up the main airstrip that for the time being it could not be used. The next night came cruisers, and under their cover the Japanese ran transports in and began unloading them in broad daylight. It was fatal to the transports, for enough of our planes remained operational to destroy them, but the enemy troops got ashore. The shortage of gasoline and ammunition in the American lines was so acute, the night bombing attacks so persistent, that there began to be doubts whether Guadalcanal could be held.

Then Halsey, recovered from his illness, was made commander of the South Pacific area. There was nothing wrong with Admiral R. L. Ghormley, whom Halsey replaced; but the former lacked both Halsey's force and his enormous popularity with everyone right down to a seaman third, and there was now a general lifting of morale all along the line. Halsey made the most fervent efforts to get the needed supplies and reinforcements into Guadalcanal, and it cost him ships —small tenders, gasoline carriers, old destroyers converted to transports, continually being caught off the island at night by Japanese ships and sunk there.

With their picked division ashore and filtering through the jungle, the Japanese now developed the full extent of their plan. It was to take the airfield by a three-pronged land attack on the night of October 25; on October 26 the main fleet, sweeping down from Truk was to destroy the American squadron that would inevitably come rushing up, and with the airfield in their hands the Americans could not counterattack with land-based planes.

The enemy had four carriers and four battleships, with all the heavy cruisers and destroyers they needed, and a light carrier detached to fly planes in to the captured airfield. On the American side there were only *Hornet* and the recently repaired *Enterprise* with a smattering of cruisers, including three of the new anti-aircraft cruisers, and one battleship. It is worth noting that the Japanese plan was fundamentally that which had been adopted for Midway—the capture of the American stronghold followed by the destruction of the reacting American forces; and it was supported by a superiority of force quite as great as they possessed at Midway, while this time the Americans enjoyed no advantage of surprise.

But the text early departed from the prepared script. At 0100 on the morning of the 26th the Japanese admiral got a radio flash from the island that the airfield was taken. He decided to go in with the fleet at dawn. Not until 0630 came an amendment that the situation on the land front was uncertain, and by this time both sides had made contact off the Santa Cruz islands from which the battle takes its name, and strikes were already being flown.

The Japanese got their planes away first and they arrived first, aiming mainly at *Hornet* in this bout. She took at least four heavy bomb hits, plus two torpedoes, and two Japanese planes that crashed into her when fatally hit and was left completely stopped, burning from end to end, when the attackers departed. Damage control parties got the fires out and the ship under tow, but she was in bad shape, and it is only slightly anticipating events to say that in the afternoon the last gasp of the Japanese attack hit her with another torpedo and she had to be abandoned.

Enterprise was a different proposition; she had not only the protection of one of the new anti-aircraft cruisers, but also that of the battleship *South Dakota,* and the Japanese learned what a very good anti-aircraft vessel a new battleship can be. They got two bomb hits on the carrier and one (which did no serious damage) on the battleship, but they lost thirty-seven planes in four minutes. The *Enterprise* search group had meanwhile found the light carrier *Zuiho* with the planes for the island and ripped her deck up with two bomb hits that put her out of action. *Enterprise* attack planes had the bad luck to run into the fighters covering the Japanese strike and became disorganized, mostly shot down; but *Hornet's* attack got in on the carrier *Shokaku* and so nearly tore her to pieces that she was not back in the war for another nine months.

The result of Santa Cruz was profoundly disappointing and even discouraging to the American high command. They had lost *Hornet* and a destroyer that fell victim to a submarine torpedo; there was only one carrier left in the South Pacific and she was damaged. But the Guadalcanal airfield was still held and Marine flyers emphasized the point by putting out from it on the day after the battle and sinking a Japanese cruiser. Moreover, though no one on the American side yet knew it, the Japanese carrier air force had been virtually destroyed. Even the instructors had been put aboard the carriers for this great effort; two hundred twelve planes left the decks of those carriers that morning and less than sixty got back. Japanese carriers

moved obscurely in the background during the rest of the campaign
for Guadalcanal, but they were an empty threat, and it was nearly two
years before they could muster enough strength to try major carrier
operations again.

IV

There was no basic strategic reason why the possession of Guadalcanal was essential to the enemy. But it had become psychologically
indispensable, if only because of the effort already put in. It is probable that the reports the Japanese leaders received from Santa Cruz
led them to believe that American carrier aviation had been eliminated quite as completely as their own. In this case it was only
necessary to put the Guadalcanal airfield out of commission long
enough to land sufficient troops to make its capture certain, and this
was the basic idea behind the next offensive, scheduled for mid-
November. A squadron built around two battleships was to move
in and shell the field on the night of November 12; the following
day a cruiser squadron would complete the work; on the day after
that eleven big transports, carrying an entire division of troops, would
move in, with the battleships again bombarding as the men landed.

This ran head-on into an American plan to reinforce the island on
November 12. That day Admiral Dan Callaghan moved in with two
heavy cruisers, one light cruiser, two anti-aircraft cruisers, and eight
destroyers, covering a group of transports. The Japanese knew that
American ships were in the area, but they assumed our forces would
clear out at night, and to encourage them to do so, launched a heavy
afternoon air attack. It failed; most of the planes were shot down, and
the only damage was to the cruiser *San Francisco*, into which one
crashed. Our ships waited for night off Guadalcanal. An hour after
midnight the Japanese were detected coming in with two battleships,
one light cruiser and nine heavy destroyers. There was precipitated the
wildest and one of the most confused actions of the war, with ships of
both nations charging in every direction, firing guns and torpedoes
at anything in sight.

No coherent consecutive account of what happened in the next
forty-five minutes is possible. But when the quick red dawn of the
tropics came over the scene, two American destroyers had gone, two

more were burning and sinking, the anti-aircraft cruiser *Atlanta* was a wreck beyond saving, the anti-aircraft cruiser *Juneau* had her back broken and would be torpedoed by a submarine while trying to leave the area. *San Francisco* was shot to pieces topside and Admiral Callaghan was killed, as well as Norman Scott, who had won at Cape Esperance. The heavy cruiser *Portland* was being towed to Tulagi with her steering gear disabled. But the Japanese had not bombarded the airfield and two of their destroyers were on the bottom and three more badly hurt, while their battleship *Hiei,* worth all the American losses put together was north of Savo Island without steering control and with her engines damaged. The flyers from Guadalcanal took after her at once with bombs and torpedoes. All day they pounded at her through what was left of her anti-aircraft fire and that of covering destroyers; at twilight her stern was glowing cherry red and she went down.

Yet the American cruiser force in the South Pacific was eliminated, and that night the Japanese cruiser squadron came down the slot for another bombardment to put the airfield out. It was only less severe than the heavy shelling of October, and only broken off because a handful of American torpedo boats—PTs—dashed out, and though they inflicted no damage, made the Japanese commander so apprehensive that he left the area.

As it turned out this was fatal. Not only were there still American planes left on Guadalcanal in spite of the shelling, but *Enterprise* had come pounding up from the south with workmen hammering and welding on her decks. While still incapable of full flight operation, she managed to send half her planes ahead to the island. At dawn they flew searches and found the Japanese cruiser bombardment squadron still within reach of the islands. Three strong strikes were flown; all the Japanese cruisers were heavily hit, and one of them went down. The enemy might have lost more if the Guadalcanal planes had not meanwhile found a much more worthwhile target. The eleven fat Japanese transports, black with troops, covered only by a destroyer ring and a handful of fighters, were plodding down the slot of the islands in full confidence that the American airfield would be out of business because their high command said it would have to be. Our planes went out and exhausted their bombs, came back and were reloaded while the pilots had sandwiches and coffee, then returned to their job. By twilight seven of the transports had gone down, the other four, all afire, were still staggering toward Guadalcanal.

With an almost incredible determination to carry through the plan in spite of the fact that serious cracks in it were already showing, the Japanese came back again that night with one battleship, two heavy cruisers, two light cruisers, and no less than ten of their out-size destroyers, determined to destroy that airfield. There was no secret about their coming, nor about the slenderness of the defensive force, which amounted to exactly two PTs, the rest all out of action. They were on their lonely patrol closing midnight when a voice they had never heard before boomed over the radio with the most dramatic message of the war: "This is Ching Chong Lee. Get out of the way; I'm coming through."

The cavalry was arriving just as the Indians closed in on the wagon train: Halsey had played his last and highest card—a task force built around the new battleships *Washington* and *South Dakota* under Willis Augustus Lee, the famous gunnery expert. With no time for coded messages to the quick-on-the-draw PTs, Lee used his Academy nickname to identify himself and drove ahead. Out ahead of the main bodies, the overwhelmingly numerous Japanese destroyers and light cruisers fired swarms of torpedoes. They sent down three of the four destroyers in the American screen and threw searchlight beams on *South Dakota,* so that an 8-inch shell from the heavy cruisers ripped through her superstructure, although she got one of the enemy destroyers. But out ahead, *Washington* tiptoed among the torpedo wakes, and as men from the sunken destroyer *Walke* hung in the water, crying "Give it to them!" she lashed out with 16-inch shell. They hit the battleship *Kirishima* and hit her again; a long flame came out of her side, she lost her steering gear, the engines would not work, there were only two guns left in action and then none. At the same time the enemy's heavy cruisers turned away, badly hurt.

The battle was over and the campaign was over. The four surviving Japanese transports did reach Guadalcanal while the battleships were fighting, but they discharged only two thousand men, more in shape for hospitalization than for war, and all four were finished by a single American destroyer that came into the lagoon next morning. The transports were irreplacable; so were the lost big transports and the air groups. "After that," said Captain Ohmae, the Japanese Chief of Staff, "I knew we could not win. I did not think we would lose, but I knew we could not win." Although the Japanese destroyers kept running in by night, they were now trying to evacuate men, not bring in reinforcements. Guadalcanal was won.

V

An important factor in the Guadalcanal victory was a wholly new Navy outfit—one created from scratch in the black weeks after Pearl Harbor to meet the special conditions of the Pacific War. To fight thousands of miles from our coasts, we were going to need bases, lots of them, built from nothing on desert islands, carved out of cliffs, slashed from jungles—and often built under fire. This was obviously no job for civilians—yet the Navy did not have the construction specialists for such a mammoth job. The answer was the Sea Bees—the Naval Construction Battalions organized by the Navy's Civil Engineer Corps. Recruited from the tough, highly skilled workers who built America's roads and dams and skyscrapers in peacetime, the Sea Bees went ashore right after the first waves and built shops, roads, landing fields, warehouses, docks, fuel tanks—all the varied buildings required to support the ships and planes of the Navy far from home.

The job was hard and dangerous. They described themselves as soldiers in sailors' uniform, with Marine training, doing civilian work at WPA wages. There were 200,000 of them, and they worked and sometimes died from the South Seas—where they built in weeks the bases for the Guadalcanal campaign—to Okinawa. At Iwo Jima they went ashore with the first waves and one battalion lost one man in four. In the Atlantic the Sea Bees went ashore in Normandy and built the beachheads that supplied the forces ashore.

Much of World War II was an engineer's war—a silent unsung battle against jungles and shifting sands and tearing hurricanes. The Sea Bees fought it for the Navy—victoriously.

★ ★ ★ ★ ★

11

Submarines

Nazi Germany declared war on the United States on December 11, 1941, but it was not until the following February that any real submarine offensive was undertaken against the American coasts. At this date the trans-Atlantic convoy system was already well organized, with American destroyers covering ships as far as the Iceland area and the British picking up from there. The early convoys of troops and supplies reached Britain with comparatively small losses. But as soon as the Germans were able to draw new operation plans and assign submarines to duty, the U-boats began to appear in numbers off the American coast and the rate of losses quickly became appalling.

This was no such diversionary campaign as that of 1918, but a major operation designed to inflict real damage. American coastal traffic was heavy, particularly in oil, since the normal method of bringing crude petroleum from the Texas fields to eastern refineries was by tanker. There was practically nothing to protect this shipping. Admiral Adolphus Andrews, commanding the Eastern Sea Frontier from Maine to Florida, had no Navy planes at all when war came, and only a handful of short-range Army craft. By April 1942, his ships afloat still included only twenty-three vessels of over 90-foot length, none as large as a destroyer, none equipped with radar, and few with depth charges. The German submarines moved in at night and sank vessels silhouetted by bright lights ashore, especially off the coast of Florida, where efforts to enforce a dim-out were resisted as bad for the tourist trade. Attacking this practically non-existent defense were many more and much better submarines than in World War

I. During the early months of 1942 the Germans had more submarines off the American coast alone than they had at sea everywhere during any month of World War I, and they were producing new ones at the rate of twenty a month. In March 1942, twenty-eight ships were sunk off the American east coast, more than half of them tankers, and fuel rationing had to be imposed on the whole Northeast, while the Florida bathers could daily see ships sinking in flames.

No statistics can tell of seamen trying to swim to safety through pools of burning oil; of shipping delayed, halted; the frantic drain on resources when the submarines began to work into the Caribbean and torpedo ships off the great oil depot at Curaçao. But the whole story is basically statistical, and is to be expressed only in the terms of gradual recovery as the means of defense increased and better methods were devised to counter the submarine attack.

1—Coastal convoys. This began by the establishment of mined refuge areas off Delaware Bay, the Chesapeake capes, and Charleston. A twelve-hour daylight run could be made between any two of these points and the submarines did not like to attack by daylight, because they were bothered by increasing numbers of planes and especially blimps. Against blimps they were helpless, because the gas-bags simply hung in the air, out of range of deck guns, calling up surface vessels until the submarine went down, sometimes permanently. As the number of available escort vessels increased, especially valuable ships such as tankers were placed in convoy and the Germans found it difficult to concentrate enough submarines to attack these convoys effectively.

2—Air patrols. One of the main American building efforts was devoted to turning out PBYs, the giant flying boats which could carry both radar and depth charges. They ranged far out to sea. At this date German submariners were almost inordinately worried by airplane attacks, and especially those that came on them without warning as a result of radar pickups. These big patrol planes worried them more; they sank as many German submarines as any other single agency. They took off at dawn, cruised all day and most of the night, with crews eating from well-supplied galleys. Many carried MAD, which located a submarine under water by means of its magnetism; the patrol plane dropped a flare at the point and came back or called on surface craft to help. The efforts of these patrol planes

were presently supplemented by those of VLR (Very Long Range)
land planes, which were able to reach out across one-third of the
Atlantic.

3—Destroyer escorts. Almost as soon as the war began there was
initiated a tremendous construction program of destroyer escorts.
They were about the tonnage of a World War I destroyer, though
with less powerful engines. The early ones were armed with three
3-inch guns and some AA pieces, with depth charges, and on the
forecastle a hedgehog, which threw a salvo of rocket-propelled anti-
submarine bombs. These had the advantage that as they descended
through the water at an angle they did not go off unless the submarine was actually hit, unlike ordinary depth charges that went off
at a predetermined depth with such a violent explosion that for some
time after all sound gear in the neighborhood was disabled. When
a hedgehog struck, the destroyer escort not only knew that it had
made a hit, but exactly where and at what distance it had been obtained. The destroyer escorts were slow in arriving, due principally
to a bottleneck in propulsive machinery. They were slow in speed
too, because they had to be given reliable but far from rapid Diesel
engines. But they were turned out in increasing numbers until there
were more than five hundred, many under the British flag. They proved
ideal convoy escorts.

4—Escort carriers. As early as 1941, the United States took over
a commercial freighter and converted her into an aircraft carrier,
with a flight deck strutted out above her normal hull. This was *Long
Island,* which delivered the first planes to Guadalcanal as soon as
the airstrip there could take them. More than one hundred twenty of
the class known as CVEs, were built, fifty-four for the British. Most
of them started as normal cargo vessel hulls and were then built up
into carriers, since this simplified the design problem. As compared
with regular carriers, they were slow, carried little defensive armament, no armor, and comparatively few planes; in a seaway their
plates wove back and forth, filling the ship with ominous groans and
bangings; they were extremely vulnerable. But they could put aircraft
in the middle of the Atlantic under any conditions. Usually they
worked with a group of four destroyer escorts in a "hunter-killer
group," their radar-equipped planes locating submarines and calling
the surface ships in for the kill if it were not made from the air. From

the moment these groups began to appear, the submarines were in deep trouble.

5—The building yards. Basic to the whole program was the tremendous production of American building yards. The need for more ships had been early foreseen and in 1941 designs were prepared for standard general cargo and tanker types that could be assembled from prefabricated parts made inland. As with the destroyer escorts, the main bar to rapid production was propulsion machinery. The earliest type, the Liberty ships, were a step backward in marine engineering technique, since they were powered by old-style reciprocating engines—which could be rapidly built—and could do only 11 knots. Later they were replaced by the turbine-driven Victory ships that could make 15. But the vital feature was that these ships were turned out by the dozens in every inconsiderable inlet of the Atlantic, the Gulf, the Pacific Coast. By September, 1942, the curve of new construction had already climbed above that of the sinking losses and it never again fell below. In November, 1943, alone ten times as much new merchant tonnage was floated out as was sunk by the submarines.

6—The technicians. During the interval between the two wars there had been intensive development of underwater listening devices, Asdic in England, sonar in the U.S. Both operated by sending out sound impulses that were reflected by the metal hull of a submarine, indicating distance as well as direction. But there were certain drawbacks to sonar: Its range was limited, which meant that the submarine had to be located within a fairly narrow area before the device could be put in operation. It could not be used by a ship traveling much over 15 knots, and the outgoing sound impulses could be picked up by a submarine, which could then take evasive action, especially by hiding itself under a water current of different temperature from those above, and sonar could pierce such a water barrier only with the utmost difficulty. Most sonar attacks were made by two or more ships, one using the gear and coaching the other in for high-speed runs on the submarine.

Radar used electric pulses in air, as sonar used sound pulses in water, measuring their reflection when they bounded back from some unseen obstacle. Germans as well as British and Americans had a form of radar as a highly secret device early in the war, and

German submarines were fitted with radar detectors. But in mid-1942 the Allies developed a completely new form of radar, using ultra-short waves, which did not register on the detectors. German scientists had told their government this was impossible, and it was the middle of 1944 before the Nazis found out how their submarines were being located by airplanes that dived on them without warning from dark or cloud.

This had a special importance, not only because long-range aircraft flying from Britain could cover the whole of the Bay of Biscay, through which the Nazi submarines made their transits to and from port, but also because of the tactical system used by the submarines themselves. As early as late 1941 they had worked out the wolf-pack method, by which one submarine located a convoy and trailed it during the daylight hours, calling on others from the area for a combined night attack. Approaches were made on the surface, where a submarine has its greatest speed. But once the new short-wave radar entered the picture, it became as dangerous to be on the surface at night as by day. But it took time to manufacture and install the new devices, and in March, 1943, the Nazi submarines, driven from the Caribbean and the American coast, achieved a record month in North Atlantic convoy sinkings. Nevertheless, in a single week two of the three leading German submarine aces were killed and a third captured, and in that same March the average sinking of a submarine per cruise had fallen from the twelve thousand tons of May, 1942, to two thousand tons. Radar deserved much of the credit.

Radar was not the only effective anti-submarine device, however. Sono-buoys began to make their appearance about the same time—buoys dropped by a plane in a circle around an area where a submarine was suspected. Their sensitive sound devices—unperceived by the submarine—picked up the noise of the submarine's engines and propellers and broadcast them by automatic radio.

7—The men. As the destroyer escorts and PCs, enlarged versions of the wooden submarine chasers of World War I, came pouring from the yards, there arose a terrific demand for crews. It had been anticipated and it was met—by training stations principally at Great Lakes, Newport, San Diego, and Norfolk. For officers there were schools at many points, chiefly the anti-submarine training command at Miami, where new officers were put through courses on

some of the most ingeniously conceived mechanical devices ever produced, to simulate all the procedures needed in anti-submarine warfare. It was a continuing process; crews containing the required
proportions of specialists' ratings—such as sonar, radar, and torpedo men—were made up while the new ships were building. They
were assembled at some central point such as Norfolk, where the
group barracked together, got acquainted, and underwent shore
training as a unit. After taking over their ship, they went to Bermuda for training at sea in collaboration with other destroyer escorts
and a "tame" submarine, which copied all the maneuvers of the
German craft.

These destroyer escort men were symptomatic of the new Navy
that was growing up after Pearl Harbor. In a typical vessel of this
class there was only one Annapolis graduate, the skipper. The exec
was a chicken farmer from Pennsylvania who had had some experience in PCs, the first lieutenant a small-boat sailor from the Great
Lakes, the gunnery officer a filling-station operator who started in
guns by duck shooting. In a crew of more than two hundred there were
not ten men who had ever seen water in anything much bigger than
a bathtub, and practically everybody was abysmally seasick on the
voyage out to Bermuda.

But they made up a team; and if in April, 1943, the Allies still regarded the submarine emergency as grave, the Germans were coming to the same opinion. That month Admiral Karl Doenitz warned
Hitler that the U-boat campaign would fail unless means could be
found of sinking more Allied ships.

II

Far different was the course of the submarine war in the Pacific.
Hampered though they were by ineffective torpedoes, U.S. submarines struck a few good blows during the retreat from the Philippines and the Malay barrier to new bases set up at Brisbane in
eastern Australia and Fremantle on the west coast. American submarines were cruising the entrance of Tokyo within a month of the
declaration of war. There also ships were sunk; not enough as yet to
cause serious worry to the Japanese, but in a manner and under
terms that gave the American command expanded ideas about what

might be accomplished. The Japanese anti-submarine people proved fairly effective at furnishing protection for convoys and they often drove submarines off, but they were not good at hunting them down. The American program for building submarines, like other construction plans, was speeded up with the outbreak of war, and in 1942 nearly one hundred were building.

These were very big submarines, nearly twice the size of the German boats, and fitted for long cruising. There were not many of them in the beginning, but in spite of the torpedo headache they had sunk eighty-two ships by July, 1942. The over-all Japanese loss for the year reached above 900,000 tons, of which only 268,000 tons was made good by new construction, with something added by seizures in the captured lands. In that July, 1942, the Japanese merchant marine stood at only 100,000 tons over what it had been at the date of Pearl Harbor. The statistical loss looked comparatively small, considering that German submarines in the Atlantic were sending down Allied shipping at the rate of 400,000 to 500,000 tons a month. But the comparative figure was not nearly as important as the fact that the whole Japanese merchant marine, including tankers, amounted to only 6,000,000 tons at the beginning of the war; if they were properly to develop the stolen island Empire, a very great increase in tonnage was needed. In addition, 3,000,000 tons of import shipping annually were necessary to maintain the ordinary civilian economy, to say nothing of the extra demands made by war.

Thanks to the submarines, the necessary increase had not been attained by July, 1942, and in August two new factors entered. The campaign in the Solomons made very greatly increased demands for shipping fuel, troops, and supplies of all kinds. At the same time American submarines began to acquire SJ radar. The radar previously carried was useful only for warning of the approach of aircraft; SJ enabled a submarine to spot a surface ship in the dark and make an approach on it from six or seven miles away without being detected by any instrument the Japanese had.

Some sixty-seven per cent of all attacks were made by night on the surface with the aid of the device, and the curve of sinkings began to rise sharply. Then the American torpedoes were improved and the curve moved up again. Between July and December, 1942, 203,000 tons of shipping were sunk within the home waters of the Empire (not

counting sinkings elsewhere), and most of this represented ships
with full loads of oil or goods from the Indies. In December, 1942,
the Japanese merchant and tanker tonnage afloat was less than it had
been at the beginning of the war, and the whole economy was trem-
bling gently, for not only were our submarines sinking cargoes of
oil, but also the coal and ore carriers that enabled new ships to be
built. By May, 1943, Japanese cargo tonnage afloat was nearly
1,000,000 tons below the pre-war figure. Japan had won her southern resources area and enclosed it in a defensive wall which for the
time being defied penetration, but she could not collect.

III

There were several reasons why the curve of Japanese losses in the
Pacific continued to go up, while the graph of Allied losses in the
Atlantic wavered and hesitantly went down. One was technical; in
the Atlantic the anti-submarine ships and planes had radar and
the submarines did not, while in the Pacific the situation was exactly
reversed. One was geographical; the Atlantic is an open ocean in
which convoys can follow any one of a number of routes, and one
of the main difficulties experienced by the Germans was in finding
the ships to attack. Quite the contrary in the Pacific, which on the
surface is so much larger; the routes from the supply areas in Malaya,
Borneo, Sumatra, and Java to Japan are relatively narrow and are
constricted still more by reefs and chains of shoals that do not even
show up on the ordinary map. An American submarine cruising
north of Formosa or off the east coast of Japan, where all the deep-
water harbors lie, could be reasonably certain that something she
wanted would sooner or later turn up. Also many of these passages
could be mined by our submarines, which thereupon hung around
to kill minesweepers or any ships that avoided their fields.

Another factor lay in training and its results. The Japanese had
good sonar gear, and as the menace of American submarines was
brought home to them, they speedily turned out large numbers of
small anti-submarine craft, so that a Japanese convoy was at least
numerically as well covered as those of the Allies in the Atlantic.
But Japan had no such elaborate training system as the British and
American setup. Perhaps they had underestimated the threat of a

submarine service that did not rank high statistically and that had accomplished comparatively little in the early months of the war. As a result there was a certain carelessness, a lack of drive, in the Japanese anti-submarine service. They located submarines, drove them down and kept them under water for three or four hours, dropping depth charges that put out electric light bulbs, jarred loose paint, smashed crockery, and gave the submariners below a very rough time —but they did not destroy submarines. In a famous action in the Atlantic the escort carrier *Card* and her attendant destroyer escorts kept after a German submarine throughout a wild gale for nearly forty-eight hours, until it was forced to surface for lack of air and battery charges. The Japanese never did anything like this. The basic fact emerges from statistics: While the Allies sank forty-one German submarines during the single month of May, 1943, and more than seven hundred all told, the Japanese succeeded in getting rid of only sixty-five American submarines during the entire war.

Yet the central and operative factor in the success of the American submarines was the men in them. In other navies, submarine duty was an assignment; the American service was entirely voluntary. No one got into it unless he wanted to, and even then he had to pass the stiffest of physical and mental examinations and go through a course of extremely rigid training. Every man, even the cooks, had to learn how to operate every piece of equipment aboard. It was a young man's service; at thirty-five a submariner was usually transferred to other duty. It was a service in which the most elaborate care was taken of the physical well-being of the crew. No ships ate so well as the submarines. When they came back from a patrol, the men were given two weeks leave in the finest hotel available. They grew beards, since fresh water for shaving is a scarce article aboard a submarine; they laughed and played uproarious pranks. Under the compressed conditions of their life, in a business where the safety of all depended upon the co-operation of all, it was impossible to observe the normal distinctions of rank, nor did the submariners try. "We're having an admiral's inspection tomorrow," one skipper was heard saying to his crew. "I'm not worried about the ship, but for Pete's sake, don't call me 'Jack' while he's aboard." And they had fantastic adventures.

The first cruise of *Guardfish* under Lieutenant-Commander T. V.

Klakring could be called typical. She left Pearl Harbor in August, 1942, for the coast of Japan. On August 19 off that coast she sighted an auxiliary and an escorting destroyer. She fired three torpedoes and heard the explosions, but they were faulty torpedoes, the explosions were premature, and the auxiliary turned away while the escort dropped two depth charges and then joined her. On August 22, three freighters were sighted, but they were too far away for an approach; that night Klakring surfaced and sank a trawler by gunfire. On the 23rd the submarine was close aboard the shore of Honshu Island; she ran in and her crew rather incredibly watched a horse-race ashore and took photos to prove it. Next morning a medium freighter came out of Kinkasan harbor: *Guardfish* hit her with two out of three torpedoes and down she went. A patrol boat came out and the submarine headed north after dodging it. On the 25th Klakring sighted another freighter and ran a submerged daylight attack. One torpedo hit the ship, but it was a dud, a second porpoised without exploding, and a third was premature. Klakring was about to surface for a gunfire attack when radar reported four plane contacts. He took *Guardfish* down to one hundred twenty feet and dodged. Bombs could be heard going off above, but there was no damage and after a while the planes went away.

At this point the weather turned to heavy rolling seas under thick fog. The boat, not yet having the new surface radar, made no contacts at all until September 2, when a freighter was sighted eight miles off amid the swells. Klakring made an approach on her and fired three torpedoes, of which two were observed to hit. The ship did not appear to be going down satisfactorily, so she was given a fourth torpedo, whereupon she broke in two. Two days later three freighters were sighted, moving in company; Klakring fired one from two and one-half miles and got a hit that sent the ship into the offshore haze, surrounded by smoke. He considered that these ships might be the advance guard of a convoy, and so it proved. That afternoon two large ore carriers showed up on which Klakring ran a submerged approach till he got within five hundred yards, where within a matter of minutes he hit one with a single torpedo and the other with two, causing both to fold up like accordions. Two other ships just coming out of Minato Bay turned back on seeing what had happened to the ore carriers, and one of them anchored. Klakring maneuvered his submarine around a series of rocks and shoals at the entrance, and finally fired a torpedo from the unheard-of distance of three and one-half miles. It hit aft and the ship went down in the shallows, with one hundred feet of her bow sticking straight up out of the water. While this was going on another freighter was seen coming up from the south. Klakring closed to one thousand yard range and fired two; at least one hit with an explosion that shook the submarine, but the ship did not seem to be going down so she was given another torpedo to hurry up the process. This proved a dud, but the freighter turned over and sank anyway.

It was now near evening, and under the descending sun patrol boats began to swarm around the audacious submarine. *Guardfish* went down to hide on the bottom, hearing the grind of propellers starting and stopping above her until after ten o'clock at night. Then, there being no further surface noises, Klakring surfaced into the starless dark and, cranking up full speed, ran a course to take his boat clear of the area. It was not sufficient; dawn showed more patrol boats on the horizon and the submarine had to be taken down for another sit on the bottom. Depth charges exploded around her, some at a distance, some nearer; and this was a process repeated during the whole of the next two days, while nineteen sound contacts were received from patrol boats. *Guardfish* slipped them all, and was making north with just two torpedoes left when she spied a fine freighter and fired both from five hundred yards. Both failed, and there was nothing to do but head back for the barn.

Not all submarines were as aggressively conducted as *Guardfish;* not all went to areas where they were as lucky in finding targets; not all captains were as clever in evasive maneuver as Klakring; but the adventures of this submarine give a fairly clear picture of submarine operations in the first two years of the war.

★　　★　　★　　★　　★

12

The Navy on the Attack

IN THE LAST ACT of the Guadalcanal campaign the Japanese were principally concerned with rescuing as many of their troops as possible from the island and setting up air bases farther north in the Solomons to seal off and neutralize the airfield they had failed to capture. The evacuation was carried out by heavy squadrons of destroyers at night. On November 30, 1942, nine of these ships entered the lagoon and Admiral Carlton Wright took four heavy cruisers, one light cruiser, and six destroyers in to hunt them. His tactics were faulty; he strung his ships out in a long close line, with the destroyers ahead, and refused to allow the latter to fire torpedoes until the guns opened. The Japanese were limited by no such restrictions; they let loose a swarm of their very fine heavy torpedoes, which sank one American heavy cruiser, blew the bows off two more, and badly holed a third, at a cost of only one destroyer.

But this notable Japanese success did not affect the general strategic pattern. As of February 3, 1943, when Guadalcanal was officially declared secure, the naval air forces of both sides had been so ground down that the United States painfully lacked carrier decks, though it had plenty of pilots, and the Japanese lacked pilots and planes for the carriers they had. The course of the war had demonstrated that no extensive overseas operations could be undertaken without air cover. And the campaign in Africa and Europe was so demanding in transports and landing craft that there was an American shortage of this equipment, too.

It was important to keep pressure on the Japanese; to attack them before they could muster for a stroke. The next move after Guadalcanal should be up the slot of the Solomons against the Japanese seal-off air base at Munda on New Georgia Island, thence toward their combined naval and air base at the southern tip of Bougainville, and then against Rabaul, which had become a key center of the Japanese operations in the South Pacific. This coincided with the strategy of General MacArthur's command, which was attacking around and across the tip of eastern New Guinea on the long road back to the Philippines. The ultimate objective was the elimination of Rabaul as an effective base.

The physical components of the new campaign were utterly different from those of the hard struggle for Guadalcanal. There were fresh Marine troops available and a new Army division. The airfield on the island now held so many planes that they dominated all operations by daylight to the limit of their range. The new American battleships had started to arrive; there were enough of them to say loud angry words to the whole Japanese Fleet if it made bold to venture through the air screen to attempt a major action. The new light cruisers were moving in; four of them under Admiral A. S. Merrill formed the famous "Hollywood Squadron," which worked alternately with Admiral "Pug" Ainsworth's three older, light cruisers. The new destroyers were coming; they furnished screens for the cruisers and ran independent missions.

The Japanese had developed a new technique of attacking ships with land-based planes, the leading aircraft dropping lines of flares to silhouette our vessels while low-skimming torpedo planes came in behind to pick them off. In this way the enemy knocked out the cruiser *Chicago* off Rennell Island in January. For the rest their light surface forces, cruisers and destroyers operated exclusively at night out of the Shortlands, which were at the very limit of American air range from Guadalcanal. The Japanese command used these ships for reinforcement, supply, surprise attacks, and evacuation; and with their high speed and superior torpedoes they had the advantage in night actions.

Yet the first brush went the American way, when three of Merrill's "Hollywood" cruisers with attendant destroyers rushed in on the night of March 8 to bombard the Japanese supply base at Vila on the shore of Kula Gulf opposite New Georgia. They caught two big Japanese destroyers at the bottom of the Gulf and sank both in a

matter of minutes; then shelled the base so effectively that they left
nearly five thousand enemy dead and wiped out huge stores of supplies.

The period from March to July was mainly one of air raids and
counter air raids: In the early days of the latter month an American
Army division was set ashore on New Georgia and began working
through the jungle toward Munda airfield. It was much tougher going
than Guadalcanal; the Japanese had foreseen such a thrust and had
strewn the whole area around Munda with pillboxes dug into the
jungle, which naval gunfire could not reach. Meanwhile they kept
reinforcing the area by the old "Tokyo Express" method—running
destroyer-loads of troops and supplies through Kula Gulf at night.

Our Navy essayed to cut off this traffic and there were clashes. The
first started at midnight on July 5; the Japanese had nine heavy destroyers in there when Ainsworth's three cruisers and four destroyers
entered the mouth of the gulf. There was a confused, milling battle in
pitch darkness; the cruiser *Helena,* veteran of Guadalcanal and many
other fights, took three torpedoes and went down, while one of the
Japanese destroyers was sunk by gunfire and another ran aground. The
enemy tried to give her fighter cover, but planes came out from
Guadalcanal, shot all the fighters down, and bombed the destroyer
into a wreck.

The New Zealand cruiser *Leander* was sent up to replace *Helena*
and less than a week later Ainsworth went in against a new Tokyo
Express, this time with ten destroyers accompanying his cruisers. The
Japanese force that night was one light cruiser and nine destroyers.
There was another muddled, flashing battle in the dark, with the
Japanese launching shoals of torpedoes, the Americans rapping out
with gunfire. We lost the destroyer *Gwin* and all three American
cruisers were knocked temporarily out of the campaign by torpedo
hits. The Japanese cruiser *Jintsu* was caught in a gunfire concentration and went down with all hands. There was a fierce air battle as
the enemy tried to attack the damaged cruisers during their retirement; there were no bomb hits and the enemy lost a number of
planes.

This second Kula Gulf was not much better than a drawn battle,
though with the new destroyers coming out we could afford the
losses better than the Japanese. But it was evident that something
more than poor torpedoes was involved when they got so many hits

and our forces practically none. There was a good deal of discussion about this in the flag bar at Purvis Bay on Tulagi, recently built and with its own zoo, consisting mainly of parrots. The destroyer men claimed they were too closely tied to the cruisers, and begged to operate on their own. The main participants in the discussion were the men of Merrill's squadron, now running almost nightly missions up the slot, and the Admiral paid attention.

In the meanwhile a large number of survivors from *Helena* were reported on Kolombangara Island, still mostly in Japanese hands. To pick them up, the Tokyo Express was tried in reverse, eleven American destroyers and two destroyer-transports moving in at night. It was a bold move, for the Japanese might come down with strong forces. In fact they did two nights later, sending in a heavy cruiser squadron in the hope of catching Merrill's lights. They missed. An American night-flying plane spotted them and they were bombed in the morning, losing two destroyers.

The Japanese were still reinforcing the islands they held and evacuating those that had gone American, using motor barges that could hide under the coasts during the day. On the night of August 6, however, they sent in a division of four destroyers. The Solomons command got word of it and rushed into Vella Gulf six destroyers under Commander Frederick Moosbrugger. He formed in two divisions, the first peeling off to the right as the Japanese approach was detected on radar, firing salvos of torpedoes, the second swinging in the other direction to engage with guns. There was a wait that seemed endless, then crash, crash, crash, explosions leaped from the Japanese line with such violence that men on an island twenty-eight miles away thought a long-dead volcano was in eruption. Three Japanese destroyers were involved in that holocaust, and as men on the American ships shouted and pounded each other on the backs, the second division finished them off. The American destroyers had caught up at last.

Now action ashore was turning more and more against the Japanese and their operational emphasis shifted to troop evacuation. The result was a long series of minor actions, involving American destroyers and PTs against Japanese barges, night-flying planes, and destroyers, which after the Battle of Vella Gulf usually avoided a fight for the sound reason that the enemy high command could not risk their loss. All through August and September these obscure combats went on and the men of the American destroyer squadrons hardly slept except when their ships were in base for repairs. On the night of October 6 came the next real battle, off Vella Lavella, when the Japanese sent in nine destroyers to evacuate troops ashore. Air scouts reported the coming movement; all but three of the American destroyers belonging to the Solomons command were on convoy duty, but Captain Frank Walker was sent in with those three, another three to follow as soon as they made the turnaround at Purvis Bay.

The battle was one of those wildly irrational Solomons night actions of which it is impossible to make any sense, even with charts of the ships' tracks. Our destroyer *Chevalier* was hit by a torpedo and went down before dawn; another destroyer had her whole bow blown off, and the third was damaged. But one of the Japanese was blown up, and though they got most of their troops off the island they were far from happy either about that night's work or the total result of the Central Solomons fighting. They had lost seventeen ships there against six American; they had lost all the islands, and American air bases were moved two hundred fifty miles nearer Rabaul.

II

Meanwhile there was action far in the north, where growing American power made it possible to consider the reconquest of the outer Aleutian Islands. All through the fall and winter of 1942 American air bases had been pushed nearer Attu and Kiska, and bombing raids took a considerable toll of Japanese vessels trying to run in reinforcements and equipment to build airstrips of their own. Early in 1943 the Japanese high command decided to put an end to this and dispatched a major supply convoy, covered by two heavy cruisers, two light cruisers, and eight destroyers. On March 26 this force encountered the heavy cruiser *Salt Lake City,* the light cruiser *Richmond,* and four destroyers off the Komandorskie Islands under Admiral Charles H. McMorris. This turned out to be one of the most remarkable battles of the war. It was a gray day with a low overcast and so cold that fuel oil turned to slush ice when the water struck it. The Japanese force, exactly double the American, was between McMorris and his bases when the fight began. The case looked pretty hopeless, but the Admiral turned away and carried the enemy into a high-speed gunnery duel at ranges between eight and twelve miles.

Salt Lake was the oldest cruiser of her class in the American Navy, but her gunners could shoot, and the first exchange landed hard on the Japanese flagship, ruining her communications system. This made the enemy cautious; they did not try too hard to close range, and when their light forces tried end runs around the line, they were driven off by *Richmond*. *Salt Lake* took a plunging hit that went through her side below the waterline, but in revenge set the second Japanese heavy smoking with another salvo. Both turned briefly, but came back. Now they hit the American cruiser badly, causing salt water to get into her fuel lines. As the destroyers made smoke for her, she gradually ground to a full stop. *Richmond* closed in to take the crew off the battered ship, but her guns kept firing through the smoke and hit the Japanese flagship again, hard, while the destroyers launched a desperate torpedo attack.

The Japanese turned away and kept right on going as *Salt Lake* got her engines working again and moved back toward Dutch Harbor. The little force had fought one of the most effective actions of the war, for the Japanese decided against any further attempt to reinforce the Aleutians or to build airstrips there. Attu was taken by an American Army task force after hard fighting in May, 1943. Kiska, under constantly growing bomber pressure, was evacuated by Japanese destroyers after the enemy had lost seven of the thirteen submarines that they sent to do this job.

During the following month the Japanese suffered another loss. Admiral Yamamoto, probably their best naval brain, decided to pay a personal visit to the Solomons. American cryptographers broke the message announcing his coming and when his plane reached the airfield, long-range fighters were already orbiting over it. They shot him down.

III

In the islands, the action off Vella Lavella marked the end of a phase. This was not immediately apparent, since the new campaign opened as though a continuation of the old, both as to ends and methods. It was another island jump—to Empress Augusta Bay on the west coast of Bougainville, the landing force a new Marine division, the cover furnished by Merrill's "Hollywood" cruisers and the eight destroyers of Captain Arleigh Burke's famous "Little Beaver Squadron," Desron 23. The landing was made on November 1, and the Marines began working inland against savage but unco-ordinated resistance, which was again according to pattern.

But there were elements in the situation unlike those of any previous campaign. One of them was that General MacArthur's forces had rounded the eastern tip of New Guinea to Lae and Salamaua on the north shore and were now in a position to work westward along the north shore toward the Philippines unless the Japanese contained them by air or surface action from Rabaul. Another was that Rabaul had lately received a great reinforcement of planes; and the third was that it was obvious to the Japanese high command that if the Americans made good their hold on Empress Augusta Bay they would set up an airstrip from which fighters could easily cover steady bombing attacks on Rabaul. At the same time the great Japanese air-naval base in the Shortlands would be completely neutralized, together with many thousands of troops.

This would alter the whole strategic situation and the Japanese reacted with violence, sending in nearly two hundred aircraft, practically all the planes of their recovering naval air force. A whole squadron of seven heavy cruisers was ordered down from Truk to Rabaul while another squadron already at that base was sent out at once to repeat the Savo Island strike against the American invaders of Bougainville. This Japanese force contained two heavy cruisers, two light cruisers, and eight destroyers and was sensibly superior to Merrill's force defending the landing.

But the invaders of Bougainville were not the unready squadron of Savo Island. Merrill steamed out to meet the enemy and shortly after midnight had them on his radar screens, coming down in three groups. His own fleet was in the classic line formation, with four destroyers ahead and four astern; at contact, he released his van destroyers to strike the enemy flank with a torpedo attack, swung his four light cruisers sharp around together and opened fire. The Japanese turned to parallel him, but their star shells were nowhere near as good as the American radar, two of their destroyers came into collision trying to dodge Burke's torpedoes, and one of their light cruisers came burning to a stop, smothered by gunfire. Merrill released his second division of destroyers for another torpedo attack and did a second simultaneous turn, cloaking it in smoke. One of the American destroyers had her stern blown off by a torpedo and another took a single gunfire hit; but when Merrill's ships made another turn together the Japanese fleet was in complete confusion, the light cruiser fatally hit, a destroyer going down, two more in bad shape and the heavy cruisers both hit. Their admiral decided to pull out, reporting that he had engaged at least seven heavy cruisers.

It was one of the best fought actions of the war, but the story was not yet over. At daybreak the Japanese sent over one hundred bombers from Rabaul to clean up on Merrill's squadron. He picked up their advance snooper on radar and asked for fighter cover, but it arrived too late, after Japanese planes were already attacking the formation. Two of the destroyers had peeled off to tow the cripples home, but Merrill kept his remaining ships in tight turns, a beautiful piece of maneuvering, and replied to the attack with one of the most furious and accurate anti-aircraft barrages yet seen in the Pacific. The formation took only one hit, on the catapult of a cruiser, and at least thirty Japanese planes were shot down, to which were added eight more when the American fighters arrived. Merrill's men had been fighting steadily for thirty-six hours.

There remained the Japanese heavy cruiser squadron now assembled at Rabaul, clearly bent on wiping out the Empress Augusta Bay beachhead, and strong enough to do it. At this point another of the new elements revealed itself in the U.S. carrier *Saratoga* and the brand new, light carrier *Princeton,* hurrying up from the south and flying off every plane on their decks while the field at Guadalcanal furnished them fighter cover. It was a risky business, for the Japanese at Rabaul had far more planes than the two carriers put in the air; but it was one of the most successful strikes ever made. The Japanese pilots, no longer as good as those at Midway, waited to catch the Americans as they split into small attack groups, but they never split, charging right through a terrific curtain of anti-aircraft fire in one continuous wave, under orders to cripple ships rather than to kill. One Japanese cruiser took a bomb down her stack which exploded in her engine-room and put her out of business for five months; another had two torpedo hits; a third suffered bad bomb damage; three near-misses left waterline holes in still another; and two of the light cruisers were hit, one by a torpedo. Only seven American planes were lost.

This ended any Japanese hope of knocking out the Bougainville beachhead by surface action, but the strong concentration of enemy planes at Rabaul remained. On November 11, *Saratoga* and *Princeton* were sent back to see about it, while three new carriers, *Essex, Bunker Hill,* and *Independence,* came down from the Central Pacific to strike in from the opposite direction. The attacks were successive rather than simultaneous, and the damage to shipping was not heavy: three Japanese destroyers and two cruisers hurt badly enough to go back to dock, and one destroyer sunk. But the real story was in the air. Japanese search planes trailed the American strikes back to the three new carriers, and about noon Rabaul flew off over one hundred eight planes. Radar gave good warning; the fighters were all up and Marine planes from the Solomons came out as the Japanese arrived. There was a spectacular air-sea battle. At the end of it not a single American ship had been hit, while the Rabaul air command had lost fifty per cent of its fighters and nearly ninety per cent of the carefully rebuilt bomber force.

This marked the real beginning of the new phase. It showed that American carriers could venture within range of land-based air strength and complete their missions—provided there were enough carriers.

The campaign had a pendant. There was a Japanese airfield at Buka, at the northern end of Bougainville, which had been inoperative for some time. The enemy decided to build it up against the Bougainville position, and on the night of November 24 rushed in a Tokyo Express—five big destroyers, three of them carrying aviation personnel. The move was spotted; against them went Arleigh "31-knot" Burke, with five destroyers of the "Little Beaver Squadron." A little after one o'clock in the morning contact was made off Cape St. George. Burke's own division of three ships fired torpedoes into the dark and swung right to avoid any counterattack, while the other two destroyers moved in. Just as the two leading Japanese took torpedoes Burke picked up the rest on radar. They ran, but not fast enough; all of them were hit by gunfire, one so heavily that she was gradually cut down and sank in a pool of flaming oil. "An almost perfect action," said the Navy evaluators, and indeed it was, for not an American ship was hit or a man lost; but when Burke's men were cheered to their anchorage as they returned to base, all they said was: "One of the bastards got away."

IV

The importance of the carrier strikes on Rabaul lay not alone in the fact that they seriously cut down the slowly rebuilding Japanese naval air service, but also in that they provided a rehearsal for the major strategic project of breaking through the Central Pacific. The Japanese theory was that from their network of airfields and bases in the Marshalls, Gilberts, Carolines, and Marianas—"unsinkables carriers" —they could at least interdict sea traffic in all areas leading up to the home islands and protect the routes to the resources of the East Indies. To this there was now opposed an American strategy that a sufficient number of carriers could overwhelm local land-based planes at any point before the arrival of reinforcements. Under cover of these attacking carriers it should be possible to seize islands or atolls in the Japanese network, put airstrips on them, and convert them into naval bases by the use of the new and very efficient mobile auxiliaries.

The Japanese fleet would be forced to come out and fight in defense of its forward island bases or see them lost one by one; and the planners at Washington and Pearl Harbor believed they were now in a position to defy the Japanese fleet.

No one yet knew how badly the enemy naval air service had been cut to pieces, but Admiral Nimitz now had at his disposal five new fast battleships besides ten of the older ones, and the Japanese gunnery line caused him no concern. He also had ten carriers, five of them the new big vessels of the *Essex* class, eight escort carriers, eight heavy cruisers, six light cruisers, and an adequate allotment of destroyers. That is, while the hard fighting up the slot of the Solomons had been going on, the U.S. had performed the astounding feat of building and manning an entire new Navy. Fifty per cent of the men of that Navy had never been to sea before; seventy-five per cent of the officers were reserves, but by the fall of 1943 they had been under an intensive course of training for months, as had the Marines and soldiers who were to make the attacks on the beaches. The whole armada was commanded by Admiral Spruance.

The big push began in the Gilberts, with simultaneous assaults on Makin and Tarawa on November 20. Battleships and cruisers furnished preliminary bombardment, carriers air cover, while troops poured ashore in the new landing craft, now used for the first time in the Pacific. Makin was an Army job; poorly defended, it was comparatively easy. On Tarawa the Japanese were thoroughly dug into underground pillboxes with interlocking fields of fire, every one of which had to be taken by individual infantry attack. The fighting was desperate and the casualties heavy before the Marines beat the resistance down. One result was to emphasize the importance of even longer and heavier pre-invasion bombardment.

At sea the Japanese reaction was too little and too late. They started a light-cruiser squadron with troops for Tarawa, but the island fell before they got there. They tried extensively the method used in the Solomons, dropping flares around a fleet at night and then coming in with land-based torpedo planes. But the American night air patrols had so improved that this did not succeed very well either and the only American ship lost was an escort carrier torpedoed by a submarine.

The next step of our advance clearly had to be the Marshalls. The Japanese had been in possession of this group since World War 1, and had four major bases on the eastern islands of the chain, all heavily defended and equipped with airfields. Nimitz boldly decided to by-pass them all and strike for Kwajalein. This was at the very heart of the Marshalls spider web, where the Japanese had a field that in its current state would house fighters but not bombers, and where the circle of the atoll was big enough to house a navy. Nimitz believed that planes from the newly-captured field at Tarawa could keep the Japanese Marshalls bases immobilized for long enough to insure the capture of Kwajalein. After this the combination of ship-borne and land-based planes would hold them down, and nothing but a major attack by a Japanese fleet at least as strong as the American could interfere.

The interlock of bases with sea and air forces was new to naval strategy; and equally novel in tactics was Admiral R. K. Turner's insistence that at least three times the amount of bombardment be provided as had been at Tarawa. New also was the organization of the fast carriers into task groups.

The last had been tried in a rather tentative way at Rabaul and in the Gilberts. Now it became the standard arrangement for a fleet, replacing the old line of battleships. These task groups usually consisted of two big carriers and one of the light type, with at least one fast battleship attached because of the tremendous anti-aircraft fire these vessels could put out; then two or three cruisers and a ring of destroyers. The other ships formed a ring around the carriers when air attack was imminent, and all maneuvered together on the tick of a watch. It took the utmost skill in ship-handling at the high speeds involved, but the men of the new Navy had now learned that skill. The important fact was that the striking force of the fleet was now concentrated around the carriers.

This was the organization when the major operation against Kwajalein began on January 29, 1944. For over a month land-based planes from Tarawa and other new strips in the Gilberts had been hammering at the Japanese Marshalls' bases and doing plenty of damage, but the enemy still had one hundred fifty operative planes on the day the carriers moved in. On January 31 each task group took one island as a target; when the landing began there was not a Japanese plane operative in the Marshalls. The American forces had achieved not mere dominance of the air, but utter control. Equally dramatic, the naval bombardment came to be known as "the Spruance haircut." It practically obliterated everything above ground on the main islands of Roi and Namur, and when some sort of ammunition dump was hit, a spotting aviator from one of the battleships saw a whole palm tree go past him at three thousand feet, moving up. The American invaders also had a new weapon for close-in support—shallow-draft landing craft converted to gunboats by the installation of 20- and 40-mm. guns and projectors for a screen of 4.5-inch rockets.

This does not mean that the landings were easy or that there was no fighting. A number of heavy pillboxes survived the bombardment; the Japanese emerged from tunnels and drains to set up machine-guns in shell holes, and as usual resisted till the last man was killed. But Kwajalein was a high point in the Pacific attack; the Japanese casualties were more than eight thousand to some two thousand of ours, and the forces moving across the Central Pacific had a new base.

Preparations were immediately made for the seizure of yet another in Eniwetok atoll, the most northeasterly of the Marshalls. On February 17, a fleet of the older battleships and heavy cruisers conducted the transports through the passes into the lagoon, while escort carriers flew air strikes and the Marines landed. The fighting ashore was severe but on the part of the Japanese disorganized. But even though resistance was mostly confined to individuals and small squads it nevertheless took six days to secure the entire atoll system.

The fast battleships and carriers were kept out of this operation not only because it was believed (correctly) that Eniwetok was less strongly held than Kwajalein, but also because it was only six hundred sixty-nine miles from Truk in the Carolines and a little more than one thousand miles from Saipan, both major Japanese bases. Four-engined flying boats from Saipan had, indeed, bombed Kwajalein sporadically and the Truk base was within easy range of land-based heavy bombers. If the Eniwetok operation were not to meet strong opposition from the air, it was essential that Truk be at least temporarily neutralized. But a neutralization attack on Truk was no light enterprise. The place was the Japanese Pearl Harbor, a mystery throughout a generation during which no white man had been allowed to visit it, the main base of the enemy fleet for its advance southward, and supposed to be of immense strength and awe-inspiring fighter cover.

It was therefore with something like nervousness that American naval men all the way back to Washington regarded the attack on this formidable stronghold. A ring of submarines was disposed around the atoll; Spruance took the two newest and fastest battleships with three carrier groups, swung wide north of Eniwetok to deceive Japanese search planes as to his destination, and descended on Truk on the morning of February 17, catching the Japanese by surprise. The first strike consisted of fighters only, to clear out air opposition; they shot down more than thirty of the planes that came up to intercept and destroyed forty more on the ground. Then came the bombers and torpedo planes, so staged from the carriers as to give a continuous flow, thirty strikes in all. That night twelve planes of a new unit went in, bombers equipped for low-level attack on radar, and next morning there was another general attack, while the battleships circled the atoll to pick up any vessels trying to escape.

Spruance and the flyers were disappointed at not catching at least part of the Japanese fleet in Truk, but they quite ruined the place and exorcised the ghost of its threat to our advance. One Japanese light cruiser was sunk by a submarine, another and two destroyers by the battleships, while in the Truk lagoon the planes took two more destroyers, three auxiliary cruisers, two submarine tenders, a plane ferry and twenty-four merchantmen, five of them tankers, for a total loss to the Japanese carrying capacity greater than that suffered in any other month of the war. There were three hundred sixty-five planes at Truk on the morning of the attack; less than one hundred remained operational at its end, and the only return blow the enemy got in was on the evening of the first day, when a stream of torpedo planes succeeded in getting one non-crippling hit on a carrier.

Moreover, the Truk attack struck a deadly blow at Japanese morale and planning. When the American assaults on the Gilberts and Marshalls began, the enemy high command decision was that these outlying islands of Empire should be used to hold down the American forces as long as possible while strength, especially naval air strength, was built up in the rear. But Truk was part of the Japanese inner perimeter, the indispensable defense line running through the Bonins and Marianas to Palau. It was also the staging point for ships and supplies bound down to Rabaul, the only point from which effective counterattack could be delivered against the MacArthur forces, now leapfrogging along the northern coast of New Guinea. After the strike on Truk, Rabaul became almost a ghost base, whose many thousands of soldiers devoted themselves chiefly to gardening.

V

When Admiral Koga, now commanding the main Japanese fleet, decided to move permanently from Truk, he retired to Tawitawi anchorage, south of the Philippines. There were two reasons for this. The shortage of fuel oil in the home islands had become so painful that it was desirable to keep heavy ships, the chief oil eaters, near the source of supply in North Borneo. At the same time the advance of the MacArthur forces along the northern coast of New Guinea was fast becoming very menacing indeed. In January, 1944, the American forces were through the barrier of the Bismarck Islands and had established themselves well down the coast; in February, the Admiralty

Islands were taken and a new American naval and air base was set up at Manus. This advance was covered by a new Naval unit, the 7th Fleet, composed of cruisers, destroyers, patrol planes, and escort carriers, which supported landings along the coast, in each case not so much attacking defended positions as gaining an area from which an airfield could be pinched out or a new one built. With each new advance the range of MacArthur's 5th Air Force bombers was extended and their fighter cover had now grown so strong that the Japanese could do little against them aloft.

At the end of March, while the new bases at Eniwetok and Kwajalein were being organized, Admiral Spruance brought his fleet down from the Central Pacific with Admiral Marc Mitscher's carriers of Task Force 58 and delivered a destructive raid on the Japanese base at Palau. Then he turned eastward and furnished air and gunnery cover for a triple landing of MacArthur's troops, half way along the New Guinea coast. This gave Koga pause to think, and the conclusion he drew was that the Americans were uniting the South and Central Pacific forces to strike toward Palau, and ultimately Mindanao, the heart of the Japanese Southern Empire, the prize for which the nation had gone to war.

It was not to be borne. He now had nine carriers with their decks full of planes and the pilots well trained at least by Japanese war-time standards; and he prepared a plan for a massive attack by his whole battle fleet against the American forces as they moved west—a greater Savo Island. In the meanwhile, he threw out a scouting line of six submarines northward from New Guinea to give him warning of the American approach. Koga had learned that he could no longer trust his search planes; they got shot down before they could report.

At this point there entered the picture one of those small factors that occasionally control major events. The American destroyer escort *England* with two others of her class had been sent to hunt a submarine supposed to be running supplies between Truk and Bougainville. They found it and *England* sank it; and the course they took afterward carried them into Koga's scouting line. One of the submarines in that line had already been knocked off without trace by a long-range search plane. *England* and her consorts struck the second member of the line, and following it down, in six days rather incredibly sank all the rest.

Added to the other evidence in hand, this convinced Koga. An American fleet so strong that his scouts did not even have a chance to report it must be operating along the New Guinea shore, and there was rather vague news of a landing on Biak Island. He called in practically all the land-based air strength from the Carolines and Marianas, even planes down from Formosa. It was the last thing he did; he was killed in a lost plane, but this made little difference, as his successor, Admiral Toyoda, went ahead with previous plans for a counterstroke. Then on June 11, 1944, came word that Spruance with the fast battleships and Mitscher's carriers had struck Saipan with their full force.

Behind them was coming a vast fleet of transports, covered by escort carriers and the older battleships. There were two days of carrier strikes on the island, followed by bombardment from the fast battleships, while two of the fast carrier groups peeled off to the north to catch Japanese air reinforcements coming down through the Bonins from the home islands, an operation in which they were outstandingly successful. In a gale, with seas so wild that there was doubt whether planes could get off the decks, an air battle was fought over the fields of Iwo Jima and Chichi Jima, and the Japanese lost heavily, both in the sky and on the ground. The two task groups turned back, reaching Saipan just as the landings were in progress.

The island had been subjected to an even heavier bombardment than Kwajalein, but here it was impossible to administer the Spruance "haircut," since the place is made up of volcanic rock, pushing toward a high mountain backbone, the whole pocked with caves and rough ravines. The Japanese had taken full advantage of the ground; they had thirty-two thousand troops in there, with tanks and artillery of all kinds among the caves. The landings were strongly opposed, the fighting heavy. All day and all night the old battleships and destroyers were firing support on call from the shore, while Spruance with the fast forces hovered out toward the west and south, placing his fleet between the growing American beachhead and the expected reaction of the Japanese Navy from Tawitawi.

The reaction was en route. Admiral Ozawa, the operative head, had good intelligence of the composition of the U.S. fleet, and knew he had but nine carriers against the American fifteen and five battleships against their seven, but he had worked out a battle plan to cancel his numerical disadvantage. He had been assured that heavy air reinforcements were coming down from the Empire through the Bonins, and these should certainly do something to reduce American strength. He was running up from the southwest against steady northeast trade winds, which would enable him to launch planes while remaining on course toward the American fleet where it was staying close to Saipan to protect the landings. He would launch from such a range that the American carriers could not strike back; the Japanese planes would land on the airstrips at Guam, refuel, deliver a second strike on the American fleet, then return to their onrushing carriers. Early on the morning of June 19 his planes began to take off.

It was an ingenious plan, but it overlooked two features of which Ozawa was ignorant. The Admiral did not know that the land-based aircraft from the Japanese home islands had been nearly destroyed, for the Japanese insistence on reporting nothing but victories had led the Saipan command to announce that these planes had been highly successful. Neither did he know that ever since he left his anchorage a concentration of American submarines northeast of the Philippines had been dogging him.

The Japanese as usual traveled in fairly separated groups, and the American submarines did not pick up all of them. Spruance, aware of the enemy's preference for coming in from several directions at once, stayed close to Saipan and Guam, lest they launch an attack on the landings from the northwest. He was only about ninety miles from the islands when at 1000 in the morning radar reported the oncoming Japanese. At once, no less than four hundred fifty fighters were placed in the air and all carriers cleared their decks of bombers and torpedo planes, sending them in with full loads to hover over the airstrips on Guam and dig them up, for Spruance had divined that the Japanese meant to use those fields. The battleships formed a screen between the carriers and the line of the Japanese advance.

The result was later called "the Marianas turkey-shoot." The four separate strikes flown by the Japanese that day ran into overwhelming fighter concentrations. The planes that got past the fighters were cut down by the battleships, and the enemy paid four hundred two planes, the largest single loss to any side in any battle of the war, for one single bomb hit, on the armor of a battleship. Only fifty-eight planes returned to the Japanese carriers; those that landed on Guam mostly crashed on runways that were kept pitted by repeated American bombing attacks.

This was not all or even the worst for Ozawa. The American submarines, released from scouting duty now that battle had been joined, bored in for attack. *Cavalla* got three torpedoes into *Shokaku*, veteran of Pearl Harbor, Coral Sea, and Santa Cruz, and she tipped over; *Albacore* put a single torpedo into the new *Taiho,* largest carrier in the world, just as she had her fuel lines running to ready planes for Ozawa's third strike, and she blew up. By evening of June 19 the painfully rebuilt Japanese Naval Air Force had been practically wiped out and although no one on our side knew it at the time, it would take more than a year to restore it.

What we did know was that the enemy had been hard hit and it was time for a counterstroke. All night, most of the next day, the American fleet steamed west and slightly north. The wind held steadily from the wrong direction; it was necessary to turn into it to fly searches and this delayed matters so that it was 4 P.M. before a search plane reported having found the enemy two hundred eighty miles distant. It was beyond the normal strike range of American carrier planes, recoveries would have to be made after dark, and to Spruance it was reported that his destroyers were running short of fuel. "If the destroyers run short of fuel, send them back," said the iron admiral. "I am going to strike that fleet and I will not be deterred by details."

The planes took off then, the pilots fully aware that they had not much more than a fifty per cent chance of getting back. It was falling twilight when they hit the Japanese fleet, which sent up all its remaining planes for defense. They got some twenty of the American bombers, and in return the flight decks of two enemy carriers were ripped up, sending them to repair yards for many months, while a third carrier was torpedoed and went down. Two tankers and a destroyer of the Japanese fleet train were sunk; a battleship sustained such damage to her engines and shafting that she was never of much use thereafter—and then the American flyers tried to find their way home.

Many of the planes were damaged and all were practically out of fuel. It was a wild night as they tried to come in, and Admiral Mitscher made the hard decision to turn on all lights in spite of the possibility of prowling Japanese submarines. Planes landed on any flight decks they could find and some of them crashed; others made water landings and their flyers had to be picked up; some never were found. But Japanese naval air power was done.

★   ★   ★   ★   ★

The Navy in Europe

In THE PACIFIC the American fighting forces were opposed by a major navy and the fighting was primarily naval, with such modifications as submarines and airplanes introduced. The Japanese would continue to fight obstinately ashore until the last man was down, but in effect naval victory meant victory everywhere in the Pacific Theater.

After the Battle of the Philippine Sea, the United States could pour land forces into Saipan, and later Tinian and Guam, until they were sufficient to wipe out resistance, with no more interference than occasional raiding planes coming down the chain of the Bonins. Admiral Nagumo, who had commanded the carriers at Pearl Harbor and Midway, shot himself through the head in a cave to conclude the operation.

In Europe things were different. The Allies had naval superiority, indeed naval control, from the beginning except for the German submarines. The problem was to get men ashore on the fortified coasts (Hitler's *Festung Europa,* "Fortress Europe") and support them inland as far as the ships' guns would reach, then to see they were adequately supplied.

This produced a form of naval war previously unknown to history; a war of the sea against the land, but one in which all the decisive actions were fought ashore and the navies supplied initial fire power and kept open the sea lanes for supplies and reinforcements. There were no great sea battles, only incidents; incidents in which men fought savagely, died bravely—and often accomplished a great deal without much benefit of history.

Aside from the fact that the British borrowed the carrier *Wasp* to fly a deckload of Spitfire planes to the rescue of hard-pressed Malta early in 1942, the first American operation in the European area was the landing on the northwest coast of Africa in November. As an undertaking in amphibious war it was a singularly pick-up affair, made without benefit of the new landing craft—which had yet to be built—and with the troops getting only the most exiguous preliminary training in Chesapeake Bay. Secrecy being a main object, the big convoy for Casablanca had to assemble at sea, its members never having seen each other before; when they reached the African coast there was revealed a painful shortage of small-boat handlers, which caused forty-six per cent of the craft in which the landing were made to be lost. At Casablanca itself the French had the new battleship *Jean Bart,* her engines inoperative but the eight 15-inch guns in her turrets working well, one light cruiser, seven out-size destroyers, and eight submarines. These put up a fight, but the new battleship *Massachusetts* knocked out *Jean Bart*'s turrets and American light craft sank three of the submarines. When the other French ships sortied to attack, they met with such fire from the old battleship *Texas* and the cruisers *Augusta* and *Brooklyn* that all but one were sunk or knocked out of action. Two days later *Jean Bart* got her turrets going again, but carrier dive-bombers quickly put her out of business and the next day French Africa surrendered.

II

Except for escort missions, very occasional fire support along the coast, and almost constant work against the German and Italian planes that came over day after day, there were no more events in European waters until July, 1943, when the Axis forces had been cleared from Africa and the invasion of Sicily was undertaken. In the meantime a considerable supply of shallow-draft landing vessels —LST, LCT, LCI, DUKW, and so forth—had become available, and there had been no little training in boat-handling by the Coast Guard. The main naval mission was conceived to be fire support for the forces on the beaches. During the training period, fire-control parties from the ships worked with the troops to learn their special language and ways of doing things, while artillery officers went aboard the ships to assess their techniques and potentialities.

There was thus achieved a high degree of co-operation at the operational level, but in the upper echelons of command things were more uncertain. Army officers insisted that preliminary shore bombardment from the water would be of little value, sacrificing the tactical surprise they hoped to attain, and they were profoundly skeptical of the value of naval gunfire support for the beachheads. The Air Force men insisted that their primary and practically only concern was striking down enemy air at its bases; they flatly refused to furnish air cover for Navy spotting planes or tactical air support for the troops. This refusal caused a great deal of trouble, for although they did succeed in doing a good deal of damage to German and Italian air bases, enemy raids kept coming in on both troops and ships throughout the operation.

The American naval support forces for Sicily consisted of five light cruisers and thirty-seven destroyers, all under command of Admiral H. Kent Hewitt. The largest overseas movement ever attempted to date, involving a half million soldiers, the invasion force got under way on the night of July 10-11, 1943. It was truly a combined and associated operation, with the British taking the southeast corner of the triangular island, the American forces the southwest. So many hundreds of landing craft and ships were involved that German radar operators on the beach thought their equipment had broken down and failed to report the armada coming in.

At the beachheads there were the foul-ups already encountered even by the more carefully trained Marines in the Pacific—landing craft grounded on offshore shoals, boats overturned in the surf, vehicles blown up by land mines or crippled by air attack or shellfire from inland. Above all there were huge untidy mounds of supplies with no one to move them, since the beach parties were totally inadequate and everyone was anxious to get inland. The tanks and artillery proved difficult to land; few of them got ashore, and these with the most insufficient supplies of ammunition. This turned out to be the Navy's opportunity. Behind the beaches Germany's Hermann Göring Division had been concentrated with a heavy force of tanks, which counterattacked at daylight. The only guns available to stop them were aboard the ships; General Patton in person climbed to the observation post to see the enemy coming across Gela plain, and spoke to the Navy fire-control officer. He called the ships; from the light cruiser *Boise* and attendant destroyers there descended a storm of shell, so accurately placed that prisoners later wanted to know what new anti-tank weapons the Americans had developed.

The Nazi tank attack was crushed and turned back in a manner that carried conviction to the Allied high command. After this every advance along the coast or inland to the limit of the range of ships' guns was carried out with the help of naval fire-control parties. However difficult it might be for the Army to land heavy guns and keep them supplied with ammunition during the early stages of an operation, a light cruiser could gallop to the spot in thirty minutes from a dozen miles away and instantly supply the equivalent of two regiments of corps artillery, while the destroyers were always on call to deliver as much fire as could be expected from a battalion of heavy guns ashore. Moreover, as is usual with artillery, guns receiving no counter-fire became very accurate, and those on shipboard were not hampered by such difficulties as moving up the ammunition supply and finding emplacements.

The total result was to reveal a fatal flaw in the concept of Fortress Europe. Naval gunfire could be concentrated on any given landing area to a degree that made shore defenses inadequate, just as concentrations of carriers in the Pacific could overwhelm any given Japanese air base. From the German viewpoint, the tactical answer to inability to defend the beachheads themselves was to assemble mobile troops inland for counterattack, but the heavy guns offshore in the ships made even this impractical. No enemy concentration heavy enough to strike through an Allied beachhead perimeter could be built up without drawing crushing fire from our ships, and the guns of an Allied light cruiser could reach twenty-three thousand yards, twelve miles inland. Within a beachhead twelve miles deep there was ample room for our invasion forces to develop all the support necessary for further advance.

It is not to be supposed that the development of invasion technique based on naval fire support was easy or without losses. Bombers came in low and destroyed landing craft at the beaches; destroyers were hit and went down; ammunition ships blew up in spectacular showers of fireworks. The troops ashore were harried by infiltration attacks, hobbled by land-mines, and violently shelled by inland artillery. But the basic fact remained: the fire of our ships could support land operations to a distance of ten or more miles inland, after which it became a matter for the Army.

This was abundantly demonstrated in the next operation after the Sicilian landing—the leapfrog to Salerno south of Naples in early September, 1943. Like the operation against Sicily, this was a joint British-American affair, with units of both nations ashore and afloat working side by side, sometimes intermingled. The landing was intended to be a surprise thrust behind the German Armies holding the Allies lower down on the Italian peninsula, but two things went wrong. The Germans, with a first-rate sense of strategic geography, had determined that if the Allies made a landing behind their lines it could hardly be at any place other than Salerno; and consequently, they mined the beaches heavily and disposed their troops accordingly. Then, the Army Air Force, which had promised to seal off the beachhead area by cutting all railroads and bridges, signally failed to make good its boast.

The result was that when the Allied troops landed on September 9, 1943, they found themselves at the bottom of a bowl of a coastal plain dominated by fortified heights, and fighting for their lives. Calls on the destroyers and two light cruisers that supported the beachhead were constant; on D-day the destroyer *Ludlow* used four hundred sixty-five rounds of 5-inch shells and the cruiser *Savannah* six hundred forty-five rounds of 6-inch, all on request. On the third morning the Germans had six hundred tanks in the area and launched an all-out drive to push the invaders into the sea, while the Allied ground commanders asked the Navy to prepare a plan for evacuation. That same day a new and fearsome weapon made its appearance—a heavy aerial torpedo, dropped by an airplane and guided by radio. One of them blew out a turret on *Savannah* and made a big hole in her bottom, while others hit transports and LSTs. Another cruiser replaced *Savannah*. On the day of the big German tank attack ashore, *Philadelphia* alone fired nine hundred twenty rounds of 6-inch, the Nazi push was turned back, and Marshal Albert Kesselring of the German command had to report: "In order to evade the effective shelling from warships I ordered a disengagement on the coastal front."

The Salerno beachhead was now secure, but nothing could pre-

vent the withdrawal of the Germans to the line of the rocky-banked
Volturno River, and they held out there through most of the winter.
The position was so stiff that the Allied high command decided on
another leapfrog operation, to the beaches at Anzio-Nettuno, just
south of Rome. The landing was made on January 22, 1944, at night.
This time tactical surprise was achieved, so that the landing forces
got ashore with little interference except from minefields while
farther south a heavy attack drew German forces to the Volturno
front. There was no need for naval support in this phase, but once
again the Army Air Force failed in the mission of cutting enemy communications to the area. When General J. P. Lucas, commanding
the American forces, was hesitant and uncertain in his movements,
the Germans worked up a concentration that held him in a pocket.
They had learned the lesson of Salerno; their artillery was sited in
hills to the rear, out of range of naval guns; they kept all exits from
the beachhead closed; and it was not until the forces in the south
broke through the Volturno line in May that the Anzio expedition
was released.

In the meanwhile a quite simple answer to the German radio-con-
trolled bombs had been found. If someone aboard the attacked ship
simply operated an electric razor as the bomb came in, it would infal-
libly avoid the ship and plunge into the water. The Germans stopped
using them.

III

The struggle for the Normandy landings was a battle of preparation
and counterpreparation. Under Hitler's personal orders the Allied
forces were to be held and destroyed at the line of the beaches. Immense amounts of steel, concrete, and labor were poured into the
project of making the whole European coast from the Hook of Holland down to around the Brest peninsula absolutely impregnable,
with underwater obstacles and mines off every accessible beach, and
pillboxes and artillery positions inshore to sweep landing areas with
fire. Above all, the Allies were to be denied the use of harbors; it was
quite clear to the German high command that no invasion of the Continent could penetrate far without vast columns of supply, the estimated need being about a ton per man per week. Such ports as the
Germans themselves did not wish to use—Dieppe, LeHavre, Cher-

bourg, Brest—were submitted to systematic and very elaborate dem-
olition programs and their waters mined, while strong forts were
established at the entrances and on the inland faces. Except for the
men occupying the beach defenses, the Army reserves were kept well
back, to be committed as mobile units when the Allies had declared
themselves. The Germans felt they could seal off any beachhead as
they had that at Anzio.

None of this was a secret to the Allied high command, and its
invasion preparations were made accordingly. Special teams of U.S.
Navy salvage experts were sent to Britain, ready to move in to clear
a port as soon as one had been taken. A tremendous bombing program was laid on by both British and American Air Forces with the
aim of disrupting communications to the selected landing area. It
succeeded far better than similar campaigns in Italy; when the invasion actually came, German troops had to move to the front afoot
or on bicycles. As for the supply matter, the British secretly designed
and prepared huge artificial breakwaters, composed partly of obsolete ships, partly of huge concrete caissons, two-hundred-foot win-
dow boxes; all to be floated across the Channel and sunk in protecting rows off the landing beaches. These "Mulberry" harbors—their
code name—were to supply shelter during unloading operations so
that supplies could move right ashore in "whales"—floating steel
roadways to landing platforms twelve hundred feet offshore—and
across the beaches until the forces ashore could win and clear a
major port.

As for the beach defenses, they were nowhere near as complete as
Hitler wished; like many another of his grandiose plans, this suffered
from the sheer difficulty of finding the men and materials to carry
them out. Along the Pas-de-Calais area, the nearest to England,
where the Germans expected the invasion must come, the defenses
were very good; elsewhere somewhat spotty. To deal with them was
the specific province of naval support; in the American landing area
it consisted of three old battleships, three heavy cruisers, and four
British light cruisers. The battleships had the special duty of knocking
out the heavy blockhouses that contained German 8- and 10-inch guns
with their own 12- and 14-inchers. Naval fire-control parties went in
with the landings.

All told there were 102,000 American sailors engaged in the

Normandy assault, with ships to the number of 2,479, including landing craft. It was one of the most massive naval efforts ever made, on
a scale that precludes any mention of individual efforts. When the
landing began at dawn of June 6, 1944, all these men and ships
were in reasonably close approximation of their assigned positions.
There were fewer calls for fire than in the Sicilian or Italian landings,
mainly because the preliminary work of the Air Force had been very
good and it provided excellent close support for the men on the
beaches. But where Navy support was wanted it worked out as it
had previously, and though on one beach there was some question
of whether the troops could get off the water's edge, they made it.
That is, the grand invasion plan worked; the troops moved inland
and fought their own battles.

By June 26, they were closing in on Cherbourg, where for the last
time in the Normandy invasion heavy naval intervention was called
for. Out of the air would come: "We are being attacked; battery at
W24-367"—"P 120"—"Very good, very good, stand by." This was
repeated a dozen, several hundred, a thousand times. At Cherbourg
the old battleships had to fight coastal batteries designed to handle
their class; they took hits and had fourteen killed among them, but
they put the batteries out of business and the place fell. It was well that
it did, for while the artificial harbor of the British beachhead was
used for months, that off the American Omaha beach was in a more
exposed position and was knocked to pieces when the worst June
storm in a half century came raging down the Channel and sent three
days of huge seas battering against its caisson breakwaters.

Compared to the Normandy invasion, that of the Mediterranean
coast of southern France to start an army operating up the Rhone
valley was achieved with ease. It was made well to the east in the
area around St. Tropez on August 15. By this date the great Battle
of St. Lô had been fought, Patton's armored columns were fanning
across northern France and the Germans had called in every available man to stop them. The forces of the French resistance were very
strong in the rear of the Mediterranean landing areas; the defenders
had practically no air cover, while the attackers flew planes from
seven British and two American escort carriers, and had a strong but
curiously mixed squadron of French, British, American, and even
Italian ships for gunnery cover. At only one of the four beaches was

there any trouble, and this was so near another where the landing
had been made against the lightest of resistance that it was speedily
pinched out. The point made was that with the backing of sea power
forces of Continental dimensions could be put ashore almost anywhere desired.

The Navy had one final job in the liberation of Europe. When the
armies come up against the barrier of the Rhine, Navy landing craft
and crews were trucked across France and given the task of moving
our troops to the far bank.

★ ★ ★ ★ ★

14

Submarines Atlantic; Submarines Pacific

I N THE AUTUMN MONTHS of 1942 Adolph Hitler and his admirals had some reason to believe that their submarine campaign would be a success. The month of the African invasion saw more Allied tonnage sunk than any other but one during the war, and German submarine production was pushing over twenty a month. German submarine losses also were growing, but not yet at an insupportable rate, and at one of the Führer's conferences it was decided that the submarines should henceforth be given increased anti-aircraft armament and orders to fight things out against planes, which seemed the chief menace. A new torpedo that, if it missed its target, would cruise in varying spirals through a convoy until it found something was already available for the U-boats, and the German scientists reported encouragingly that they had just about solved the difficulties attendant on the development of the acoustic torpedo, which would home on the sound of a ship's propellers.

The Nazi conferees agreed that a submarine of much greater underwater speed was needed. Designs for a boat of heavy battery capacity that would provide such speed were already at hand, and Professor Walther reported success in preliminary experiments with his radical new submarine powered by hydrogen peroxide, which would yield an underwater speed of 25 knots. There was also a new device called the "Pillenwerfer," which ejected a cloud of bubbles that lasted for fifteen minutes and gave Allied sonar so strong a reaction that their ships depth-charged the bubbles. Better yet, there was the "Schnorkel," found on a Dutch submarine during the invasion of Holland. It had a floating tube which enabled the U-boat to take in air while well below the surface, and thus to operate continually on Diesels, and it was hardly bigger than a periscope, so that detection was extremely difficult. Wolf-pack tactics were working well; one large Allied convoy was attacked by no less than twenty submarines.

Five months later, in the key month of May, 1943, these bright prospects had suddenly turned grim. The new Allied micro-wave radar, of whose very nature the Germans were unaware, was bringing planes in on submarines under all weather conditions, and most destructively in the Bay of Biscay, which the growing range of patrol planes enabled the British Coastal Command—with the aid of U.S. Navy Liberator squadrons—to cover at all times. When the German submarine commanders asked for air cover, Marshal Göring only talked vaguely of a new airplane type that would be ready in a year, and did nothing. The heavier anti-aircraft armament of the submarines and the order to fight it out on the surface against planes had produced little but losses; after a few planes had been shot down, pilots learned the trick of watching from out of gun range, while calling up more planes or ships to assist in the attack.

The Nazi weaving torpedo was never much of a success; their acoustic torpedo did not become fully operational until the fall of 1943, but after a few preliminary achievements (six ships were sunk out of one convoy) it ran head-on into the fact that American scientists had foreseen its development and already had in production four separate devices for countering it. Experienced sound operators soon learned to tell the reflection of "Pillenwerfer" bubbles from those of a submarine. The big battery submarine, Type XXI, had been designed for production in sections all over Germany, with the final assemblies to be made at ports, but the tolerances were so large that the sections often failed to fit, and Allied bombing interrupted both transportation and assembly. It was the end of 1944 before the first of the new type took her trials, and only one ever became operational. As for the Walther submarines, they were still unfinished at the end of the war.

The Germans also made a dismaying discovery about the "Schnorkel." It did indeed help a U-boat to evade detection, but it was of no assistance at all in the attack phase, where improvement was most needed, while alert Allied radar operators began to pick up "Schnorkel" indications on their instruments. When twelve Italian and six German submarines attempted to interfere with the Sicilian invasion nine of the Italians and three of the Germans were sunk.

And the Allied anti-submarine measures continued to increase, both in numbers and intensity. Early in the war the Allies had developed "huff-duff," the high-frequency direction finder; now rising production made it available in quantity for both shore stations and ships, and the German regulation that submarines should report their positions every night gave it admirable opportunities. Nazi wolf-packs located convoys and prepared to close in on them only to find their intended victims making unexpected and inexplicable changes of direction away from the submarines. Often, submarine concentrations gathered for attack found themselves attacked instead by an entirely new type of formation, the hunter-killer groups. Rather than merely escorting convoys, these groups of fast light craft went to areas where "huff-duff" had pinpointed the U-boats and sought out the enemy.

This was ruinous to the German submarines. The escort carrier *Bogue* and her accompanying destroyer escorts sank six; the destroyer escort *Frost,* working with the carrier *Croatan,* got two in a roaring gale where men had to clutch lifelines as they operated their gear; planes from the escort carrier *Guadalcanal* bombed *U-505* to the surface in the South Atlantic, and she was captured by boarding from the destroyer escort *Pillsbury,* as in the old days of sail. Life aboard the destroyer escorts was hard, incidents were various and dramatic, but the statistics tell the story. In mid-1943 the Germans abandoned the attempt to deal with convoys off either the British or American coasts and took most of their submarines to the mid-Atlantic west of the Azores, using submarine tankers, or "milch cows" for refueling. But the hunter-killer groups got after them there, too, sinking all but one of the "milch cows." In 1940, twenty-six Allied vessels were destroyed for each submarine lost; in 1942 the ratio had been cut down to thirteen to one, still serious because there were so many more submarines. But in 1943 the rate of exchange had fallen to two of our ships lost for every German submarine sunk and the merchant marine building yards were producing vessels so fast that at the end of the year all the Allied losses since the beginning of the war were more than made good. In 1944, Admiral Doenitz of the German Navy advised his Führer that the only hope was to carry on as best as possible until new boats and new devices should tip the balance again. They never did; after January 1, 1944, more than one submarine was sunk for every ship the Nazis destroyed, and the effort that had made the German Navy into a practically undiluted submarine service had collapsed in utter disaster.

I I

In June of 1943 things began to pick up for American submariners. Admiral Charles Lockwood, head of Submarines Pacific, conducted experiments which revealed the defects in American torpedoes, and U.S. submarines at last began to get reliable weapons. In fact, they had more than one, for a captured German electric torpedo had been picked up and turned over to Westinghouse to copy. But some parts of the copy could not be produced by American methods and the torpedo as a whole could not be fired from American tubes, so Westinghouse proceeded to build its own on the basis of the German device. It took a year to develop, and even then was not wholly satisfactory: The new missile ran hot in the tubes and slow in the water, its guide-fins were weak, and submariners were skeptical of the whole business. But Admiral Lockwood's people worked hard at ironing out the bugs, and though the use of the new torpedo was wholly voluntary, thirty per cent of all torpedoes carried by the end of 1943 were electric. They were slower than the conventional steam torpedoes, but their utter silence, the fact that they left no warning wake to be traced so that the target ships and escorts never even knew from what direction they came, made them rapidly more popular in the service. Toward the end of the war more than two-thirds of all torpedoes fired were electrics.

With this improvement in weapons and the steady growth in numbers of new submarines, Japanese shipping losses began to mount. While the absolute figures did not match those sent down by the Germans in the Atlantic, the losses were far less supportable. The Japanese merchant marine was not only smaller than that of the Allies to begin with, but the very materials of which it was built had to be brought from overseas in the ships that were going down. At the end of 1943, the year that saw the Allied building yards replace all the losses since the beginning of the war, the total Japanese merchant marine had fallen from 5,400,000 tons to 4,100,000 tons, and there began to be acute shortages not only of oil, but of rubber, ores, bauxite, and especially coal.

In 1944, the American submarines began to run wild. *Sandlance*, for instance, sank two freighters off Honshu in the midst of drift ice and freezing fogs in February; then got into a big troop convoy bound for the Marianas. Her first periscope look showed ships all around the horizon; *Sandlance* fired two from the bow at a light cruiser, two from the stern at a troopship, then swung around and fired another pair at a second transport. The depth-charging was wild and aimless; the submariners had time to see all three ships go down before they were driven to take refuge on the bottom for eighteen hours, then head home with all torpedoes exhausted. A convoy from Shanghai to New Guinea ran foul of two submarines, lost twenty thousand tons of shipping and so many soldiers that Japanese defense plans in the area were materially affected.

In May, a unit of three American submarines, operating like a German wolf-pack, got after a convoy carrying a heavily reinforced Japanese regiment to Saipan and sent down four ships; the survivors reached the island without the weapons, the construction equipment, or the twenty-two tanks that their convoy was carrying. Off Formosa the submarine *Parche* completely broke up a large Japan-bound convoy, firing nineteen torpedoes, nearly all of which hit, and sending down several ships, including two valuable tankers. The whole South China Sea had become unsafe for enemy shipping.

Nor was the attrition of Japanese merchant ships the only result of our submarine operations. Early in 1944 it became evident to Washington that Japanese destroyer losses in the fighting for the Solomons had been very severe while their rate of replacement was low. Destroyers were moved up to second priority on the list of submarine targets, just below battleships and carriers. Seven Japanese destroyers went down in a month and more followed. The effect snowballed, each destroyer sunk reduced the number of available convoy escorts and made our submarine attack still more successful.

The pace of sinking accelerated; and after the fall of Saipan, when tenders could be moved up to that island to give our submarines a shorter run to the hunting grounds, there was another jump in kills. From then on Japanese convoys from the southern resources area had to move up the comparatively narrow channel past the tip of Luzon and around Formosa. Every step of the way they were dogged by American submarines, operating singly or in groups. Statistics: in January 1944, Japanese oil imports were still 1,000,000 barrels for the month; in August they had nose dived to 300,000. In December 1944, the total Japanese merchant marine had fallen to under 2,000,-000 tons, a million less than the tonnage estimated necessary to maintain the pre-war civilian economy. The tonnage figure kept going down. At the end of the war, while the Germans were losing more than one U-boat per ship sunk the Japanese were losing twenty-six ships for every American submarine they sent down.

Mostly the American submarine attacks were made by means of radar bearings on the surface at night, but there were exceptions, as when *Sailfish* began such an attack on the carrier *Chuyo*, got one torpedo into her during the dark, and came up to find a typhoon so furious that when the submarine reached periscope depth she could see nothing but walls of raging green water. She persisted, and at dawn hit the staggering carrier with a second torpedo, which brought the victim to a halt. At nine o'clock in the morning, with the typhoon driving white water off the tops of the waves and destroyer masts occasionally visible through the welter, *Sailfish* fired two more torpedoes that finished her victim.

Examination of the detailed records of these submarine actions brings out the fact that the most decisive factor in their success was the persistence and aggressiveness of the attacks. Thus *Harder,* spotted on the surface by a Japanese destroyer which made straight for her, instead of diving fired three torpedoes in a "down-the-throat" shot and killed off the destroyer. She also sank four other destroyers, two of which were specifically hunting for her, before herself being sunk, and caused Admiral Toyoda to report to Japan that there was a massive concentration of submarines around his anchorage.

Multiply such incidents and the reasons for the attrition of the Japanese merchant marine and destroyer force becomes visible. Nor were the exploits of American submarines limited to direct military action. As long ago as the loss of the Philippines, submarines had been employed to bring out the stock of gold from Manila and many nurses from Bataan. Thenceforth our submarines ran regular shuttles into the islands, carrying supplies, ammunition, and leaders for the expanding guerrilla movement.

Another activity began with the preliminary air raids on Wake and Marcus in September, 1943, when the carrier admirals asked that a couple of submarines be stationed off the islands to rescue aviators who might be forced down. The submarine *Skate* rescued no less than five, and submarine life-guards became a regular feature of every air strike, whether flown from carriers or land bases. Later when Saipan had become a center for the B-29 strikes on homeland Japan, a regular submarine patrol was set up along the line of their flight; the undersea craft rescued dozens of aviators and in one case pulled a man right out of Tokyo Bay. There was no more important contribution to morale during the war. Any pilot starting on a mission could be sure that if he were forced to ditch there would be a submarine not far away from where he came down, and even if it did not sight him immediately, it would be coached in by other planes.

The first submarine photographic reconnaissance was conducted in the Gilberts prior to the attacks on Makin and Tarawa. *Nautilus*, under Commander W. D. Irvin, had the job. There had been tries at this sort of thing before, but it was found that the periscope vibrated, it transmitted light at low efficiency, or something else went wrong. Irvin's exec, Lieutenant-Commander R. B. Lynch, was a photography enthusiast who insisted that the only thing wrong was the camera. He himself had a very fine special camera of German make, and when it was tried from *Nautilus* the result was so clear a panorama of beachheads, showing machine guns and artillery positions, camouflage and other dangers, that every commander of an amphibious assault from then on demanded submarine photos of the beachheads. They always got it; though the most careful research failed to disclose in the country more than ten of the German cameras that were the only ones that could do the job, and they had to be kept in a safe at Pearl Harbor to be doled out for each mission.

At the outset of the war the Japanese submarine service was numerically one of the strongest in the world, and it had the advantage of remarkably good torpedoes. It also had eleven submarines carrying float-planes for reconnaissance, to which nineteen more were added later, and a supply of two-man midget submarines, to be launched from larger craft. Indeed, the high command counted more heavily on the midget submarines at Pearl Harbor than on planes from the carriers.

The results were far from commensurate with the equipment. Only one midget got into Pearl Harbor and it was promptly sunk; the others never returned. In fact, the total contribution of the midgets for the whole war was the sinking of one ship and damage to a British battleship in the Indian Ocean. Nor did the larger Japanese submarines do much better. Twice they hit the carrier *Saratoga* without sinking her; a battleship was hit once, the moribund *Yorktown* was sent down in the last act of the Battle of Midway along with a destroyer; the carrier *Wasp* and another destroyer were sunk during the Guadalcanal campaign and an escort carrier in the Marshalls. As to the war on commerce, the sum total of Japanese submarine sinkings of American ships was not more than twenty vessels. Against this, American submarines sank one thousand, one hundred fifty Japanese merchant ships, three carriers, four escort carriers, one battleship, twelve cruisers, and about half the Japanese destroyer service.

A good part of the poverty of the Japanese submarine record was due to the fact that the Imperial Army was in control of all major policy lines. After the American invasion of Guadalcanal, Japanese Army officials insisted that the first and almost the only duty of the submarines was to carry supplies to garrisons in the increasing number of islands that were cut off and beleaguered. The Japanese submarine service thus became substantially a department of undersea transport and supply, and in the last days of Guadalcanal the Japanese troops that remained were kept alive only by the almost nightly arrivals of rice-carrying submarines. Another factor was the failure of the Japanese to develop an efficient surface search radar until near the end of the war, when it was too late. There was also the Japanese fondness for seeking short-cut solutions, such as fleet submarines carrying midgets, and toward the end of the war, "human torpedoes," to be guided to their targets by suicidally-inclined naval men. They never accomplished anything important and the human torpedoes, which had to be carried outside the submarine hulls, were always breaking down.

But when all allowances are made, the utter failure of the Japanese submarines throws a tremendous reflected light on the achievements of their American opposite numbers. The Japanese sent twelve of their biggest and best submarines to lie off Pearl Harbor during the Midway operation, in a situation strategically not too different from that of the five American submarines that watched the Tawitawi anchorage in the preliminaries to the Battle of Philippine Sea. The aggressive American submarines reported on the whole Japanese fleet movement and sank two carriers; the twelve Japanese submarines made no reports but: "Patrols too alert; no prospects." The Japanese had a high sense of duty and a fanatical sense of devotion, but it was the initiative and drive of the men in the tin boxes beneath the surface that made the difference.

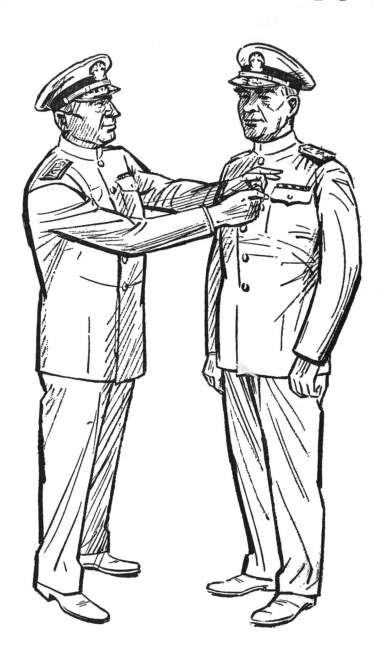

15

Transit from Formosa to Okinawa via Leyte

W HEN SAIPAN had been taken to the accompaniment of much hard fighting and Tinian to the south of it with relative ease, the strength of the American amphibious forces was thrown against Guam, and resistance there collapsed within a month. This was in August, 1944, and a new strategic plan became in order, since in the meantime the MacArthur forces had hippity-hopped along the whole northern coast of New Guinea to Morotai Island, from which they could run bombing raids to the Southern Philippines. Their obvious next step was the invasion of Mindanao. The operation was planned for late November. In the meantime Halsey had taken over for Spruance in the Central Pacific, and 5th Fleet became 3rd Fleet by the change. Halsey's ships supported the operation against Peleliu, the anchor of the western Carolines, whose seizure was insisted on because the Japanese might use the airfield there.

The attack was probably a mistake. Peleliu has a rocky spine of hill, shot with caves, which the Japanese had connected through intercommunicating passages and fitted with artillery behind steel doors. It was only after the most desperate fighting and ten thousand casualties that the place was subdued and then it was of very little use. But in the meantime Halsey with the carriers conducted a heavy raid on the central Philippines to keep the enemy from interfering with the Morotai-Peleliu operations, and the results were such as to change planning ideas all the way back to Washington. Halsey lost only eight planes; he destroyed more than two hundred Japanese aircraft, sank twelve merchant ships and a tanker, and he reported that the central Philippines were far weaker than areas north and south. He believed the enemy could be attacked there, and at once; and MacArthur lent full support to the argument. It convinced Roosevelt and the Chiefs of Staff. The revision of plans caused the assignment of the Central Pacific ground forces to the temporary command of MacArthur, the advancement of the assault date from late November to October 20, and orders to the 3rd Fleet to support the invasion.

Halsey decided to begin his support operations by cutting off the Philippines from land-based air reinforcements, and on October 11 he hit the staging fields on Okinawa. Next morning he was off the big island of Formosa, where there were important air bases. Admiral Fukudome, in charge of the Japanese air forces on Formosa, had foreseen such an attack. Thinking to imitate Spruance in the Battle of Philippine Sea, he had cleared his fields of all but fighters. He expected to cut the American attack forces to pieces as they came in over his anti-aircraft batteries; then counterattack at night with torpedo planes staged-in from the north and China.

What Fukudome failed to calculate on was the superior training of the American flyers, and the fact that on the morning of October 12, when they began coming over, there were present the strike formations from four full carrier groups, sixteen carriers. The air combat was intense, and forty-three American planes went down, but the Japanese lost more than two hundred, and American dive-bombers cut up nearly every hangar and fuel and ammunition dump on Formosa. That night the first of the Japanese torpedo planes came in on the Fleet and they got one hit, on a cruiser. Next day there was another attack on the fields and on the night of the 13th a second massive Japanese air torpedo attack. Another cruiser was torpedoed (both of them eventually got home), but Japanese flyers, seeing their own planes flame on the water and then disappear, reported a great victory to Tokyo, with at least eleven carriers sunk, and parades were held in the Japanese capital. Actually, in exchange for two torpedo hits on cruisers and seventy-nine American planes down altogether, the Japanese had lost six hundred fifty aircraft, and the chance of serious air reinforcement to the Philippines had vanished.

I I

The Japanese were not noted for their sense of realism, and the practical destruction of the American fast carrier task force had been confirmed by Imperial rescript. Nevertheless there must have been some men near the sources of command who were not satisfied that Halsey's carriers were eliminated from the combination when the huge fleet of MacArthur's transports moved into Leyte Gulf on October 20 and began to land troops, under air cover from a dozen escort carriers, the cruiser fire of 7th Fleet, and six old battleships. The enemy had no choice, however; as one Japanese admiral expressed it, if the Philippines fell to the Americans the Japanese fleet would be cut off from its supply of fuel if it remained in the north and its supply of arms and ammunition if it remained in the south. Thus it was meaningless to talk of saving the Fleet at the expense of the Philippines. The whole remaining strength of the Japanese Navy was committed to wiping out the beachhead in Leyte Gulf.

The plan was as complex as any the intricate Japanese strategists ever hatched, with three distinct attack forces: south, central and north. The central force was the main Japanese fleet under Admiral Kurita, which would leave its anchorage off western Borneo with five battleships, including the giants *Yamato* and *Musashi,* largest battleships ever built and carrying 18-inch guns, ten heavy cruisers, and a complement of destroyers. After coming northwest of the Philippines, this fleet would work through the Sibuyan Sea south of Luzon, north of Leyte, and emerge from San Bernardino Strait to fall on the assembled American transports in Leyte Gulf. Meanwhile a second Japanese force, a southern group of two battleships, one heavy cruiser, and four destroyers under Admiral Nishimura would cross the Sulu Sea and penetrate Surigao Strait south of Leyte, aiming at the same objective. The American preference for concentration was well known; against whichever of these forces we concentrated, the other should be able to break through.

Down from Japan itself came the northern force. Admiral Ozawa was sent down far to the northeast of the Philippines with four carriers, two battleships whose afterdecks had been made into flight decks, and a force of cruisers and destroyers. Their basic mission was to draw

Halsey north and away from Leyte Gulf. This process would be aided by the fact that the first act would be an attack on Halsey's carriers by all the land-based air that could be assembled, followed by a shuttle attack launched from the carriers and coming in from the east. The Japanese carrier air groups were thin because so many of the pilots and planes destined for them had been lost in the battle off Formosa, but they ought to accomplish something, and next morning they would take off from Philippine fields and fly back across Halsey to their own decks. That is, Ozawa's was a decoy mission—with teeth in it.

Still another enemy group under Admiral Shima, with two heavy cruisers and one light cruiser as its main units, had started from the home islands to pick up American cripples after the air battle off Formosa. There were no cripples to pick up; Shima's force was shunted on southward to cut in east and south of Luzon and to follow Nishimura's southern force through Surigao Strait. Shima and Nishimura were on such bad terms they were not speaking to each other, and the Japanese Admiralty forgot to tell either that the other would be there.

On the American side there were more than five hundred transports and landing craft deep in the bight of Leyte Gulf between the islands of Samar and Dinagat, covered by three groups of four escort carriers each, plus the six old battleships and their supports, all under Admiral Kincaid. Halsey was a little eastward with the battle line of six fast battleships and four carrier groups under Admirals John S. McCain, F. C. Sherman, G. F. Bogan, and R. E. Davison. Aircraft from these groups had been striking at airfields all over the Philippines and had destroyed some two hundred Japanese planes besides sixty-six knocked down by the escort carriers. There seemed to be plenty more enemy aircraft where those came from, however, and the American beach-heads were subject to constant harassing attacks. One airstrip at Tacloban was nevertheless nearly ready.

This was the situation when the first contact was made, just in the gray of dawn on October 23, west of Palawan Island. The contactors were the American submarines *Darter* and *Dace*, which since midnight had been running parallel to Kurita's main body, the Japanese central force, seeking attack position. In the misty light they found it; four torpedoes from *Darter* smashed into the heavy cruiser *Atago* and she went down in nineteen minutes, two more hit the heavy cruiser *Takao* and she had to be escorted back to Singapore to take no further part in the war. As the Japanese turned from that deadly menace, more torpedoes from *Dace* hit the heavy cruiser *Maya* and she sank in four minutes. *Atago* was Kurita's flagship; he transferred to the battleship *Yamato* and pressed on without making a submarine hunt because of the urgency of his mission. He had suffered a loss the importance of which only appeared later, for *Atago* carried down with her his staff communications personnel.

Kurita pressed on then, and at dawn of the 24th was in Sibuyan Sea, south of Mindoro. Nishimura's smaller force to the south had taken a crooked course to avoid searches, but that same dawn found it passing through Sulu Sea, and there it was spotted by a heavy air search from Davison's carrier group, which immediately attacked and succeeded in getting a hit on one battleship and burning out a turret on a destroyer. Nishimura doubtless expected to be attacked again, and wondered why his southern force was allowed to make a peaceful voyage all that day through the Sulu Sea.

There was a good reason. Halsey's flyers had now spotted Kurita's central force coming through Sibuyan Sea, and all four fast carrier groups turned on it. The whole Japanese plan depended on timing; when Kurita called for land-based air cover he got no reply at all because all the land-based air was already out to attack the American carriers. This wave did succeed in finding one of Halsey's groups and badly damaging the light carrier *Princeton* with bombs, but meanwhile Kurita was without air cover under the American attack, and took damage all through his fleet, particularly to the heavy cruiser *Myoko*, which was so hard hit she had to be sent back, and to the battleship *Musashi*, which took a torpedo as well as bombs. About noon a second strike came in; this time *Musashi* took two heavy bomb hits and two torpedoes and began to settle by the head, while Kurita filled the air with complaints about the lack of planes.

He knew nothing of what had happened to the other forces in the combined attack. Actually Ozawa's carriers of the northern decoy force had reached position east of the American fleet and launched their strike—seventy-six planes only, all the depleted Japanese carrier force could muster—but word of this never got through to Kurita because of the loss of communications personnel. Of that strike only three planes got back to the carriers; and they accomplished nothing but to cause the suspension of damage control and salvage operations on *Princeton,* whereupon that light carrier blew up. They did not even hamper a third strike on Kurita, in which *Yamato* received two heavy bomb hits and *Musashi* four, while the latter picked up three more torpedoes, which left her speed at nine knots and her forecastle almost awash. Then came the fourth attack, which concentrated on the damaged battleship; *Musashi* received ten more bombs and four torpedoes, and at 1510 capsized, while Kurita, unable to get any replies to his messages, turned his central force back in the direction from which it had come.

This turnaway was duly reported to Halsey, whose searchers had meanwhile located Ozawa's northern carrier force. He turned north and east toward it with three carrier groups, sending McCain's, which was very low on oil, into the offing for refueling. In view of the criticism that has been leveled at what was later called "Bull's Run," it is worth looking at the state of his knowledge and ignorance at the time. He knew that the Japanese battle line had been turned back; he did not know that the seventy-six-plane strike of the afternoon represented all the attack strength Ozawa had. The best intelligence at the date and place was that instead of four carriers with nearly empty decks, Ozawa had eight very full ones, since no one on the American side was yet aware that the two hit by submarines in the Battle of Philippine Sea had gone down and it was supposed that two of the new enemy carriers then building were ready for action. Since the beginning of the war the main Japanese danger had been from carrier air, and it was vital to shunt those carriers away from the sensitive beachhead. During the night therefore, Halsey turned north and east.

But the Japanese central force had not really turned back. Under the shadows of evening, with all the battleships more or less damaged, Kurita reversed course again and at midnight was slipping through San Bernardino Strait toward the Leyte Gulf beachhead. One night-flying plane reported this turn, but there was no confirmation.

III

At this hour Nishimura was already entering Surigao Strait toward Leyte Gulf, spinning his southern force out into a column, and the reception committee was waiting. It consisted of Admiral Jesse L. Oldendorf with the full surface strength of 7th Fleet. A little after 2 A.M. Nishimura's ships were attacked with the torpedo by no less than twenty destroyers from both flanks of the strait; beyond that they came under the fire of eight American heavy cruisers and six of our older battleships. The torpedoes disposed of two of the Japanese destroyers and probably one of the battleships; the rest came under the storm of shells from the American battle line and the second Japanese battleship went down, while the heavy cruiser was so crippled that she did not last till daylight and another destroyer had her bow blown off. Nishimura and his force were gone; only a single Japanese destroyer escaping down the Strait. In behind this mess, with burning and sinking ships and drifting smoke in the night, suddenly came the detached Shima force. It progressed far enough to discover it was in a death trap before turning away, the light cruiser taking a crippling torpedo hit (she was sunk by planes next morning) and one of the heavy cruisers gunfire damage that sent her to Manila, where carrier planes sent her down early in November before she could be repaired. At dawn, the men of 7th Fleet, thoroughly happy with their performance, were taking ships into Surigao Strait to mop up cripples and find survivors when there came a message from Admiral Kincaid. It spelled trouble, real trouble. The main body of the Japanese fleet—Kurita's central force—was attacking the escort carriers off the beachhead in Leyte Gulf.

There the enemy had been suddenly sighted at nearly 0700 of a somewhat misty morning, with rain squalls chasing each other across the sea. The American northern formation of six escort carriers was east of Samar and northeast of Leyte Gulf, readying strikes for troop support and anti-submarine patrol. At once every plane was sent off the decks as fast as it could go, while the other escort carrier formation set up strikes against the Japanese heavy ships. Simultaneously, urgent messages, some in clear, went to Halsey and Oldendorf. Kurita, without air spotting, was almost as much surprised as the Americans when he sighted a number of what he took to be regular carriers to the south of him and it cost him some time and confusion before he straightened his line and got his ships swinging around a circle with the idea of pressing these carriers back into Leyte Gulf. The survivors of Kurita's central force were four battleships, six heavy cruisers and eleven destroyers, and the Japanese Admiral opened fire from his biggest ships at thirty-five thousand yards.

The American escort carriers, protected only by destroyers and destroyer escorts, turned westward into a rain squall, then south, the ships making all the smoke they could as salvos from the big Japanese guns fell all about them. For something like half an hour, there was fitful firing at the American ships, half-hidden in rain and smoke, and a single-handed counterattack by one American destroyer, which got herself cripplingly damaged in the process. Meanwhile the escort-carrier planes kept on the offensive, not with co-ordinated attacks, but in groups of two or three, driving in with the utmost resolution. The Japanese evaded most of the torpedoes, but one hit the heavy cruiser *Kumano* aft, and Kurita released his ships to act independently. They dodged a second surface torpedo attack, smashing up two of the little destroyer escorts, but in turning away from it, they lost valuable sea room.

It was now 0800. The rain squalls had lessened and most of the American light ships were gone or crippled. Although persistent air attacks had damaged the Japanese ships a good deal topside, they were still in good shape and the four heavy cruisers leading their line had pressed the American escort carriers off their southerly course toward the southwest. Two of the Japanese had clear firing range and were hitting the carriers again and again, often with armor-piercing shells that went right through the thin sides without doing any damage but making holes. But *Gambier Bay* took hits in her engine room, dropped back, and was sunk under violent shelling. By 0830 the Japanese heavy cruisers were shepherding the carriers around to the west, their destroyers were in a position to make torpedo attacks, and off to the south a single enemy battleship had sighted the second American escort-carrier group and was firing on it at extreme range.

At this juncture a really well-co-ordinated American torpedo plane attack came in on the heavy cruisers, getting a torpedo hit on *Chikuma* and a heavy bomb hit on *Chokai* that put both ships out of action. Kurita was five miles to the north of this and could see nothing of what was going on, the observation planes from his flagship had been shot down early, and his communications were extremely poor. He ordered the fleet to reform on a northerly course toward the flag, and while he was doing it, there came another wave of American torpedo planes that got no hits, but forced him to take strong evasive action and increased confusion. Watching the Japanese turn back on the flag bridge of the escort carrier *Fanshaw Bay,* a signalman who had expected nothing but death that morning, said: "Hell, they got away."

This was not quite the story. Around 1100 Kurita had his ships in fair order again, close to the coast of Samar. *Chikuma* and *Chokai* were so badly hurt that they were disposed of, and with the rest he headed back toward Leyte Gulf. But about this time he received a new strong strike from carrier planes, in which the heavy cruiser *Suzuya* took bomb hits that started fires which soon reached the torpedo compartment and blew her sides out. Kurita could not but assume that these planes came from the main American fleet, the task groups following Halsey. (Actually they were a pick-up group, many of which had refueled on the half-finished Tacloban airstrip.) Thanks to communications failures the Japanese Admiral never got messages from Ozawa saying that Halsey had been drawn well away to the north, and since Nishimura was dead under the waters of Surigao Strait there were no messages from him. The opposition was too heavy; Kurita made one final turnaround, and headed his central force back through San Bernardino Strait.

Off to the north Ozawa expected his decoy force to be hard hit, and so it was. Not long after dawn American search planes began to appear, and just after 0800, when the serious trouble for the escort carriers was beginning back off Leyte Gulf, the strike came in. There were only eighteen Japanese fighters to meet it, and they were quickly disposed of. All four of the carriers were hit, the light carrier *Chitose* by heavy bombs forward and near misses that opened so many of her seams that she presently tipped over and sank. Two other light carriers were not seriously damaged, but the big *Zuikaku* got a hit that disabled her steering gear and the light cruiser *Tama* took a torpedo that caused her to drop out of formation and try to reach home independently. It was no use; a submarine got her on the way in.

About 1000 came the second wave of American planes; they concentrated on the light carrier *Chiyoda,* set her afire and brought her to a halt. Salvage parties worked frantically over her, but an attempt to take her in tow failed because of the presence of American planes. This attack caused Ozawa to get off a comforting message to Kurita, saying that he had drawn at least two and probably more of the American carrier groups after him and it was safe to proceed into Leyte Gulf; it was one of the messages that never got through. In the meantime, appeals for help from Leyte Gulf had been reaching Halsey, but for the time being they only annoyed him; he assumed that 7th Fleet had plenty of strength to deal with any force that had broken through San Bernardino Strait. But now came two messages that changed everything; one from Kincaid of 7th Fleet, saying his battleships were far from the scene of action and almost out of ammunition and fuel; one from Nimitz back at Pearl Harbor asking where the fast battleships were. The latter was not an order, but to Halsey it had the force of one; he reluctantly turned back with the fast battleships at their best speed.

It was unquestionably a mistake. Halsey's battleships arrived back at Leyte Gulf only at twilight, when all they could do was mop up a damaged destroyer and a crippled light cruiser trying to follow Kurita's retreat, while the chance to wipe out all Ozawa's force was lost. As it was, the third American air strike, coming in the afternoon, sank the light carrier *Zuiho* and finished *Zuikaku,* the last survivor of Pearl Harbor. Under the twilight the American cruiser force covering the carriers formed line, sank what was left of *Chiyoda* by gunfire, and put down another destroyer.

The battle for Leyte Gulf was over, all three sections of it, with downed pilots and the survivors of sunken ships spread all through the Gulf in life rafts, flashing lights and hoping for rescues. It was the greatest sea fight in American history, or in any history, on any basis of comparison. The Japanese lost three battleships, four carriers, seven heavy cruisers, four light cruisers, and nine destroyers—an entire navy. Perhaps more enemy ships might have been sunk under exactly the right combination of actions and reactions, but the battle was decisive just as it was. The Japanese Navy as such was never heard from again.

But there was one ominous portent of things to come. At the height of the battle, just as Kurita was reorganizing his fleet on a course north, there had appeared over the southern escort-carrier group twelve Japanese planes. They made no attempt to bomb or torpedo; instead they dived vertically out of the low overcast and deliberately crashed decks with their loads of bombs. The carrier *St. Lô* was blown up by one; *Suwanee* and *Kitkun Bay* were badly damaged.

The attackers were the "kamikazes," or special attack units of volunteer suicide pilots, whose motto was "One plane, one ship." At that time hardly anyone but the highest levels of Japanese command even knew of their existence. They were not to remain in obscurity long.

IV

With the elimination of the Japanese Navy except for occasional sporadic sneak attacks, the naval situation in the Pacific became rather strikingly like that which had obtained during much of the Civil War. Our Navy had attained its strategic objective of complete dominance of the seas. Its frontier was the enemy's coastline, and henceforth it functioned in support of shore-going forces delivering attacks on that coastline.

There were differences, to be sure, the obvious one being the addition of the air element, and it was this last that decided the next operation after the Battle for Leyte Gulf. Nimitz and the Pearl Harbor planners wished to push forward the Central Pacific offensive, to seize bases from which the Japanese home islands could be bombed under fighter cover in preparation for a landing. But the struggle for the Philippines was now in full swing, and the Japanese had decided to make their main defense on Leyte, the battle for which became a contest to bring in reinforcements, just as it had been on Guadalcanal. And as on Guadalcanal, air strength was necessary for close support of troops, to interdict Japanese attacks from the air, and to harry the convoys that brought enemy reinforcements across the narrow passages to Leyte. The two airstrips set up inside the beachhead were not very efficient. More airstrips could not be built right away because the engineers were desperately needed to find means to move vehicles and supplies through the Leyte combination of jungle, steep slopes, and deep mud. Air support had therefore to come from the sea, and the Battle for Leyte Gulf had left our escort carriers badly battered, short of both planes and flyers. Under the circumstances Halsey could hardly refuse to keep the fast carriers in the area for the time being.

They shot down more than seven hundred Japanese planes and cut enemy surface movement to pieces, but there was no such complete command of the air as that obtained in the Central Pacific operations. The enemy had dozens of small, well camouflaged airfields scattered through the islands. The "kamikaze" movement, so perfectly adapted to the Japanese temperament, spread like a disease while the foul weather and low clouds of the rainy season gave the planes opportunities to slip in undetected until the last minute. The headquarters estimate was that the average firing time against such an attacker was twenty seconds. Fighter patrols were not the complete answer either, because the kamikazes came by ones and twos, at any hour of the day or night, and a man determined to give his life for the Emperor was careless of proper tactics.

It was not until December, when MacArthur got a whole division ashore on the west coast of Leyte (at the cost of two destroyers sunk and one hit by a kamikaze) that the situation on that island cleared up. MacArthur was a general who never let the enemy get set for the next blow. He instantly struck through Sibuyan Sea for a landing on Mindoro. The Japanese reacted by sending one hundred fifty kamikazes in a group from South China. They smashed up a light carrier and a destroyer, but all the rest were shot down without inflicting damage.

Nimitz was now growing impatient to have his fleet back, but MacArthur persuaded him to let the carriers stay for one more operation—the landing in Lingayen Gulf on Luzon, which should lead to the reconquest of all that mattered of the Philippines. Halsey's part was to stand in north of Luzon, bombing the Formosa fields and the shores of South China to keep air assistance from being staged in. The landings would be covered by 7th Fleet, with much the same ships that had gone in at Leyte, the whole converging along a variety of routes through the Philippines.

The kamikazes also converged from every possible direction. During the advance to Lingayen it was not too bad, for it was often possible to dodge a suicider once he had committed himself to his dive. Only one American escort carrier was lost in the advance. But when Kincaid's squadron reached the comparatively restricted waters of the Gulf and began to fire support missions it was a different matter. When two American battleships, three cruisers, and several smaller vessels had been hit by kamikazes on the single day of January 6, 1945, Admiral Oldendorf took his fire support groups out of the Gulf and signaled that more air cover was absolutely essential.

The fact was that the Army Air Force from the southern Philippines had been charged with the duty of keeping the Luzon fields out of business and had not done so. There was a call for Halsey and the fast carriers and he came rushing down the flank of the Philippines. At a cost of twenty-eight planes, he hit the enemy fields so hard that major raids ended, though occasionally one or two Japanese planes would slip in, and they hit another battleship and two escort carriers before the actual landings took place. Our naval gunfire support was so heavy that MacArthur's troops were unopposed at the beaches; Halsey took his squadron into the South China Sea on what became known as "The Long Cruise," thirty-eight hundred miles in eleven days. Off the coast of Indo-China his planes sank forty ships and shot down about one hundred Japanese aircraft; at Takao thirty-four more enemy planes went down and the installations were smashed. Hong Kong got a going over and then Formosa again before Halsey turned through the Strait of Luzon, southeast to base at Ulithi. One of his carriers was badly hit by a kamikaze in the last act, but that was the only damage.

V

At Ulithi the fleet passed over to Spruance and Mitscher under the designation of 5th Fleet, for operations in the north. A major attack on Okinawa to close the iron ring around Japan was already in the stage of planning and training, but before it could take place there was an essential task the Navy must perform for the benefit of the Air Force. Long-range planes flying from Saipan had to go in at twenty-eight thousand feet because the enemy gave warnings from their bases in the Bonin and Volcano islands, and fighters came up to interfere. The only solution was to establish an American fighter base in the chain and Iwo Jima had been selected, both because of its location and the fact that it offered the best possibility for airfield development. Now Iwo Jima was an extremely tough nut; intelligence and aerial scouting showed it to be composed entirely of volcanic rock heaving up in caverned terraces, filled with gun positions, and almost

certainly with connecting tunnels like those on Peleliu. Heavy bombers from the Marianas had been giving it almost daily strikes, but the
Marine officers who were to make the attack shook their heads when
they studied the before-and-after photographs. The big bombers, they
said, were only tossing rock around; they wanted not less than ten
days of flat trajectory gunfire preparation, pinpointed on specific
targets.

They could only have three days, thanks to Halsey's retention in
the MacArthur area, and the fact that that general would not release
the old battleships that had been supporting his landings. There had
to be a carrier strike in the Tokyo area to isolate Iwo Jima from support during our landings, and on February 16-17, 1945, Spruance
made it with the whole fleet, the first time American ships had attacked Japan's homeland since the Doolittle raid of 1942. The material damage was small compared to other operations, but confusion
was introduced into Japanese councils. When the American fleet
peeled off in the direction of Iwo Jima on the way back from the
strike, effective Japanese air interference was blocked almost as completely as at Kwajalein.

Just the same, the Marines ran into plenty of trouble after securing a beachhead on the Iwo shore. There was a steep rise from the
beach, covered feet deep with volcanic ash that stalled every sort of
vehicle, and the Marines had to work their way through by hand
under heavy fire from mortars and machine guns. When routes for
tanks were built to the top of the rise, there was still the problem of
dealing with the rocky, gullied, fortified rises beyond, each hole a
fortress. It took a month to capture Iwo Jima, and the casualties
were higher than in any other island operation of the war, both directly and proportionately. Once it was taken, however, the big
planes for Tokyo could go most of the way under fighter protection
and find an emergency landing station halfway back. Okinawa's
turn had come.

Okinawa is a long, tortuous island with a wasp waist at the center,
supposed at the time to be inhabited by sixty-five thousand Japanese
troops, which turned out to be a gross underestimate. The American
attack force was four Army and three Marine divisions. In addition
the whole strength of the Pacific Fleet was to be thrown into the
operation.

A massive carrier strike was launched against Kyushu, the southern island of Japan, from which air opposition would principally come, on March 18, 1945. It turned into one of the big air-sea battles of the war; some two hundred twenty enemy planes were destroyed on the ground and another three hundred six shot down over the fleet. The Japanese got two bomb hits on carriers with slight damage, but a pair of hits on the carrier *Franklin* caught her launching planes. There were fires and explosions on the hangar deck that killed eight hundred men and nearly ruined her. The engine spaces had to be evacuated; the carrier could not be steered, and she steamed through the Pacific without direction for hours until two of our cruisers got tow-lines aboard. Yet the battered ship was brought safely home, which is a measure of how far damage control had advanced since the early days of the war. And back at Kyushu, Japanese were hit hard enough to prevent their interfering with our invasion wave that swept across the narrowest part of Okinawa on April 1.

Ashore the operations of the first few days were relatively easy. The Japanese had decided to defend the wild hilly section in the northern peninsula of Okinawa, and most especially the southern end of the island. Here the country was all limestone projections, filled with caves. The enemy had made a regular fortified system of the whole area, with tunnels running inside the hills, so that the occupants could fire from any of the numerous exits and duck back into caverned chambers forty feet deep. The fields of fire were interconnecting; it was not enough merely to silence a gun at one of these holes, the whole mountain had to be taken inch by inch and every exit plugged.

The Japanese objective in this system of defense was not merely holding out, as on most of the other islands, but to hold the American fleet within reach of the kamikazes, which were to gradually wear it down to destruction. For the kamikazes had now become official; the Japanese high command issued an amazing order that all air operations were to be conducted in this fashion, whether the pilots liked it or not. They usually came in groups of six, with as many fighters as could be provided for cover and a fast two-engined plane as guide. They provided the American Navy with one of the stiffest problems it had during the war.

A major kamikaze operation was scheduled for April 8, one that should really drive the Americans from Okinawa. All available kamikazes were to take part in it, and it would be backed by a naval raid by the giant battleship *Yamato,* with a light cruiser and eight destroyers, about all that remained mobile of the once-great Japanese fleet. But Spruance's scout planes detected signs of unusual activity on Kyushu and on April 4 he hit the airfields there. Some Japanese planes got off the ground and two hundred forty-eight of them were shot down; kamikazes made hits on an American carrier and a destroyer that caused both to go home with major damage.

Fearing another such counterattack the Japanese stepped up their movement to April 6, sending out what planes were ready, three hundred fifty-five in number, while the ships put out. That was a hard day in 5th Fleet. Admiral Turner, in charge of amphibious operations, had set up a line of destroyers and destroyer escorts with special radar in a circle around the area of operations ashore. About half the suiciders were shot down by fighters from Spruance's ships, but the rest plunged into the picket vessels and the ships of the amphibious groups ashore. They sank three destroyers and two big cargo ships with part of their load; three more destroyers took two kamikazes apiece and were towed out as wrecks; seven destroyers, 2 destroyer escorts, and two minesweepers were hit, and the old battleship *Maryland* so heavily damaged that she had to leave the area. That night a scouting submarine sent word that the Japanese fleet was out. Admiral Spruance, roused from sleep to hear the news, glanced at the chart, said: "Tell Mitscher to go take 'em," and went back to his bunk.

In the morning the planes from two American carrier groups were over *Yamato* and left her staggering, with four bomb hits and eight torpedoes in her, and one of the accompanying destroyers gone. Half an hour later a strike from another carrier group arrived; *Yamato* got four more torpedoes, which was too many. She turned over. The light cruiser and three more destroyers sank. Japanese naval activity was at an end.

All the same it was clear that if the assault of April 6 were repeated often, the U.S. Navy would soon run out of destroyers. Spruance and Turner reorganized the picket line, with a pair of destroyers on each station, accompanied by four of the larger type of landing craft converted to gunboats, their personnel accommodations replaced by heavy batteries of 40- and 20-mm. guns, vessels too small and low to attract kamikaze attack themselves, and very useful in close-in work. The 5th Fleet was to continue to cruise in the area—a mobile fortress.

From that day to the end of the campaign in June, it was slow, slugging, dogged work, ashore and afloat. The expected repetition of the massive attack of April 6 failed to materialize, though there were several lesser versions. The Japanese could not get enough men and planes together for another major effort; their organization was falling apart. But every day and all day there were kamikaze warnings out on the picket line. The planes would come tumbling through the overcast with their deadly charges and a pillar of flame and smoke would mark another hit, with dead men and wounded aboard and damage-control parties struggling to keep her afloat. Of those ships sixty-eight were sunk (though none bigger than a destroyer) and three hundred sixty-eight damaged, including carriers of various sizes; 4,907 Navy men were killed, or more than either Army or Marines lost on Okinawa, in spite of the hard going against caves and tunnels.

But the fleet stayed; the Marines and soldiers stayed, and they did not lack for supplies or arms or ammunition or anything else that could be brought overseas. And when the campaign was over and what Japanese records were left could be examined, it was found that besides more than one hundred thousand men who died defending the island, Okinawa had cost Japan nearly seven thousand planes. It was too much; it was so much too much that, even before the first atom bomb dropped, the decision had been taken to surrender.

Yet in the long view the epitaph of the Empire was that pronounced by Raymond A. Spruance: "The submarines beat Japan."

★ ★ ★ ★ ★

16

A Kind of Peace

AT THE CLOSE of World War II there was the usual American rush to whittle the armed services back to peacetime status. It was a different world, however, from any we had ever known. The United States had acquired responsibilties not merely in keeping the seas, but the shores beyond the seas. These were accepted by all but a few isolationists, and the only way we could discharge this duty was by continuing to be a great sea power, incomparably the largest in the world.

The Navy that came out of the war was a Navy of specialized ships, which becomes most obvious by comparing it with the Navy of sailing-ship days, when warships differed only in size. In the American Navy of 1945 there were differences not only of size, but of function; the LSD (Landing Ship Dock) was larger than a destroyer, but neither fulfilled anywhere near the same office as the other, nor could. Destroyers themselves branched out into specializations— radar picket destroyers with reduced armament; ocean escorts with strong anti-submarine equipment; anti-aircraft destroyers; fleet destroyers to cover the flanks of a task force; destroyer transports to run landing forces quickly to a beachhead. Even carriers had to split up into escort carriers to cover convoys; anti-submarine carriers, having planes with elaborate radar for locating submarines and others with the necessary bombs and rockets for fighting them; and attack carriers with search planes, dive-bombers, and torpedo planes. That is, the U.S. Navy was not only the largest, but by its nature had become the most varied force of its kind in the world.

A fleet of such extent and differentiation implies a personnel of specialists. In spite of the inevitable demobilization shrinkage in total numbers, this was exactly what the post-war Navy became. The old generalized seaman who could pull a rope on any station disappeared in favor of the young boot, who even in his first enlistment was studying electronics or sonar or fire control. The old razor-edged fence between officer and enlisted tended to be more and more broken down. It was increasingly held that the officer function is one of leadership and correct delegation of technical responsibilities. This is not to say that technical matters were neglected in the training of naval officers; they got more rather than less, and the average lieutenant-commander of the 1950s had formal schooling for something like seven years, including his specialized postgraduate courses. But officer duties became more supervisory.

At the same time there was maintained and even augmented a feature of the naval service dating back to John Adams, one which caused British sailors visiting our ships to describe them as "luxury liners." The seamen aboard an American warship ate better, were better paid, and furnished with more comforts than any others in the world. When the technique of air-conditioning became practical, all the new ships were air-conditioned.

There was thus developing a new type of Navy, one in which not only the individual ship, but also the force of which it was a part, and the men aboard the ship were formed with a view to performing a specific task. But before this development could become complete there rose round the Navy a storm equal to that of the gunnery controversy of the 1900s. It was provoked by the (then) Army Air Force, which demanded not only status as a separate service, but also the place as the first line of defense on the theory that strategic bombing of an enemy's resources could win a war without the intervention of the other services. In accord with this theory, the Air Force wished control of all flying operations, even including those of carrier planes.

The results of World War II hardly supported the deduction as to the value of strategic bombing, but the simplicity of the concept gave it a wide popular appeal, and it was driven home by an adroit and vigorous propaganda. In the "unification" bill which set up the separate Air Force, the Navy was fortunate to secure a provision to keep its carrier air. But the story was not yet over. In 1948 the Navy obtained an appropriation for building a new carrier, large enough to house planes that could carry an atom bomb. The Air Force protested acrimoniously that this was an invasion of its field of action, that carriers were obsolete, and they made so much noise over it that Secretary of Defense Louis A. Johnson canceled the carrier. There was a violent controversy, in the course of which the President dismissed Admiral Louis Denfeld, Chief of Naval Operations, but neither bitterness nor the undercover struggle died down until June 25, 1950, when the United States suddenly found itself at war again.

The occasion was the sudden violent invasion of the southern half of Korea from its northern section, where the Soviets had set up a well-armed puppet government. Under the auspices of the United Nations, American forces rushed to the defense. That war became entangled with issues of international and domestic politics which have nothing to do with the Navy, but its effect on strategy and on the service needs notice.

The main strategic feature was that the North Koreans drove rapidly southward until they had confined the U.N. and U.S. forces to the southeast corner of the peninsula, the Pusan perimeter. The methods of transport used by the North Koreans were primitive, but they were adept at concealment, moved mostly by night, and had no large supply dumps that could be attacked. In spite of an air superiority that amounted to domination, Air Force planes found few points of attack and could not effectively interrupt enemy communications. On the other hand, the small air force of the Marines, to which there had been strong objections during the controversy, provided close tactical support for the ground troops in a manner the Air Force was quite unwilling or incapable of giving the Army.

The central part of the Korean peninsula is composed of wild tumbled mountains with few lateral and no vertical roads. The major support lines for the North Korean forces thus ran close along the two coasts. That along the eastern shore could be, and was made almost impassible by gunfire from the sea, delivered by battleships, cruisers, destroyers, and even gunboats. But the west coast roads, which cut farther inland, permitted of no such interruption. Under the circumstances General MacArthur determined on a massive shore-to-shore amphibious landing at Inchon, a major Korean port far up the west side of the peninsula and far to the rear of the main enemy forces. It was delivered on September 15, 1950, under cover from carriers and cruisers, and it was a complete success, the troops being put ashore in the heart of the city. The communications of the North Koreans were effectively cut, their forces began to break up and were driven in confusion to the far northern end of Korea, where they would have been destroyed but for the intervention of the Chinese Communists.

The importance of the operation lay in the continuing demonstration that the Navy could intervene successfully in a campaign ashore; in fact, some distance inshore. Thus out of the Korean war there began to grow a new concept of the service, not merely as a force to obtain command of the sea in the classical sense, but to employ the sea for projecting force to any distance that could be reached from it. New weapons—the atomic bomb, guided missiles—are merely elements of that force; the new means of propulsion—high temperature steam, atomic power—are merely parts of the complex. The old concept of sea power was to "make the frontier the enemy's coastline"; the new is that in the face of sea power coastlines no longer exist.

I I

As with all new concepts—including the idea of the Navy itself—it is taking time for a new concept of sea power to be understood.

The frontier Congressmen of our new Republic saw no need of a Navy when we had squirrel-hunting Kentucky riflemen ready to repel invasion ashore. Later there were demands for a Navy limited to commerce-raiding cruisers, official privateers. The 1870s found the public tolerating the Navy only as a coastal defense force; while as recently as the 1920s, there were voices proclaiming that since we ourselves didn't want war, we didn't need a Navy at all and should scrap our ships.

So today there are voices raised to declare that the nuclear bomb makes ships and ship-based aircraft obsolete. But these critics are just as shortsighted as their predecessors in the 'coonskin caps. If anything, the atom bomb has magnified the importance of the Navy to our survival. Three ships of the New Navy—*Forrestal, Boston, Nautilus*—tell the story.

Forrestal—the nameship of a class which we are laying down at the rate of one a year—with her sisters is the heart of our atom-age fleet. This latest offspring of old *Langley* is a carrier that displaces 75,000 tons fully loaded, which not only makes her class the largest warships in the world but gives them thousand-foot decks—long and strong enough to handle bigger aircraft than any carrier before them. They are packed with every innovation. Escalators rush air crews to their planes. Steam catapults hurl them into the air. Angled flight decks, jutting awkwardly from one side, provide a second runway, so that planes can take off and land simultaneously. They are designed specifically to handle planes big enough and fast enough to deliver nuclear bombs.

As Secretary of the Navy Charles S. Thomas pointed out, there is no safe refuge from the deadly brood of such super carriers. No point on land is more than seventeen hundred miles from the ocean, and more than half of the people of the world live within fifty miles of blue water. These carriers are our strategic ace-in-the-hole, floating nuclear bases, able to dispatch the ultimate weapon to any point on the face of the earth.

Of course carriers can be sunk—just as shore bases can be blasted. But before a ship can be sunk it must be found and its air defense must be penetrated. The location of the land bases is fixed and known, but a carrier base is always on the move anywhere in millions of square miles. A would-be aggressor must face the fact that dreadful retaliation is certain unless those sea-going bases are first hunted down on the vast waters of the earth.

As long as the airplane remains the primary method of delivering an atom bomb, *Forrestal* is the Navy's answer to today's war—to keep it from coming; to fight it if it comes.

Boston is a cruiser, lineal descendant of *Constitution*. *Scorpion* might be a better name for her: her sting is in her tail where she mounts an after battery unlike that carried by any American cruiser before her. The conventional turret rifles are replaced with launching racks, for *Boston* is the Navy's first guided-missile cruiser. And guided missiles are replacing conventional artillery today as they may well replace the bomber tomorrow.

Boston is armed with Terriers—slim, needle-nosed missiles that can strike down an enemy plane thirty miles away. And Terrier is only one of a whole family of Navy guided missiles. Talos and Tartar are also anti-aircraft weapons—Talos a long-range missile for continental air defense; Tartar small enough to be used in the anti-aircraft batteries of a destroyer. Regulus is a surface-to-surface weapon—designed to replace some day the great 16-inch guns of the battleship—resembling the conventional wingswept jet. Sparrow is air-to-air, carried in Navy fighters, guided by electronic signals to seek out the most evasive aircraft. Petrel, an air-to-surface weapon, allows Navy pilots to attack surface targets from far outside the range of ground batteries. Still under development is Polaris, a so-called intermediate-range missile—that is, it is to be launched against targets fifteen hundred miles away.

These are the weapons that have been made public. It is a safe guess that even deadlier ones are under development, including presumably the most devastating of all guided missiles, one that is launched under water and proceeds to the surface, climbs into the air, and seeks out its target: The Germans had begun to develop such weapons by the end of World War II. Thus armed, a submarine will not risk even a momentary appearance on the surface to launch her missile. Instead, she can lurk unseen in the depths and speed nuclear missiles against a target deep in the heart of an enemy country.

Boston already has a sister ship, *Canberra,* with the fleet. The first guided-missile destroyer is in commission. Sooner or later there will be guided-missile submarines. All spell out a Navy the salvos of which will reach far across the world.

And finally the submarine *Nautilus,* already a historic ship even if she never fires a shot in battle. On that January day in 1955 when she first went down the Thames past New London and to the sea, a new kind of sea power was born as surely as when Fulton sent *Clermont* up the Hudson. First atomic-powered vessel in the world, *Nautilus* has demonstrated convincingly what this means: two years and fifty thousand miles without refueling, long cruises submerged, astonishing speed under water.

Already the Navy has displayed sketches of atomic-powered cruisers and destroyers. In fact, a nuclear-powered cruiser is under construction and an aircraft carrier with nuclear engines is on the drafting boards. As Admiral Arleigh Burke—the "31-knot Burke" of World War II, now Chief of Naval Operations—has pointed out, atomic power enables the Navy to design ships "around their power plants and weapons rather than around their fuel-carrying capabilities."

Atomic power at last frees the sailor from dependence upon frequent refueling, the price he had to pay for escaping the vagaries of the winds. Overseas fuel bases or fleet oilers that crawl after the battle forces and refuel them at sea are alike unneeded by atomic-powered ships: The cruises of *Nautilus* and her successors will be limited only by their supplies of food and ammunition. And with no need to economize on oil they can run constantly at high speed.

III

With such ships and weapons to develop, it is no wonder that the Navy sees big changes coming, despite a six and one-half billion dollar program that has already brought one hundred new combatant ships and rebuilt four hundred old ones since World War II. At some point in the decade of the 1960s, we will have a brand new Navy. Built from scratch, it will be atomic-powered, ready to use nuclear weapons against targets at sea or ashore. And ready, by every indication, to send these deadly weapons hundreds or thousands of miles by guided missiles.

Yet fundamentally, of course, the important things in the Navy are not ships or aircraft or guns—even atomic ships and atomic missiles—but people. In its long history, the Navy has been manned by men as varied as the country they served. The impetuous bravery of Cushing and the caution of Hopkins, the icy intellect of Spruance and the hotheadedness of Wilkes, the bravura flair of Paul Jones and the dogged puritanism of Foote—all these are part of the Navy and its history. So, too, are thousands whose names are recorded only on crumbling muster rolls or in dusty BuPers files—men who lived the life of the Navy in every billet from ship's boy to commodore; men who battled the boredom of peace and often died unnoticed in the turmoil of war.

Is there a distinctive pattern running through these personal histories? If there is any one thing, it is perhaps a willingness to take a chance when hardheaded calculation shows the game is worth the candle. This is something different from blind bulldog courage or suicidal disdain for death. This is the doctrine of the calculated risk that paid off so notably when Farragut took his wooden ships past the New Orleans forts, when Decatur led a tiny commando force into the midst of an enemy harbor to blow up *Philadelphia,* when a handful of destroyers and escorts took on the whole Japanese battle fleet at Leyte Gulf.

The men of the Navy will take such risks again. If the past is any guide to the future, they will succeed. That success may mean the survival of our country.

★ ★ ★ ★ ★

Index

THE AUTHOR AND HIS BOOK

FLETCHER PRATT *was born in Buffalo, N. Y., on April 25, 1897. Author of more than fifty books covering a wide variety of subjects, he was best known for his work as a naval historian. He attended Hobart College for one year and then went to work in a public library. His first writing job was as editor of a house organ for the Curtiss Airplane Company. He later became a reporter for the Buffalo* Courier-Express. *In 1919 he went to New York where he free-lanced for various trade journals. It was eight years later he first started writing fiction and contributing to various publications, among them detective story and science fiction magazines. His first published book,* The Heroic Years *(Smith and Haas, 1934), was a history of the Madison administration and the war of 1812. Thereafter he was usually working on three or four projects at the same time. As an acknowledged authority on military affairs, he found himself back in journalism during World War II years as military expert for the New York* Post. *The long list of his historical and fictional works includes:* The Cunning Mulatto *(Smith and Haas, 1935);* Hail Caesar! *(Smith and Haas, 1936);* The Navy—a History *(Doubleday, 1938);* The Lost Battalion *(with Thomas Johnson, Bobbs-Merrill, 1938);* Road to Empire *(Doubleday, 1939);* Sea Power and Today's War *(Harrison-Hilton, 1939);* Secret and Urgent *(Bobbs-Merrill, 1939);* Fighting Ships of the U. S. Navy *(Garden City, 1941);* Naval War Game *(Harrison-Hilton, 1941);* America and Total War *(Smith and Durrell, 1941);* The Incomplete Enchanter *(with L. S. de Camp, Holt, 1941);* Land of Unreason *(with L. S. de Camp, Holt, 1942);* What the Citizen Should Know About Modern War *(Norton, 1942);* The Navy Has Wings *(Harper, 1943);* The Navy's War *(Harper, 1944);* A Short History of the Army and Navy *(Infantry Journal, 1944);* My Life To the Destroyers *(with L. A. Abercrombie, Holt, 1944);* Fleet Against Japan *(Harper, 1946);* Empire and The Sea *(Holt, 1946);* Night Work *(Holt, 1946);* Man and His Meals *(with Robeson Bailey, Holt, 1947);* The Marine's War *(Sloane, 1948);* Ordeal by Fire *(Sloane, 1948);* The Well of the Unicorn *(as George W. Fletcher, Sloane, 1948);* Eleven Generals *(Sloane, 1949);* Empire and Glory *(Sloane, 1949);* Preble's Boys *(Sloane, 1950);* The Third King *(Sloane, 1950);* War for the World *(Yale, 1951);*

The Monitor and The Merrimac *(Random House, 1951);* Double in Space *(Doubleday, 1951);* World of Wonder *(Twayne, 1951);* Carnelian Cube *(with L. S. de Camp, Gnome, 1951);* Rockets, Jets, Guided Missiles and Space Ships *(with Jack Coggins, Random House, 1951);* Castle of Iron *(with L. S. de Camp, Gnome, 1952);* A Short History of the Civil War *(Pocket Books, 1952);* Double in Jeopardy *(Doubleday, 1952);* Blue Star *(in Witches Three, Twayne, 1952);* By Space Ship to the Moon *(with Jack Coggins, Random House, 1952);* Petrified Planet *(Twayne, 1952);* Stanton, Lincoln's Secretary of War *(Norton, 1953);* Undying Fire *(Ballentine, 1953);* Tales from Gavagan's Bar *(with L. S. de Camp, Twayne, 1953);* My Diary, North and South *(Harper, 1954);* Famous Inventors and Their Inventions *(Random House, 1955);* All About Rockets and Jets *(Random House, 1955);* The Civil War *(Garden City, 1955);* The Civil War in Pictures *(Holt, 1955);* Battles that Changed History *(Doubleday, 1956); and* Civil War on Western Waters *(Holt, 1956). Despite his prodigious writing chores, he found time to collect and raise monkeys and make detailed maps for his own use. An accomplished linguist, he also found time to translate many books, mostly from French and German. He died at Long Branch, N. J., June 10, 1956, a few days after he completed the manuscript for this book. He is survived by his widow, the former Inga Stephens whom he married in 1926 and who illustrated a number of his books, and a brother, Robert Horton Pratt.*

THE COMPACT HISTORY OF THE UNITED STATES NAVY *(Hawthorn, 1957) was designed by Sidney Feinberg and completely manufactured by American Book–Stratford Press, Inc., and illustrated by the late Louis Priscilla. The body type was set in Times Roman, originally designed for use by* The Times *of London.*

A HAWTHORN BOOK